Rule Britannia

Also by Deirdre David:

Fictions of Revolution in Three Victorian Novels:
"North and South," "Our Mutual Friend," and "Daniel Deronda"

Intellectual Women and Victorian Patriarchy:
Harriet Martineau, Elizabeth Barrett Browning, George Eliot

RULE
BRITANNIA

WOMEN, EMPIRE, AND
VICTORIAN WRITING

Deirdre David

CORNELL UNIVERSITY PRESS
Ithaca and London

First published 1995 by Cornell University Press.

Printed in the United States of America

♾ The paper in this book meets the minimum requirements
of the American National Standard for Information Sciences—
Permanence of Paper for Printed Library Materials, ANSI Z39.48-1984.

Library of Congress Cataloging-in-Publication Data

David, Deirdre
    Rule Britannia : women, empire, and Victorian writing /
Deirdre David.
        p.   cm.
    Includes bibliographical references (p.   ) and index.
    ISBN 0-8014-3170-0 (cloth : alk. paper)
    1. English literature—19th century—History and criticism.
    2. Great Britain—Colonies—History—19th century—Historiography.
    3. Women and literature—Great Britain—History—19th century.
    4. Imperialism in literature.   5. Colonies in literature. 6. Women
in literature.   I. Title.
PR468.I49D38   1995
823'.80932171241—dc20   95-32733

To the memory of my mother, Phyllis Mary Whitaker (1909–1989),
who knew how to run a Brixton barrow.

And to the memory of Bruce Ruddick (1915–1992), who taught me
to understand Brixton, and almost everything else.

CONTENTS

ILLUSTRATIONS

PREFACE

L ondon. Implacable November weather. Mud in the streets, soot in the air, fog in the nostrils. But this is not 1852, the year of publication of the first monthly number of Dickens's magnificent novel of the metropolis, *Bleak House*. I am evoking a historical moment in 1952, in the seedy suburbs of a city little changed from Dickens's London. The soon to be crowned Elizabeth has returned from Kenya, and Buckingham Palace is planning more royal tours to shore up the crumbling colonies; Jamaican calypso singers are singing about their island in the sun; and the first black West Indians to arrive in Britain after World War II are accommodating themselves to dreary life in lower-class South London. Having fled large-scale unemployment, postwar inflation, and miserable living conditions, black people from the Caribbean found the imperial metropolis entering upon its age of austerity. Given Britain's class-bound society, the age was more austere for some than for others, just as, in *Bleak House*, the "ill-favoured and ill-savoured" neighborhood that houses the Smallweed family differs significantly from the St. Albans countryside that surrounds the quaint coziness of Bleak House itself. The few hundred West Indians who settled in the grimy late-Victorian suburb of Brixton joined a working-class population skilled in coping with the clothing, coal, and food rationing that continued well beyond the end of the war. Brixton is roughly ten miles from the center of London's Mayfair, but in terms of social class in the raw winter of 1952, when the postwar immigration to Britain began to manifest itself in working-class London neighborhoods, it might as well have been in Tobago. The cultural distance between, say, Brook Street, W.1., and Coldharbour Lane, S.W.16, site of Brixton's outdoor market and also of the Labour Exchange that in the early 1950s was supplying London Transport with a fleet of West Indian bus conductors, was immense. What happened during the next decade—how the class distance between Mayfair and Brixton became the grid for the race map of the metropolis, how a vastly diminished empire continued to define metropolitan experience, how a few hundred West Indians became many thousand—was affirmed for me one afternoon in the mid-1960s when I visited the ladies' room in Claridge's Hotel. At that moment, I understood the enduring material reality of the British empire.

Ladies' room attendants in hotels of this sort are cautiously chatty, ready to exchange a few circumspect murmurs about the weather but always conscious of the social gulf between themselves and their customers. This particular afternoon, in response to my casual remarks about the vagaries of London Transport, the attendant told me she lived in Brixton. "Oh" I said, "I know Brixton. My mother used to have a second-hand clothing stall in the market—right after the war, up until the early fifties." The woman looked at me suspiciously. Dressed appropriately for lunch in a posh hotel, my London intonations now part of a socially mobile transatlantic accent, I did not look, nor did I sound, like the daughter of a woman who ran a stall in one of London's working-class outdoor markets. When I mentioned my mother's name, my schoolgirl talent in selling used clothing, my father working as a placement officer in the Labour Exchange on Coldharbour Lane— in sum convincing her that I *knew* Brixton—she wistfully announced, "Well, dear, Brixton's changed. They're selling tropical fruit now in Brixton." There it was—the empire come home to South London, the mangoes and papayas of the tropics on sale next to the cauliflower and brussels sprouts.

I began with an evocation of *Bleak House* to suggest what I regard as a quite precise link between a Victorian novel and the material alteration of a London street market. Essentially, I will argue in *Rule Britannia* that the two cultural moments I have just conjured up—the first in 1952 when Elizabeth and Philip were in Kenya and West Indians were settling in London, and the second in the mid-1960s when a "changed"

Brixton became a vivid metonyn for the immense geopolitical changes wrought by British military and cultural power—are partially created, along with innumerable other cultural moments in the history of Britannia's ruling of the waves, by the textual construction of empire to be found in Victorian writing. If, in the words of Benedict Anderson, the nation is "an imagined political community" (6), then this writing helps to "imagine" the Britannic nation. In sum, I've looked at how Victorian writing about empire helped to get the tropical fruit to Brixton, and my particular interest has been in the significant participation of women in this textual enterprise: women as writers, as subjects of representation, as images of sacrifice for the cause of empire. In writing this book, I have always had in mind the way fictional and nonfictional texts produced during the Victorian period construct, in part, the material reality of a historically transformed fruit and vegetable stall in South London.

An earlier version of portions of Chapter 2 appeared in my essay "Children of Empire: Victorian Imperialism and Sexual Politics in Dickens and Kipling," which was published in *Gender and Discourse in Victorian Literature and Art,* ed. Antony Harrison and Beverley Taylor (De Kalb: Northern Illinois University Press, 1992), copyright © 1992 by Northern Illinois University Press. I thank the publisher for permission to reuse this material.

My greatest debt is to the graduate students in seminars dealing with Victorian culture and empire I have taught for the past decade or so at the University of Maryland, College Park, and at Temple University. To name all would take up more space than one is allotted on these occasions and to name some would fail to register properly a gratitude for so many insights shared with me in seminar discussion. Yet I must record my appreciation of the research assistance provided by Sherry Whitlock and Martin Wurdemann at the University of Maryland; their capable work has contributed much to this book. As a department chair, I have found the give and take of the classroom excellent relief from the administrative crises and bureaucratic tangles sometimes involved in such work—my deep thanks, therefore, to all my students for a bracing encouragement to keep on writing. I have also been fortunate in receiving from colleagues and friends helpful and pointed readings of some or all of the chapters; in particular, I am grateful to Dan O'Hara and Barry Qualls. In the final stages of manuscript preparation, the excellent editorial skills of Carolee Walker and Kay Scheuer were very helpful to me; and I feel privileged to be included for the second time in a group of authors guided by Bernhard Kendler, the most gifted of editors.

Edward Said's name appears several times in this book, as the critic who more than any other has created the possibility of talking about culture and empire. But it is as a dear friend that I wish to acknowledge him here, as someone who for some twenty years has prodded me to read more, think harder, write better. Whatever contribution this book makes to the study of women, empire, and Victorian writing is due, in large part, to his warmth and generosity.

DEIRDRE DAVID

Santa Fe, New Mexico

Rule Britannia

INTRODUCTION

TROPICAL FRUIT IN BRIXTON

> Our landscape was as manufactured as that of any great French or
> English park. But we walked in a garden of hell, among trees, some still
> without popular names, whose seeds had sometimes been brought to
> our island in the intestines of slaves.
> —V. S. Naipaul, *The Mimic Men* (1967)

In *Bleak House,* Dickens imagines the empire in various ways. Jo, for
instance, comes out of the reeking court that is Tom-all-Alone's
and decides to eat his breakfast ("his dirty bit of bread") on the
doorstep of the Society for the Propagation of the Gospel in Foreign
Parts, all the while admiring "the size of the edifice" and knowing nothing of the "spiritual destitution of a coral reef in the Pacific" (221). In
historical actuality, that the Society for the Propagation of the Gospel
could venture into "Foreign Parts" depended upon British military and
civil protection. That there is in the metropolis an "edifice" built and
protected by empire upon whose doorstep Jo can sit shows how Victorian people were surrounded by material evidence of their imperial
power and that Dickens may juxtapose the domestic neglect of Jo with
missionary zeal to convert the heathen suggests how his enduring concern for the abused child that begins with *Oliver Twist,* gains in *Bleak
House* imaginative force by the material existence of empire, just as,
of course, his criticism of besotted philanthropy is heightened by the
figure of a neglected boy. Most obviously, it is Mrs. Jellyby's desire to
settle "a hundred and fifty to two hundred healthy families cultivating
coffee and educating the natives of Borrioboola-Gha, on the left bank
of the Niger" (37) that provides Dickens's critique of a philanthropy
obsessed with Africa and neglectful of domestic misery. Less obviously,
however, that the Bagnet children in *Bleak House* are named Quebec,
Malta, and Woolwich for the military barracks in which they were born

and where their artillery-man father was either protecting British interests (in the case of Quebec and Malta) or preparing to do so (in the case of Woolwich) reveals how possession of foreign territory is registered in the daily lives of ordinary Victorian people in modest, and, I would argue, significant ways. *Bleak House* constructs ideas about empire for Dickens's reader, both in its large moral critique and in its small acts of representation.

When literature and colonialism became a visible subject of cultural study some twenty-five years ago, critics tended to concentrate upon Renaissance travel narratives and were influenced primarily by the work of Frantz Fanon.[1] Since that time, however, the colonial and imperial practices of the Victorians have also become the object of literary analysis, and what follows clearly demonstrates that I have situated my readings in an already rich field of study.[2] In a memorable moment in one of the most frequently cited texts in this field, Conrad's *Heart of Darkness*, Marlow derives comfort from seeing large chunks of the world colored red on British maps of imperial possessions. That he can feel this way signals, of course, his immersion in late Victorian imperial culture, however ironically he may view his situation, and his sense of security rests upon British geopolitical power at the end of the nineteenth century. To put this in another and necessarily circuitous way, the privileged cultural milieu of civil discourse that fosters Marlow's ambivalence was enabled by military and civil forces that invaded and took over various territories around the world, ranging from chunks of the African continent to small islands in the West Indies. The wealth derived from empire served to create a curious and mainly middle-class reading public: the audience

---

[1] See, in particular, Stephen Greenblatt's important essay "Invisible Bullets: Renaissance Authority and Its Subversion, *Henry IV* and *Henry V*" and Fanon's *The Wretched of the Earth* and *Black Skin, White Masks*.

[2] I have in mind such works as Alan Sandison's *The Wheel of Empire* (1967); Benita Parry's 1972 examination of late-Victorian Anglo-Indian fiction, *Delusions and Discoveries;* Martin Green's influential *Dreams of Adventure, Deeds of Empire* (1979); Edward Said's by now indispensable *Orientalism* (1978) and his *Culture and Imperialism* (1993); Gayatri Spivak's essays of the mid-1980s on issues of feminist individualism and subaltern voice; and the essays published in the autumn 1985 and autumn 1986 issues of *Critical Inquiry*, collected and edited by Henry Louis Gates, Jr., under the title *"Race," Writing, and Difference*. All these books and more recent studies such as Patrick Brantlinger's *Rule of Darkness: British Literature and Imperialism, 1830–1914* (1988), Jonathan Arac and Harriet Ritvo's collection, *Macropolitics of Nineteenth-Century Literature: Nationalism, Exoticism, Imperialism* (1991), Suvendrini Perera's *Reaches of Empire: The English Novel from Edgeworth to Dickens* (1991), and Jenny Sharpe's *Allegories of Empire* (1993) constitute the foundation for further work in the field.

for Victorian writing about Britain's geopolitical power, whether in the form of political essays, travel narratives, missionary tales, or novellas that question the imperial project. In turn, this writing imaginatively collaborates, consciously or not, with structures of civil and military power to constitute and secure the red spaces that prove so comforting to Marlow, and to Conrad's British readers. And those red spaces contained the indigenous peoples who were to be transported by economic need after the Second World War to the working-class areas of a damp and foggy metropolis.[3] In an ironic reversal of the pattern of British invasion and subjugation of lands and peoples throughout the Victorian period, the colonized begin to invade the imperial center, bringing with them tropical tastes nurtured, perhaps, by eating fruit from the nameless trees evoked in the epigraph for this chapter. If one imagines, with Naipaul, that from the intestines of Africans brought across the Middle Passage to Trinidad in the early 1800s come trees whose fruit is exported to Britain to be sold in a South London suburb in the 1960s, then the extraordinary geographical and historical scope of the British empire becomes harrowing, vivid, awesome, as it did for me when I learned from a ladies' room attendant about a "changed" Brixton.

In the literary texts that are my primary subject in this book, together with no less significant cultural documents such as political essays, parliamentary reports and speeches, missionary literature, and travel narratives,[4] I have aimed to trace a small part of the immense Victorian "discourse" (a seductively capacious term) of colonialism and imperialism. In saying I am interested in such discourse, I mean something very close to Peter Hulme's lucid explanation of his project in *Colonial*

---

[3] See Peter Fryer for useful details of black immigration to Britain after World War II. Fryer notes that the miserable living conditions for black people living in Barbados, British Guiana, British Honduras, Jamaica, the Leeward Islands, and Trinidad and Tobago that were documented in the Moyne Commission Report of 1938–39 remained essentially unchanged ten years later. Submitted to the government at the end of 1939, the report was not published until June 1945: its revelations of substandard housing, schooling, and medical care were considered too unsettling to be published during the war. As Fryer observes, it was to escape such conditions that in 1948, several hundred West Indians emigrated to Britain, to be followed in 1951 by one thousand more and in 1952, by two thousand (*Black People in the British Empire* 32, 118).

[4] In examining the cultural work performed by texts defined differently according to formal convention, I believe it helpful to bear in mind what Bakhtin has to say about literary form: "After all, the boundaries between fiction and nonfiction, between literature and nonliterature and so forth are not laid up in heaven. Every specific situation is historical. And so the growth of literature is not merely development and changes within the fixed boundaries of any given definition: the boundaries themselves are constantly changing" (33).

Encounters: the study of "an ensemble of linguistically-based practices unified by their common deployment in the management of colonial relationships" (2). Where Hulme's interest is in how, in the seventeenth and eighteenth centuries, "large parts of the non-European world were *produced* for Europe" through such a discourse, my focus has been upon how Victorian writing created that nation-defining construction on which the sun was said never to set: the British empire. At the end of a dazzling parliamentary speech delivered in July 1933 (which I discuss at some length in Chapter 1), Thomas Macaulay speaks of an empire "exempt from all natural causes of decay . . . the imperishable empire of our arts and our morals, our literature and our laws" (718). Where Macaulay evokes this imperishable empire of culture in contradistinction to the vulnerable empire founded upon military conquest, I intend to show their constitutive reciprocity and absolute inseparability. Necessarily, this has been a selective enterprise, and in a moment I shall explain why I have been interested, say, in Macaulay rather than Mill, *Dombey and Son* rather than *Vanity Fair,* Haggard rather than Kipling.

What follows, therefore, is not just about how colonialism and imperialism are represented in Victorian writing but also about a paradigm of reciprocal relationship between political and textual practices. What Edward Said claimed for Orientalist discourse in the book that in so many ways initiated the kind of work I have aimed to do here — "its very close ties to the enabling socioeconomic and political institutions" (*Orientalism* 6) — is something I see as indispensable for an understanding of Victorian writing about empire. In particular, Stephen Greenblatt's perception that the colonialist text seeks to control through recording the behavior of alien cultures has illuminated my readings of those cultural documents I have related to the literature. Greenblatt observes that recording indigenous practices serves to constitute an alien culture and that the culture is thereby "brought into the light for study, discipline, correction, transformation" (27). The missionary literature and travel writings I discuss demonstrate, especially, one culture's desire to control and thereby transform another. In thinking about the textual labor of empire building, I have also tried to address an issue usefully examined by Chris Weedon in her integration of the theoretical perspectives of cultural materialism and feminism: for Weedon, the primary task for all critics must be to "tackle the fundamental questions of how and where knowledge is produced and by whom, and of what counts as knowledge" (7). How knowledge of empire is produced in Victorian writing, for whom this knowledge is produced, and the purposes for its production are questions fundamental to my readings. Without doubt, Victorian regimes of political power and cultural knowledge produce the enormous social institution of Britannic rule, which was always being defined differently according to different historical moments.

Consequently, this book seeks to identify and elaborate what Homi Bhabha has termed "writing the nation." In particular, I have been concerned with that Victorian "writing the nation" which is produced by women and which is about women as resonant symbols of sacrifice for civilizing the "native" and women as emblems of correct colonial governance.[5] By the beginning of the Victorian period, gender differences within British society were becoming part of the cultural furniture, and it is possible to see how writing about empire both appropriates and elaborates Victorian gender politics in a construction of national identity defined by possession of "native" territory and control of "native" peoples. Victorian writing about empire thus becomes an increasingly imbricated discourse, reliant upon powerful attitudes and values regarding women in culture and society. Powerful codes governing the middle-class British woman—her importance in cultivating the private, domestic sphere, her imagined moral superiority and capacity for sacrifice, her supposed incapacity for sustained intellectual activity (to name the most familiar)—were sufficiently in ideological place at the beginning of the Victorian period for them to become available to an emerging and adjacent discourse: that of writing the imperial nation. This discourse deploys a constellation of overlapping race and gender ideologies that discloses their mutual constitution. And within this writing the nation about women, women themselves, of course, participated in its construction: sometimes in enthusiastic consonance with praise of Britannic rule, sometimes in a contrapuntal voice that speaks skeptically alongside the primarily androcentric voices that articulate ideal governance of the empire. For these reasons (primarily to do with history), women, empire, and Victorian writing form a rich ideological cluster and a compelling subject for cultural analysis.

As an instance of the reciprocal making of gender and race politics, consider the common political metaphor of mother country and dependent children/colonies that one finds so often in nineteenth-century

---

[5] Throughout this book, I am making a distinction between Victorian writers' usage of the term "native," almost always pejorative and patronizing, and my own references to indigenous peoples controlled by the British.

"MAGNA Britannia: her Colonies REDUC'D" (1766). By permission of the Library Company of Philadelphia.

writing about empire and that derives from earlier images of Britannic rule such as the eighteenth-century "Magna Britannia." In the Victorian period, the allegorical female figure "Reduc'd" by the loss of her American colonies has become the actual queen plumped up by the acquisition of vast amounts of territory. The metaphor of mother country evokes, of course, Victoria herself as the great Britannic mother, ruling with maternal severity and sympathy her own eminently respectable large family, her own British subjects, and her own subjugated natives.[6] Victorian women derive their gendered authority to rule colonized peoples within the domestic realm of their Simla bungalows and Jamaican plantations and to write travel narratives and missionary literature relegating the "native" to his lazy, pagan place from Victorian ideas about race. What Diana Rivers says to Jane Eyre when Jane is contemplating a future as St. John's missionary wife shows the way Vic-

[6] See Peter Burroughs for a valuable discussion of the stages leading to colonial self-government in Canada, a process modeled on the mother country/child colony relationship. Burroughs traces what was seen by the British government in London as an "evolutionary process leading inexorably through representative institutions to local self-government" ("Colonial Self-government" 39). Mary Poovey makes the interesting argument that in post-1857 British imperial rhetoric, India is figured as poor, brutish, and sick—in sum, in need of curing "by an efficient head nurse cum bourgeois mother (England, middle-class woman)" (196).

torian culture placed women in imperial spaces and authorized their function within those spaces. When Diana declares that Jane is "much too pretty, as well as too good, to be grilled alive in Calcutta" (441), she means that Englishwomen who go out to India are sacrificed to the climate and to native threats of molestation precisely in response to Victoria's imperative, articulated through the ideology and practices of her subjects, to civilize barbaric societies.[7] As evidence of the power of these intersections between race and gender politics—Victorian women may rule the Britannic empire, may "write" the empire, must suffer for the empire—it is interesting to see how they resonate in a postmodern text such as J. M. Coetzee's revision of Defoe's *Robinson Crusoe*. In *Foe*, when Susan Barton describes to Friday her ancillary work in producing Defo's [*sic*] fiction and likens her writing to Friday's labor upon Cruso's [*sic*] island, she says, "think of each mark as a stone, and think of the paper as the island, and imagine that I must disperse the stones over the face of the island" (87). In different and unequal spheres of labor, Susan Barton's task symbolizes the work of the Victorian woman writer in the textual shaping of empire, and Friday's physical exertion symbolizes, needless to say, the native labor that creates the geopolitical fact of empire. The textual narrative of imperialism is made through Susan's labor, and the material narrative of imperialism is made through that of Friday. What's more, Susan Barton's postcolonial awareness of woman's discursive work for androcentric colonialism implicitly interrogates the literal and imaginative demands made upon Victorian womanhood in the cause of furthering Britannic rule. In addition to rewriting *Robinson Crusoe*, *Foe* also revises the demand for female sacrifice in the cause of civilizing the barbarian that is expressed in *Jane Eyre* (which I shall explore at length in Chapter 3), albeit in smaller and less obvious ways.

In what follows, I have built upon the essential work of identifying strategies deployed by Victorian writers to justify Britain's occupation and governance of its acquired territories. Primarily, such work entails unpacking the rhetorical and ideological moves that displace the unquestionable link between empire building and commercial profit into political fictions of a barbarism waiting at the gates. I also hope to complicate some established ideas about the Victorians: that they believed in their own cultural and racial superiority and that they disguised, con-

[7] Calcutta continues to signify a place of suffering and disease, a place where one does not want to be. On 5 January 1990, the president of the Dallas Gay Alliance was quoted by the *New York Times* as saying that Dallas is "the Calcutta of the AIDS Epidemic."

sciously or not, their oppressive practices as fables of paternalistic improvement. My readings cannot fail to concur in these assessments, but they go on to suggest the inherent variety of the disguise and thereby refute a monolithic approach to understanding Victorian empire. Among other things, Victorian attitudes toward empire are almost always unambiguously racist, occasionally worried about the European erosion of native customs, often uneasy about the domestic prices demanded for the maintenance of distant territories, frequently fearful of the consequences of British invasion and subjugation, sometimes infatuated with the exotic delights of alien cultures, and periodically attentive to what is construed as the moral responsibility of imperial rule.[8]

To be sure, every chord of what I regard as a pluralistic chorus of justification may be termed a unified and unifying masking, a mystification, if you will, of the violent oppression and material exploitation of enormous numbers of non-British peoples. What I hope to get at in this book is a sense of the discursive density of these mystifications, a feel for how some cultural documents worked to create, explain, and negotiate the difficulties attendant upon possession of an immense and always changing empire. In the process of doing this cultural work, Victorian writing takes on some of the qualities of what Mikhail Bakhtin, in developing his theory of the dialogical nature of the novel, terms heteroglossic discourse. As Bakhtin observes, "The living utterance, having taken meaning and shape at a particular historical moment in a socially specific environment, cannot fail to brush up against thousands of living dialogic threads, woven by socio-ideological consciousness around the given object of the utterance; it cannot fail to become an active participant in social dialogue" (276-77). Bakhtin's image of an organic web of ideological meaning created from "living dialogic threads" evokes almost perfectly my own sense of how the Victorian discourse of empire shifts its meanings, repeats itself, contradicts itself, and periodically recovers its stability at the discursive moments when it is most visibly weaving British national identity. While always at root a justification of its subject, the writing the nation that deploys Vic-

---

[8] For an informative discussion of Victorian ideas about race, see Christine Bolt's *Victorian Attitudes to Race* and her essay "Race and the Victorians" in Eldridge; see also Douglas Lorimer's *Colour, Class, and the Victorians* for the useful distinction he draws between a pre-1860s enthnocentric attitude that assumes cultural superiority but admits the possibility of native races conforming to so-called civilized norms and a post-1860s view that British culture and society are superior by virtue of biological inheritance.

torian gender politics varies according to its historical moment, as one sees, for instance, in the different affiliations of women and empire.[9] In the early-nineteenth-century nostalgia for a masculine spirit of adventure imagined as enfeebled by calls for moral improvement of the natives, women are tolerated as necessary but meddlesome; in the mid-Victorian Liberal emphasis upon the cares and duties involved in such imagined improvement, women are required, in historical actuality and in symbolic representations, to perform sacrificial roles; and in the late-nineteenth-century questioning of British engagement abroad, worries about empire and race are inseparable from patriarchal worries about female cultural assertion.

IMBRICATED DISCOURSE

The arrival of West Indians in Brixton, their tropical fruit fragrant evidence of their presence in the imperial metropolis, suggests a significant image to which I shall return frequently: that of invasion. In one way or another, this image informs almost all the writing I have chosen to discuss, most of which is concerned, predictably, with India. The tremendous importance of that lucrative trading colony to Britain's global prominence in the nineteenth century is registered everywhere in Victorian writing about empire, and the actual penetration of British troops into India in the eighteenth century is a literal instance of the trope of invasion. But it is also to be found in the transportation of bricks carried as ballast in slave ships to Naipaul's fictionalized Trinidad in *The Mimic Men* (bricks that are then used to build sugar plantations) and in the arrival of fortune-seeking Rochester in creole Jamaica and the counterarrival by his wife in the isolation of the rural midlands. And, of course, it is manifested in the presence of tropical fruit in Brixton after World War II. In *Heart of Darkness*, Marlow observes of Kurtz that "the wilderness had found him out early, and taken on him a terrible vengeance for the fantastic invasion" (59). Contextually, Marlow's judgment is grounded in his discovery of Kurtz's unrestrained gratification of what remains unspecified desires; metaphorically, however, Marlow's judgment also resonates with Kurtz's literal invasion of

---

[9] What I have in mind here is something similar to Mary Poovey's conclusion about Victorian ideologies of gender: "the middle-class ideology we most often associate with the Victorian period was both contested and always under construction; because it was always in the making, it was always open to revision, dispute, and the emergence of oppositional formations" (3).

Africa for the looting of vast amounts of ivory. The sequential figuration of invasion, subjugation, and occasional self-interrogation is a recurrent motif in the texts I have studied. All of them, I should note, are written from the British perspective on Victorian empire, however critical their implications.

Chapter 1 explores the resonant imagery of invasion and counterinvasion as it appears in Wilkie Collins's *The Moonstone* and goes on to juxtapose Macaulay's well-fortified parliamentary rhetoric of colonial conquest and pacification of India with the letters of Emily Eden written home to England when she accompanied her governor-general brother to India in the late 1830s. Eden's private, rueful, epistolary take on the British imperial project that is glorified in Macaulay's public, parliamentary rhetoric suggests how early Victorian gender politics begins to shape formal and political differences in male and female modes of writing the imperial nation. Chapter 2 examines Dickens's *The Old Curiosity Shop* and *Dombey and Son* to illustrate the moment of emergence in Victorian culture when women become freighted with the moral task of civilizing the colonized. More than any other Dickens novel, *The Old Curiosity Shop* and *Dombey and Son* disclose the intimate, constitutive relationships between fragile, pale Englishwomanhood and demonic, African savagery, and between domestic tyranny and colonial subjugation.

In Chapter 3, I examine the Victorian novel that has received the most critical attention in terms of its narrative appropriation of the empire in its story of female individualism: *Jane Eyre*. Building upon Homi Bhabha's theorization of the categories of the pedagogical and the performative in the construction of a nationalistic individualism, I have argued that the ideological contradictions of Brontë's novel may be traced to Jane Eyre's complex governess sensibility. In this chapter, as in all the others, I have incorporated a close reading of nonfictional texts (here travel narratives about Jamaica and sensationalist literature about the practice of suttee) into my analysis of fiction to claim a confluence at certain historical moments in the Victorian period of powerful and prevailing ideas about gender and race in culture and society.

Chapter 4 offers a historical reading of a legal case conducted in the Calcutta courts in the mid-1880s concerning imputed loose behavior on the part of a woman missionary and combines this reading with discussion of the Anglicist and Orientalist debate regarding the education in English of Indian natives and the emergence of the babu figure in

British Raj culture. The dangers to the imperialist nation posed by assertive women in the metropolis, which were felt by androcentric patriarchy in British Calcutta, continue to govern late-Victorian writings about the so-called new imperialism and popular adventure fantasies exemplified in the fiction of H. Rider Haggard. Discussion of this danger and a contemporaneous fear that the laboring body of the native and the laboring body of the British woman were taking on a rebellious life of their own make up the focus of Chapter 5. In this chapter, I have concentrated upon Haggard's *King Solomon's Mines* and *She* and also upon Tennyson's poems of empire. Their nationalistic gestures having proved, it seems, too embarrassing for serious attention from his critics, these poems reveal a yearning for social order modeled on that of Victoria's impeccable domestic and imperial governance. In my concluding chapter, I have shown that the character of Emilia Gould in Conrad's *Nostromo* is a synthesizing figure embodying the multiple ways in which writing the Victorian nation deploys resonant ideas about gender difference for constructing Britannic rule.

Before I move to my initial arguments about invasion and counter-invasion, about gender difference and imagining the nation, I want to look briefly at the invasion, as it were, of literary studies by the historical fact of empire. The critical and theoretical work of intellectuals such as Edward Said, Gayatri Spivak, and Homi Bhabha since the late 1970s has laid the groundwork for what is now an established and rapidly growing field of critical and theoretical inquiry. Dissertations abound on topics in postcolonial literatures and black British studies. From my perspective as a critic interested in links between metropolitan culture and the material practices of empire, and the reciprocity of gender and race politics, this is a fine thing. But I think we need to be vigilant that, in documenting repellent colonial practices, tracing the formal geography of travel narratives, gathering the ideological threads of missionary literature, and analyzing how Victorian writing constructs empire, we do not lose sight of those subjects who were objects in the creation of British colonial and imperial supremacy. I mean the West Indians who are deformed into pumpkin-loving Quashee in Carlyle's "Nigger Question," those bearers who march in the margins of all Victorian travel literature, the West Africans saved from slavery by the Church Missionary Society and prominently featured in the Society's literature, and the English-educated babu figures who turn up in the fictional form of Ezra Jennings in *The Moonstone* or Babu Hurree Chunder Mookerjee in *Kim*. Victorian women travel writers, some have argued, were freed from the Victorian domestic constraints of gender into sympathetic understanding of indigenous peoples, and thus into a less masculine and therefore less aggressive mode of asserting their presence on the landscape through travel writing.[10] But we must not forget that the social freedom of these women was purchased through class privilege and that their understanding was enabled by an apparatus of subjugation of indigenous peoples. This is not to diminish their achievements but to illuminate what made them possible.[11]

As a historically attentive critic, in my most recent work, I dealt with the position of the Victorian woman intellectual in a male-dominated culture. In what follows, my analyses of the Victorian woman as writer about empire and as a figure of empire have built upon the thinking that went into that book.[12] In the earlier project, I tried not to lose sight of the female subject who is so often the object of feminist criticism; it was important, on the one hand, not to sentimentalize the writings of Victorian women as records of heroic essentialist struggles, and, on the other hand, not to see these women as fatally imprisoned by patriarchal modes of discourse. Now, it seems important not to lose sight of

[10] See, for example, Shirley Foster who argues that the woman writer "often represents foreigners sympathetically, as individuals with whom she tries to identify rather than as symbols of an alien 'otherness'" (24).

[11] An insidious myth of glamorous women travelers is central in western advertising. Ralph Lauren's "Safari" advertisements show women lounging on zebra skins somewhere in Africa with not a black face in sight. The Ghurkha leather company promotes its handbags with the claim that "Ghurkha recalls the romance of an era when privileged women with servants in tow, traveled half way round the world by train and steamer to the elegant hotels of Bombay and Jaipur to wait for their gallant, titled gentlemen and officers to finish their military campaign, or their polo match or the elephant hunt"; subduing what the Victorians called the natives is indistinguishable from wielding a polo mallet. The Petersen catalog touts its "Out of Africa" shirt with the following fantasy: "Between the years 1906 and 1939, a trickle, then a light rainfall, then a downpour, of Englishmen, Germans, Scots, and some remarkable women, began to fall upon the immense gorgeous plateau of East Africa"—falling apparently into a world entirely uninhabited until their arrival. In a different but equally racist key, the "Media Business" column of the *New York Times* on 20 May 1993 noted the success of a television commercial for Acura cars: "Four aborigines lope across a cracked desert floor toward a parked Acura. Dressed in loincloths, alligator-tooth jewelry and body paint, they exchange puzzled looks as they approach the gleaming car. Once they figure out how to get in, they take off—in reverse." Without editorial comment, a creative director's enthusiasm for this advertisement was quoted by the *Times:* "It was so original, so arresting, so entertaining . . . I marveled at every second." One marvels, in turn, at the unexamined racism of these advertisements.

[12] See my *Intellectual Women and Victorian Patriarchy: Harriet Martineau, Elizabeth Barrett Browning, George Eliot.*

those peoples who helped to create the European subjectivity that both produced and was produced by Victorian writing about empire, or, to bring this chapter back to its beginning, in exploring the imagined and actual worlds of empire, I have always had in front of me the important story of how the tropical fruit got to Brixton.

In the practice, then, of a historically grounded cultural criticism, I want to complicate the gloomy essentialist position that a master culture/master discourse must always in monolithic fashion appropriate counterculture/counterdiscourse, or, to put this another way, I hope to have made a contribution to Edward Said's critical project of avoiding a politics of blame and a politics of confrontation. In addition, I have aimed to avoid sterile acquiescence in acknowledging nothing beyond the indeterminacy of discourse itself. Even if we only *have* discourse, according to Michel Foucault, then we must remember that discourse is about people who lived, who still live, and about events that happened, continue to happen. I am hopeful that this book will disclose a theoretical alignment with those poststructuralists who connect the signifying system to social forces and with those cultural materialists who admit disruption of the hegemony, if not its transformation. If I have been successful, then *Rule Britannia* will have filled a gap in current colonial and postcolonial cultural studies through reconciliation, in Said's words, of "an isolated cultural sphere, believed to be freely and unconditionally available to weightless theoretical speculation and investigation, and, on the other, a debased political sphere, where the real struggle between interests is supposed to occur" (*Culture and Imperialism* 56–57). But I should emphasize that all my readings are grounded in a belief that the British empire was, at root, shaped by an economic self-interest sometimes baldly articulated, sometimes subtly negotiated, and sometimes wishfully erased.

An article in *The Times* on 6 January 1848, for instance, discloses a straightforward linking between empire and the national economy characteristic of the politics of the wealthy middle class that constituted *The Times*'s primary readership during this period. Addressing itself to "the state of deepest depression" to which the West Indian proprietors have been brought by the fact that slave labor in Cuba continues while they must reconcile themselves to a postemancipation plantation economy, *The Times* declares "We have, then, two objects before us which are generally and reasonably sought by the community at large. We wish for a commodity at its natural price, and we wish to extinguish a certain method of producing this commodity" (*Select Documents on British Colonial Policy* 434–35). Since, *The Times* continues, the "West Indian interests are our interests"—that is to say, cheap sugar benefits the domestic economy—then "it is necessary to set our own planters on their legs again," which may be achieved by discouraging slavery since it presents the only competition to be feared by "the free labourer" (435). I do not mean to suggest that the antislavery movement was driven entirely by commercial interests, or to say that all Victorian writing about empire lacks significant agency. Rather, I have tried to negotiate a critical position that sees Victorian writing about empire as an imbricated discourse constituted by different forms that are enabled but not always entirely determined by economic and political forces.[13] *The Times* article may be said to endorse unambiguously economic development of the empire, whereas *Bleak House*, by virtue of its formal existence as Victorian novel, not newspaper leader, may be seen as the product of a literate culture enabled by the economic development embraced by *The Times*, yet also as a complex work of the literary imagination that defies easy categorization as coherent ideological defense or criticism of Britannic rule. To be sure, as I suggested earlier, Victorian writing about empire imaginatively collaborates with structures of civil and military power to secure Marlow's red spaces, but it is the different formal shapes and the reciprocal relationship between race and gender politics to be found in this collaboration that I have aimed to elaborate.

Thomas Macaulay's parliamentary rhetoric and Emily Eden's private letters, to which I shall turn in a moment, have behind them an immense body of actual people. Macaulay is addressing the issue of maintaining direct control over some 540,000 square miles (at the height of its power the British Raj ruled a population of some ninety million Indians). Emily Eden is describing people who were, for her, sometimes mere background, sometimes disconcerting evidence of poverty, and sometimes vivid reminder of the frightening fact that a tiny group of British officials was governing, literally, millions of Indian natives (in 1835, there were approximately twenty-four thousand civil servants,

---

[13] My sense of form here is derived from Fredric Jameson's dialectical model of ideological containment and utopian desire as elaborated throughout *The Political Unconscious: Narrative as a Socially Symbolic Act*. Jameson sees literary form determined by contesting ideologies and engaged in constructing strategies to contain this contestation.

military officers, and troops in India).[14] The labor of indigenous peoples built the British empire; the wealth of the empire produced a metropolitan culture; this in turn, produced the novels, poems, essays, travel narratives, missionary memoirs that I have grouped and studied in adjacent relationships. These indigenous peoples are the subjects represented or occluded in Victorian writing about empire. There *was* an East India Company, a scramble for Africa, a Great Game played on the Northwest frontier. And rapacious Englishmen such as the despicable Colonel Herncastle in *The Moonstone* actually did loot diamonds, bring them home as rightful plunder, and bestow them on their nieces. The invasion of empire began, after all, with armies, weaponry, and violence, even if it ended up with tropical fruit in South London.

[14] See John Pemble's introduction to *Miss Fane in India* for details of the astonishing numerical disparity between British government officials and the indigenous population. *Miss Fane in India* is an edition of letters written by Isabella Fane in 1835–38, when she accompanied her father to the Punjab.

CHAPTER ONE

THE INVASION OF EMPIRE:
THOMAS MACAULAY
AND EMILY EDEN GO TO INDIA

All work in India which concerns itself with the moral and physical welfare of its women is work that will tell in the long run; for woman is the lever, the only infallible lever, whereby sunken nations are upraised.
— Maud Diver, *The Englishwoman in India* (1909)

Far from the India whose different meanings for Thomas Macaulay and Emily Eden I shall explore in the principal part of this chapter, we find Gabriel Betteredge, primary narrator of *The Moonstone* and veteran house steward on the ruling-class Verinder Yorkshire estate. His thinking shaped by *Robinson Crusoe*, that core work of territorial conquest which returns the rebellious individual from foreign risk to domestic security, he steers the reader through the first part of Collins's novel, all the way punctuating his narrative with comical waves of the union jack. From his xenophobic perspective, Britons never will be slaves, and it is always nasty foreigners who most threaten a domestic social order founded on upstairs benevolence and downstairs loyalty. By his lights, those inquisitive, loitering Indians (familiar to all readers of Collins's novel as the dedicated protectors of a diamond wrenched by a British officer from the head of an Indian statue) can only be in search of the family silver. In terms of his suspicion of anything beyond Yorkshire, to say nothing of what lurks across the English Channel, however, it is significant that the plot of *The Moonstone* proves him correct. It *is* foreign Indians, arriving mysteriously on the stage of Collins's masterpiece of sensation fiction, who disrupt the social system so dear to Betteredge's imperial heart, who fracture the domestic social harmony secured by half a century of British colonial conquest.

As prelude to Betteredge's version of the events that seem to have precipitated the disappearance of the diamond from the Verinder household, Collins provides a Prologue. In a suggestive yoking of narrative sequence and political meaning, he couples the Prologue and the subsequent individual narratives that have been generated by a need to establish "a record of the facts," which is how Franklin Blake describes the assembly of subjective versions of these "facts" that is *The Moonstone*. The Prologue relates a tale of wanton murder and naked greed on the part of a Verinder ancestor (a Colonel Herncastle) at the battle of Seringapatam in 1799. Herncastle's villainous deeds dramatize what Abdul JanMohamed has usefully termed the "dominant" phase of British subjugation of foreign territory and appropriation of the resources of indigenous peoples. The events described in the Prologue occur in late-eighteenth-century India, before Evangelical imperatives of duty, responsibility, and hard work, coupled with agitation for parliamentary reform and abolition, begin to replace Nabob thinking's unembarrassed sanction of material gain. As JanMohamed describes the process, with the early-nineteenth-century beginnings of a transformation in the means of subjugation, from coercion by economic practices to consent because of an internalization of Western cultures, and in the aim of the colonizer from profit making to civilizing, we see the emergence of a "hegemonic" phase (80–81). The Prologue to *The Moonstone*, then, is both a late-eighteenth-century political prelude to Victorian attitudes toward empire and a fable of individual brutality erased by a subsequent and coherent sequence of individual stories gathered in the cause of a common good. In addition, the methodical narrative structure of *The Moonstone*, which sequentially decodes the mystery, suggests the mid-Victorian reliance on evolutionary, unfolding explanation as a means to the eradication of political and moral disorder. *The Moonstone* thus displays what Peter Brooks describes as the Victorian "confidence in narrative explanation," a belief that "history can be and should be a tracing of origins" (275–6).[1] At the end of the novel, we see the reestablishment of a social order that has been agitated by the presence

---

[1] As Frances Mannsaker observes, "The second half of the nineteenth century was dominated by various evolutionary theories of human development in almost all areas of study—the political, ethnological, anthropological, psychological, sociological, religious—which carried certain corollaries in the discussion of racial characteristics" (128). In particular, Mannsaker refers to the work of the anthropologist Edward B. Tylor who, she observes, "propounded a well-regarded theory that the human race as a whole followed a certain sequential pattern of cultural development" (128).

of the diamond in Yorkshire, a place far from Marlow's red spaces of empire but close to the metropolitan center that is their point of origin.

From Betteredge the reader learns that the diamond has been inherited by a Colonel Herncastle's niece and that when the stone is placed in her possession, ruling-class country-house life begins to unravel. Betteredge confides, "here was our quiet English house suddenly invaded by a devilish Indian Diamond—bringing after it a conspiracy of living rogues, set loose on us by the vengeance of a dead man. . . . Who ever heard the like of it—in the nineteenth century, mind; in an age of progress, and in a country which rejoices in the blessings of the British constitution?" (67) The "living rogues" are, of course, the three Indians in pursuit of the stone, a counterinvasive trio produced by the intrusion of British forces into India in the latter part of the eighteenth century, forces whose material reason for being there in the first place is symbolized in Herncastle's looting of the diamond. The Orientalist of the novel, Murthwaite, groups these shifty-looking "natives" with other Indians living in England by characterizing them as sharing a "secret sympathy" with those of "their own religion, as happen to be employed in ministering to some of the multitudinous wants of this great city" (330–31), which would seem to be a dark allusion to drugs. Metaphorically linked, then, with the opium given to Franklin Blake as a scientific experiment cum practical joke, the Indians are inseparable from the diamond in a trope of colonial return. In *The Moonstone*, we can see that the colonized enters the territory of the colonizer, the slave the space of the master, and, in the case of Gabriel Betteredge, the repressed the imagination of the repressor. Through his amazed description of a quiet English country house being "invaded" by an Indian diamond, Betteredge articulates, altogether unconsciously, a paradigm of British intrusion and counterintrusion in the developed hegemonic phase of Victorian imperialism.[2]

Betteredge's stunned recognition of invasion suggests multiple meanings in the Victorian culture of empire. First, and most obviously, one thinks of the historical, actual invasion of India, Africa, Australia, Burma, Malaya, the West Indies (and more) by British military and civil forces in the nineteenth century. Second, almost simultaneously

---

[2] John R. Reed was the first critic to discuss in a substantial way the presence of empire in Collins's novel. He also argues that *The Moonstone* provides a critique of imperialism, a view contested by the arguments of this chapter. See "English Imperialism and the Unacknowledged Crime of *The Moonstone*."

with this territorial intrusion, one discovers in *The Moonstone* and in many of the other texts I shall discuss, a pattern of counterintrusion by subaltern figures, their complex agency produced by British forces, into spaces thought safe from foreign intervention. Brontë's Bertha Mason Rochester and Dickens's Abel Magwitch are two figures who immediately suggest this pattern of disruptive resistance from the edges of empire; in *The Moonstone,* the trope of counterinvasion gathers together in Britain the Indians, the diamond, and the opium, all produced through the British appropriation of large parts of the Indian subcontinent and all wrested, as it were, from their own ahistorical "natural" places. Third, *The Moonstone* is but one Victorian piece of writing that reveals the imaginative intrusion into British literature by the thematic material of empire, and as a corollary and later development, the appearance in the disciplines of historical, cultural, and literary studies of the topics of colonialism and imperialism.

Victorian colonialism and imperialism, however, are by no means new subjects of analysis in historical research and cultural criticism, even if they are relatively new topics in literary study. For example, the question of whether Britain's imperial policy took a whole new, scramble-for-Africa turn after 1870 has long been a matter of debate, together with the affiliated issue of when colonialism ends and imperialism begins.[3] Discussion of these terms will serve to clarify their pervasive usage in this book. In 1902, J. A. Hobson distinguished between colonialism as benevolent transportation of European culture to foreign places and imperialism as bellicose acquisition of territory. While later historical analyses question the benevolent nature of colonialism, Hobson's definition of imperialism as an internationally competitive and militarily supported land-grabbing operation has remained in place. For Hobson, colonialism places no drain upon English material and moral resources "because it has made for the creation of free white democracies, a policy of informal federation, of decentralisation, involving no appreciable strain upon the governmental faculties" (132).

---

[3] The argument set forth by Ronald Robinson and John Gallagher in *Africa and the Victorians* (1961) initiated this latter question. Robinson and Gallagher claim that late-nineteenth-century British expansion originated in fear and pessimism rather than in self-confident assertion and that the post-1870 speed-up in colonial annexation should be seen as an intensified expression of what had been occurring throughout the Victorian period rather than as a new development. Paul Kennedy also argues that British imperialism forms a continuum throughout the nineteenth century and that it should be seen as an ongoing process of interaction between the metropolis and the colonized periphery. See "Continuity and Discontinuity in British Imperialism, 1815–1914."

By contrast, imperialism is "the very antithesis of this free, wholesome colonial connection, making, as it ever does, for greater complications of foreign policy, greater centralisation of power and a congestion of business which ever threatens to absorb and overtax the capacity of parliamentary government" (132). Situating his views in the context of late-nineteenth-century fears that running the empire was draining the mother country of domestic vitality and that the bloody subjugation of "lower races" by "white races" (133) squandered British resources, Hobson sternly indicts imperial practices. Echoing Marlow's scorn in *Heart of Darkness* for Roman colonists in Britain as mere "conquerors" dedicated to "a squeeze," not to "an unselfish belief in the idea" (50), Hobson speculates that if "incomes expended in the Home Counties" were to be traced to their sources, "it would be found that they were in large measure wrung from the enforced toil of vast multitudes of black, brown, or yellow natives, by arts not differing essentially from those which supported in idleness and luxury imperial Rome" (160).

In the Victorian period, this association of the British and Roman empires, while sometimes serving to glorify a British achievement thought to excel anything managed by the Romans, is more often the means of creating a moral lesson (as we see in Hobson's alignment of the "enforced toil" exacted by Rome and Britain).[4] In 1854, for example, three years after the Great Exhibition displayed its vast visual narrative of British mercantile power,[5] and three years before the Indian uprising disclosed the complicity of this narrative with military forces, Elizabeth Barrett Browning disdained the imperial glory that had, in her view, been purchased at the price of domestic misery.

The speaker/poet of "A Song for the Ragged Schools of London" evokes a cautionary contrast between the English and Roman empires and asks, "Shall we boast of empire, where / Time with ruin sits commissioned?" (ll. 26–27).[6] She warns, "Lordly English, think it o'er, / Caesar's doing is all undone!" (ll. 33–34). England should remember that she already has "ruins worse than Rome's" in her "pauper men

[4] In 1808, however, as Tricia Lootens notes, the fifteen-year-old Felicia Hemans in *England and Spain* hails "Albion" as "Thou second Rome, where mercy, justice, dwell, / Whose sons in wisdom as in arms excel!" (Lootens, 248).

[5] For an excellent discussion of the great commodity that was the Great Exhibition, see Thomas Richards, *The Commmodity Culture of Victorian England*, chap. 1: "The Great Exhibition of Things."

[6] All citations to the poetry of Elizabeth Barrett Browning are to *The Complete Works of Mrs. Elizabeth Barrett Browning*.

and women." And in the two-part "Casa Guidi Windows," an impressionistic meditation on Italian culture and politics, Browning disdains Britain's celebration at the Crystal Palace in 1851 of her commercial victories and indicts her refusal to support Italian national aspirations. This conjunctive attack upon worldly greed and upon Britain's isolationist politics, both fed by imperial expansion, suggests how Victorian writing about empire emerges from particular historical moments, and, in the case of Browning, how it is further characterized by the politics of the writer, a politics that conjoins resistance to mercantile materialism with celebration of Italian idealism:

> But now, the world is busy; it has grown
> A Fair-going world. Imperial England draws
> The flowing ends of the earth from Fez, Canton,
> Delhi and Stockholm, Athens and Madrid,
> The Russias and the vast Americas,
> As if a queen drew in her robes amid
> Her golden cincture, — isles, peninsulas,
> Capes, continents, far inland countries hid
> By jasper-sands and hills of chrysopras,
> All trailing in their splendours through the door
> Of the gorgeous Crystal Palace.
>
> (2:577–87)

In the conservative distaste for mercantile colonialism, which I shall analyze in discussing Dickens and Tennyson, these two writers evoke the figure of a young Queen Victoria in their creation of female characters who reject middle-class materialism in favor of a less secular social order. Dickens's Florence Dombey, for example, possesses an almost unnatural spirituality that paradoxically flowers in the grit of the grubby metropolis and that serves to chasten the granitelike materialism of her father, whose power gathers nations from empire. And Tennyson's Maud scorns a "new-made lord" whose mine-owner grandfather laid "his trams in a poison'd gloom" and favors the speaker of the poem, the conservative gentry son of the Hall who has been displaced by changing times and values. Maud possesses the finely tuned moral rectitude and girlish vitality with which early Victorian culture invested the young female monarch, whose succession in 1838 followed a long period of Regency flamboyance and a short span of rather dull kingship.[7] Browning,

---

[7] Margaret Homans argues that Queen Victoria embodied "wifeliness" for her subjects, that the more she appeared "a bending, yielding, wifely figure," the more her subjects granted her "the

by contrast, implicitly faults the queen for failing to curb the ambitions of "Imperial England," whose power gathers nations together at the Crystal Palace in a manner similar to that of a queen drawing in as much of the globe as she can manage to fit within the figurative circle of her "golden cincture." But however differently they may appropriate the image of Victoria for their critiques of mercantile materialism, Dickens, Tennyson, and Browning all lament the loss of values imagined as once present in a preindustrial, preimperial Britain, and, at root, elaborate the figure of Victorian woman as moral reformer of a materialistic culture. In addition, each writes in the early to middle decades of the Victorian era when to write about empire was ambiguously to hail Britannic rule and sentimentally mourn the passing of a phantom social order: in sum, to fathom ways in which Britain might enjoy the wealth brought by empire without having to acknowledge the brutal means of its acquisition.

By contrast, Conrad's late Victorian interrogation of empire in *Heart of Darkness* avoids sentimental nostalgia, even if it depends, at heart, on the unexamined association of Africa with barbarism and Europe with civilization, however corrupt that civilization may become when tainted by an embrace of African "horror." Voiced most pointedly, perhaps, in Marlow's observation that "The conquest of the earth, which mostly means the taking it away from those who have a different complexion or slightly flatter noses than ourselves, is not a pretty thing when you look into it too much" (50), Conrad's view expresses in part a British weariness with foreign engagement. It is in this context, too, that one should hear Hobson's insistence that imperialist land grabbing must be abandoned, that the domestic economy is bled rather than nourished by competition with other European powers for African territory, resources, and labor. But Hobson, needless to say, is a far less anguished political critic than Conrad, whose indictment of Western exploitation and celebration of the British no-nonsense decency embodied in Marlow eventually suggest to the reader that although imperialism is nasty, the British manage it less nastily than most. Hobson's unambiguous purpose is to demonstrate the thrift of colonial societies in contrast to the excess of imperialist ones.

It is interesting to discover that earlier in the century, the values with which Hobson invests colonialism are to be found in literature pre-

---

power to model their lives" (19). Victoria's conventionally feminine subordination to Prince Albert implicitly allows her to reign supreme over him and everybody else in Victorian Britain. Such actual and imagined subordination is affiliated, it seems to me, with nineteenth-century ideologies of middle-class female rejection of the material and cultivation of the spiritual.

scribing emigration to Canada, Australia, and South Africa as medicine for domestic ills. For example, Charles Rowcroft's *Tales of the Colonies* (1843), related through the sagacious voice of a former Australian magistrate, provides practical advice about emigration procedures, securing land, and living alongside a large and frightening convict population. Politically grounded in the hard times of the 1840s and in fears that Britain might go the revolutionary way of France, Rowcroft's *Tales* exemplifies writing about empire characterized by contemporary historical conditions. The union workhouses of the 1840s, Rowcroft declares, are "nurseries of Chartism . . . schools of plots and treasons," and he aims his *Tales* at conversion of the "wretched half-starved pauper" into a "contented well-fed colonist" (vii). Similar to Harriet Martineau's *Illustrations of Political Economy* (1832) in their didactic style and chin-up message, the stories are usefully instructive: middle-class readers, for instance, worried about finding suitable occupations for their children who have been "incited" by society to push their way into professions, are urged to remember that although there may be surgeons on every street corner in London, in Australia there are few. The domestic struggles of a corn trader, pressed by the recession that followed the Napoleonic wars to pay "rent, and rates, and taxes, and tithes" at a time of falling prices, are eventually resolved in his emigration to Van Diemen's Land. We learn of his happy receipt upon arrival of twelve hundred acres, his ease in securing a female convict servant, and his profitable retooling as a sheep farmer. Successful in his colonial enterprises, he in turn relieves the government of the expense of maintaining convicts by employing them as servants and agricultural laborers. The reader learns about the state of the soil, the price of sheep, and the essential tools for Australian fresh starts, such as axes, candle molds, screws, pistols, pewter basins, and vegetable seeds. Alert to the incentives to committing crime in an 1840s society riven by "uncertainty of subsistence" (231), the narrator shows how offenders are placed in a condition of "progressive improvement" in the colony—very much like the colony itself, which was transformed rapidly in the first quarter of the nineteenth century from penal settlement to flag-flying British outpost.[8] In Rowcroft's entertaining *Tales*, pickpockets become shepherds, drunken cooks sober silversmiths, and impoverished cob-

---

[8] For excellent documentation of this process, see Paul Carter, *The Road to Botany Bay*, and Robert Hughes, *The Fatal Shore*.

blers bullock drivers, just as in *David Copperfield,* Wilkins Micawber, armed with the knife of "a practical settler," is transformed from financial failure to prosperous colonial citizen. These figures may be seen as rehabilitated social losers who provide, it is worth noting, historical evidence for George Eliot's agreement in her 1856 essay "The Natural History of German Life" with Wilhelm Heinrich von Riehl's views on emigration. Endorsing Riehl's call for colonization as the remedy for "perverted civilization" (281), Eliot welcomes "colonization as presenting the true field for this regenerative process. On the other side of the ocean, a man will have the courage to begin life again as a peasant, while at home, perhaps, opportunity as well as courage will fail him" (281).

Taken as a whole, Rowcroft's *Tales* relates the building of a colony. When the dispirited corn trader first arrives in Van Diemen's Land, similar to Robinson Crusoe in his lack of resources, and dependent on the beneficence of colonial government just as Crusoe is dependent on the providence of a higher power, there is virtually no colonial presence. Throughout the years of the former corn trader's budding success as a sheep farmer, the colony grows through the building of a church, a counting house, a government building, and a bank, just as, of course, Crusoe's colony grows through the building of his castle and his summer retreat, and the proliferation of his crops and his flock of goats. There is a recurrent problem, however, in Rowcroft's story of colonial expansion and achievement, a disruption of the narrative of incremental acquisition of land, money, and status, just as Crusoe's perfected world of self-sufficiency is disrupted by the arrival of the cannibals. In Van Dieman's Land, escaped convicts turn bushrangers, dress themselves up in kangaroo skins, attack settlers, steal sheep, and form alliances with aboriginal groups. Here we see expressed a primary fear to be found in many Victorian narratives of colonial triumph over barbarism and domestic discipline of criminals: rebellion by the subjugated figures whose labor feeds the empire or sustains the domestic economy. In a pattern similar to that of Collins's vanquished Indians who return to disrupt the metropolitan heart of an empire dependent upon their subordination, and in a journey similar to that undertaken by the most moving of all "returned" colonial figures, Abel Magwitch, the convicts who are physically building the colony flee their road-making sentences, move out to the liminal spaces of uncolonized territory, and threaten those settlers whose existence depends on the large laboring population. Whether to be traced in Rowcroft's uncomplicated narratives of colonialism, in the formally sophisticated suspense of Collins's sensation novel, in the family and class romance of Pip and Magwitch, or in the presence of tropical fruit on sale in Brixton, images of the oppressed intrude upon the settled territory of the oppressor.

In the distinctions drawn by Hobson between colonialism and imperialism some sixty years after Rowcroft's *Tales,* we see both similarities and differences between the two texts. In Hobson's polemic and in the early colonialist literature designed to encourage emigration, colonialism relieves domestic problems of unemployment, temptations to crime, and so on. Considered in the larger political sense, however, colonialism and imperialism differ little in terms of a shared essential meaning: the arrival of individuals from one country in another for the purpose of appropriating land and subjugating indigenous populations, or, as Edward Said puts it, "thinking about, settling on, controlling land that you do not possess, that is distant, that is lived on and owned by others" (*Culture and Imperialism* 7). Although there is no fully developed military occupation of Australia in Rowcroft's 1843 *Tales,* British acquisition and redistribution to colonizers of aboriginal land are ordered and protected by the state.[9]

REFORMING THE RAJ

Except as female convicts rehabilitated into servants or as the resilient wives of ambitious immigrants, women play little part in Rowcroft's narrative of colonial invasion. In general, the early Victorian discursive participation of women in the construction of empire is to be discovered more prominently in travel narratives, memoirs, and letters written from Britain's paramount trading colony, India, than in the genre, exemplified by Rowcroft's *Tales,* produced to encourage the colonies of white settlement.[10] Primarily, this is to do with issues of social class and

---

[9] Patrick Brantlinger has correctly argued that the distinction between colonialism and imperialism becomes irrelevant when one considers the larger political picture: the grabbing of land and the subjugation of indigenous peoples by invading forces. Brantlinger also observes that "early and mid-Victorians expressed imperialist ideology in their writings" (8). However, it is worth bearing in mind Edward Said's point that "'imperialism' means the practice, the theory, and the attitudes of a dominating metropolitan center ruling a distant territory; 'colonialism,' which is almost always a consequence of imperialism, is the implanting of settlements on distant territory" (*Culture and Imperialism* 9).

[10] Mary Louise Pratt makes the interesting argument that the work of nineteenth-century women travel writers differs from that of men not merely because they describe domestic settings

the difference between settlement and temporary occupation. Quite simply, the lower-class woman settling in the colonies had little time to record her experiences, whereas the more privileged woman—the sister of an army officer posted to India, say, or a missionary wife stationed in Jamaica—possessed the leisure and education to write letters to her family, to attempt a travel narrative, to keep a journal. The privileged and educated woman may be said, however, to perform a kind of textual labor in the service of empire which is analogous, in an imaginative and far less demanding way, to the physical labor of lower-class women such as Kim's washerwoman mother in Kipling's novel or the unrecorded work of women who labor in Van Diemen's Land in the 1840s.

Almost always, the travel narratives, memoirs, and letters produced by Victorian women disclose a more domestic and therefore different picture of empire than that to be found in conventionally male genres such as the essay, the government report, and the public speech. But this is not to argue, I hasten to add, that male writers championed empire and women lamented it, that army officers, colonial officials, barristers, and so on, raucously endorsed colonial and imperial practices, or that army wives, residents' sisters, and governor-generals' daughters were wringing their hands about the injustice of Britannic rule. If nothing else, this book will, I trust, refute such a view. I am interested in the ensemble of discursive differences that construct particular forms of knowledge about Victorian empire: differences of gender, race, social class, and historical moment. As a way of beginning to unpack some of these differences, I would like to compare the rhetoric of two quite similar yet very different individuals who wrote about empire in the nineteenth century. Thomas Macaulay, famous Whig politician, and Emily Eden, not-so-famous sister of a governor general, both traveled to India in the 1830s. The language of Macaulay's parliamentary performance and of Eden's letters home to her sister suggest how attitudes toward empire are inflected by differences in political affiliation and gender, although I think it important to recognize that Macaulay and Eden have more in common than the simple opposition of Whig/Tory and male/female would seduce us into believing. Macaulay and Eden are ruling-class individuals who exercise the different forms of

---

but because from "these private seats of selfhood [women travelers] depict themselves emerging to explore the world in circular expeditions that take them out into the public and new, then back to the familiar and enclosed" (*Imperial Eyes* 160).

cultural power allotted to them by virtue of gender politics, and rather than presenting a consistent common front or staging a stark opposition, they inhabit and possess different rhetorical arenas and styles, each in its own specific and sometimes contesting way serving to construct British national identity. Most of all, what their writing reveals is that an unease about empire, however tentative and small its expression, is virtually simultaneous with its glorification.[11]

For Macaulay, India possessed an early fascination. He recalls that as a boy he used to stare "with the greatest interest" at a "daub of the taking of Seringapatam" in a shop-window in Clapham (Trevelyan, *Life and Letters* 265).[12] When he rose in the House of Commons to make his great Charter speech in July 1833, he was only seven months away from assuming his duties in Calcutta as a member of the Supreme Council, from whence he returned three and a half years later, never again, in the words of John Clive, having "to give a thought to his financial situation (289). The occasion for the 1833 speech was the second reading of a Commons bill that contained certain economic and administrative reforms proposed by the cabinet as essential for renewal of the East India Company's Charter (hence the naming of his July 1833 performance as the Charter speech). Macaulay's ideas thus become central in early Victorian efforts to erase the memory of colonial corruption, exemplified, for instance, in Wilkie Collins's Colonel Herncastle at Seringapatam.

By the 1830s, the group that formed the core of Britain's late-eighteenth-century presence in India—merchants, British officers and troops, and the officers and troops of the East India Company's own private army—had been replaced by a much larger military and civil presence. V. G. Kiernan observes that the late-eighteenth-century standards of conduct "could hardly be elevated. . . . Men were as completely emancipated from conscience or criticism as the Spaniards in their worst years in America. . . . Those 'Nabobs' who did get home with their ill-gotten gains were welcomed for their money but detested for their insolence, and for the dissoluteness that was said to be infect-

[11] George Levine claims that if Macaulay could have written a novel "he would have wanted it to have the classical pretensions of Fielding and the symmetry and precision of Jane Austen" (*The Boundaries of Fiction* 117). This affiliation of Macaulay with Jane Austen forms a further connection with Emily Eden, who herself very often writes as if under Austen's ironic influence.

[12] John Clive notes that when Macaulay arrived in India, he made a trip to Seringapatam and recalled how his uncle, Gen. Colin Macaulay, had been imprisoned there and had distinguished himself during the siege (293).

ing English society and even subverting the Constitution" (*The Lords of Human Kind* 34-35). The Indian territories had, throughout the eighteenth century, been governed by employees of the East India Company, resident in India, as John Clive observes, "not in order to found a permanent Empire nor as a ruling caste, but for the purpose of enriching themselves and the company's proprietors" (306). By the time of Macaulay's speech, ideals of disinterested discipline had begun to replace informal codes of casual debauchery, and it was time to complete the process with a kind of Utilitarian cleanup. His argument is saturated with this historical and moral difference.[13] Grounding himself in the principles of free trade and Utilitarianism developed by James Mill and relying upon the primary thought of Mill's *History of India* (a work, incidentally, that Macaulay had attacked in the *Edinburgh Review* some four years before his 1833 speech), he examines the early stages of British invasion of India. As he soon makes clear, the primary task for Britain is to make official the hitherto less formal business of going out to the East, to rehabilitate and thus transform the "dominant" stage of imperialism, which we see, of course, in Herncastle's snatching of the diamond in *The Moonstone*, into a "hegemonic" stage of consent rather than coercion in the relationship between colonizer and colonized.

Macaulay begins with a capacious history of how the East India Company has created a union of commercial and military forces, with the messy result that in 1833 the Company is a "political monster of two natures" (694). Brilliantly deploying a rhetorical tactic whose effect is to elide the Company's history of corruption, he dwells at length on answering two questions: "In what state, then, did we find India? And what have we made India?" (702), or, as we might translate these questions, in what state did Britain find India when it invaded that subcontinent? Macaulay finds that history scarcely furnishes a parallel for the condition of "invaded" India. Groping for a comparison, he comes up with fifth-century Europe—despotic, anarchic, shifting, restless, rife with treason, revolution, and parricide. "Society was a chaos," he concludes (702-3). But in the middle of the eighteenth century, the Company initiated "the reconstruction of a decomposed society": regrettably, but perhaps unavoidably, Macaulay declares, this was an effort

---

[13] For indispensable analysis of the influence of Macaulay and his fellow Evangelicals and Utilitarians upon British policy in India, see Eric Stokes's commanding study, *The English Utilitarians in India*.

Thomas Rowlandson, *The Grand Master or Adventures of Qui Hi?* (1816). By permission of the British Library Oriental and India Office Collections, V2179.

tainted by "guilt and shame" (703). Because untrained men were transformed in a few months from clerks drudging over desks or captains in marching regiments into civil and military tyrants prone to extortion and corruption by their lack of professional preparation, he argues, India remained subject to what was perceived in the Victorian popular imagination as oriental despotism unchecked by British discipline.[14]

Having laid the justifying ground for reformation, Macaulay, as one might expect, proceeds to outline the stages of the necessary

[14] A full flowering in the Victorian popular imagination of Macaulay's myth of British "duty" and Indian "chaos" appears in Harriet Martineau's book on India, hastily cobbled together after the uprising in 1857. Enumerating British sacrifices for the empire, Martineau wonders "whether the history of any nation presents a picture of a more virtuous devotion to public duty" (*India* 106). Historical research, however, reveals that India was not quite the economic mess of British imperial ideology. As Peter Fryer points out, "When European adventurers first reached India they did not find an industrial or technical backwater. . . . India was not only a great agricultural country but also a great manufacturing country. It had a prosperous textile industry, whose cotton, silk, and woollen products were marketed in Europe as well as elsewhere in Asia. It had remarkable, and remarkably ancient, skills in iron-working" (21). Fryer argues that British imperial practices transformed the economic base from combined agriculture and manufacture into an agricultural colony that exported to Britain raw cotton, wool, jute, oilseeds, dyes, and hides.

moral, political, and administrative transformation. Fundamentally, these changes characterize the administration of the British Raj for the rest of the century.[15] Strongly in favor of one provision of the 1833 bill that introduced competition for places in the Indian Civil Service previously awarded through patronage, Macaulay emphasizes that Britain's empire must be staffed by superior minds. In a manner consistent with his (male) public school education, Macaulay claims that these minds will be recognized as such by outstanding academic achievements in Latin, Greek, and mathematics. It is difficult to imagine, though, that even the most brilliantly assiduous of these intellects could ever match that of Macaulay. He records that on his four-month voyage out to India, he read "insatiably; the Iliad and Odyssey, Virgil, Horace, Caesar's Commentaries, Badon de Augmentis, Dante, Petrarch, Ariosto, Tasso, Don Quixote, Gibbon's Rome, Mill's India, all the seventy volumes of Voltaire, Sismondi's History of France, and the seven thick folios of the Biographia Britannica" (Trevelyan, *Life and Letters*, 269).[16] Having in mind, then, the intellectual laziness of earlier colonial administrations, Macaulay articulates the second, indispensable stage of successful colonial occupation: to sustain the control acquired through military power, the empire must initiate an ancil-

[15] I do not mean to embellish the myth of Macaulay as the sole individual force in the partial transformation of Indian indigenous culture to British ways of thinking and doing business. In his essay on John Stuart Mill's service to the East India Company, Abram L. Harris offers a sensible brake to such glorification of the individual and accompanying neglect of pertinent historical processes: "Historians who have credited Macaulay with having exercised a tremendous influence on the future development of Indian education, contending, in some cases, that he was an originator of India's modern educational system, seem to overlook two facts. The first is that the Bentinck resolution [which Macaulay's Minute of 2 February 1835 preceded by one month] which he probably did influence, was repudiated by the Court of Directors in a dispatch ordering him to adopt no new measures or to pass any new laws materially affecting the civil or military arrangements without previous reference to the court. The second fact is that India's modern educational system was inaugurated by the famous dispatch of 1854, the authorship of which is attributed to Sir Charles Wood, President of the Board of Control, the East India Company" (196–97).

[16] In *The Life and Letters*, Trevelyan provides Macaulay's extraordinary "reading accounts" while in India. For a thirteen-month period beginning in December 1834, Macaulay notes that he read "Aeschylus twice; Sophocles twice; Euripides once; Pindar twice; Callimachus; Apollonius Rhodius; Quintus Calaber; Theocritus twice; Herodotus; Thucydides; almost all Xenophon's works; almost all Plato; Aristotle's Poetics, and a good deal of his Organon, besides dipping elsewhere in him; the whole of Plutarch's Lives; about half of Lucian; two or three books of Athenaeus; Plautus twice; Terence twice; Lucretius twice; Catullus; Tibullus; Propentius; Lucan; Statius; Silius Italicus; Livy; Vellenius Paterculus; Sallust; Caesar and, lastly, Cicero" (32). Jonathan Arac refers to Macaulay's rereading and love of classical literature in making a case for Macaulay as both an "archaic cultural icon" and a "modern individual subject" ("Peculiarities" 197).

lary, civil method of developing discipline and maintaining power. This method depends upon a class of civil servants trained in an English public-school curriculum.

In a related expression of this second, hegemonic stage of colonialism that initiates civil structures of control, Macaulay, in his well-known 1835 "Minute" on Indian Education (discussed more fully in Chapter 4), demands the creation of "a class who may be interpreters between us and the millions whom we govern; a class of persons, Indian in blood and colour, but English in taste, in opinions, in morals and in intellect" (729). Although no Indian entered the Civil Service until 1864, Macaulay, in 1835, calls for a class of native civil servants, trained in British methods of administration and culturally formed by British androcentric ruling-class ideals propagated at Oxford and Cambridge (Spear 180). Obviously, Macaulay could not have possessed the political prescience to see that his calls for an educated class of "native" bureaucrats would, in part, lead to the removal of the educators. Nor could he have foreseen that the implementation of his call for a uniform code of laws, included in the July 1833 speech, was partly instrumental in the events of 1947. The existing legal system, according to Macaulay, clearly needed reformation: Hindu law, Mohammedan law, Parsi law, English law, are all, as he puts it, "perpetually mingling with each other and disturbing each other, varying with the person, varying with the place" (713–14)—a state of affairs that would horrify Gabriel Betteredge, master of the pantry and laundry book, those exemplary records of the perfected discipline of the Verinder household.[17] The uniform code of laws for India was, of course, drafted mainly by Macaulay himself as Legal Member of the Supreme Council from 1834 to 1838, and the legal profession in India was thus established on a predominantly British model.

Concluding his dazzling rhetorical performance with what Eric Stokes terms "a torrent of eloquence" (45),[18] Macaulay mandates the education of Indian natives so that they may become customers for British goods, as well as efficient servants of the imperial enterprise: "To trade with civilised men is infinitely more profitable than to govern

[17] In this connection, see D. A. Miller, *The Novel and the Police*, chap. 2: "From *roman policier* to *roman-police:* Wilkie Collins's *The Moonstone*."

[18] Macaulay wrote to his sister Hannah on 11 July 1833 that an old member of the House of Commons praised him as follows: "Sir, having heard that speech may console the young people for never having heard Mr. Burke" (Trevelyan, *Life and Letters* 225).

savages" (717). As many historians of the British Raj have observed, the socioeconomic change from Indian self-sufficiency to a dependence on British goods, particularly cotton, proved as binding a form of subjugation as abandoning the vernacular in favor of the English language.[19] Governing savages can be done with brute force, but civilizing them requires Europeans trained in the practice of civil invasion; needless to say, the government of savages belongs to the dominant phase of imperialism, and the civilization of them belongs to that of the hegemonic. Macaulay is an originator of the political foundations of the latter phase, and the closing passages of his Charter speech cast Britain as selfless benefactor to "a great people whom God has committed to our charge." British rulers owe to the Indian ruled "the most sacred duties" of education in freedom and civilization; duty demands that the colonizer give "knowledge" to the colonized so that "the public mind of India may expand" under the British system until it matures, guided by the firm, paternalistic, and not so invisible hand of empire. These are Macaulay's concluding questions: "Are we to keep the people of India ignorant in order that we may keep them submissive? Or do we think we can give them knowledge without awakening ambition?" (717). Making some adroit rhetorical moves that justify British control through prediction of its glorious relinquishment, he pragmatically ventures that "The sceptre may pass away from us."[20]

Later in the century, as I have already suggested, the figure who came to play some part in arranging the passing of the scepter is the British-educated native civil servant: the babu, a subaltern figure trained in the practices of cultural translation who is produced by the empire for its maintenance and reproduction.[21] Coached by the British professional

---

[19] See, especially, Stanley Wolpert, who observes that as the demand for Indian cloth diminished in London and Lancashire and as Britain stepped up the export of cheap, machine-made cottons to India, a "quiet revolution from economic self-sufficiency to foreign dependence" occurred (214). In a useful essay about the central significance of India to the British economy in the nineteenth century, R. J. Moore notes that the "possession of India was vitally important in the success of the Lancashire cotton industry, the key to Britain's emergence as the workshop of the mid-nineteenth-century world" ("India and the British Empire" 76).

[20] See William A. Madden for discussion of Macaulay's rhetorical styles, one of which he associates with his "pragmatic cast of mind": "This habit of mind appears everywhere in Macaulay's prose and affects his handling of almost every topic of which he treats" ("Macaulay's Style" 132).

[21] "Babu" is a Hindi word, whose first deployment by the British, according to the *OED*, was in 1782. A title of respect in Hindi, roughly signifying "Mr." or "Esquire," "babu" was used by the British to refer to a native clerk who wrote in English.

class of teachers, lawyers, and missionaries resident in India in the Victorian period, the babu becomes pivotal in the orderly administration of territories being rapidly acquired and incorporated into the Victorian imperial system.[22] Ironically, of course, the babu also participates, albeit unconsciously, in a process of recording and thus transforming his own land and culture similar to that described by Stephen Greenblatt, whereby colonized territories and territories are "brought into the light for study, discipline, correction, transformation." The subaltern babu figure in India may be said to have been trained in a master language of imperial administration, which he then repeated, politically redefined, and eventually deployed for the purpose of overturning that administration. This development is similar to that described by Homi Bhabha in his reading of native repetition of missionary teaching. For Bhabha, working from a poststructuralist Derridean perspective, the sign of colonial authority is continually defined and redefined through its repetition of the process of differentiating itself from the colonized "other." The subaltern figure interrogates the master text in such a manner that the colonizing power must endlessly re-form itself against the native de-forming mimic countertext. As Bhabha observes, "the colonial presence is always ambivalent, split between its appearance as original and authoritative and its articulation as repetition and difference" ("Signs" 169). In representing empire, either explicitly as a chosen subject, say in *Kim*, or implicitly as an assumed aspect of Victorian life, say in *Vanity Fair*, the novels, letters, essays, and other texts that constitute a discourse of empire contain within themselves their own unsettling potential.[23]

[22] Kenneth Ballhatchet, in his study of race and sexual politics in India under the British Raj, observes that the "justification of foreign rule was generally assumed to be that it was bringing not only material but moral progress" (123). He quotes from the *Friends of India*, which suggested in 1835 that Indians should be edified at "conversation parties," where, " 'With very small expense, they might in this way be brought under the full power of the courtesy and intelligence of superior minds' " (12). Ballhatchet notes that by the second half of the nineteenth century, Indians had seen enough of British rule to realize the hypocrisy of such plans for cultural elevation of the so-called native. It is interesting to see how Karl Marx unhesitatingly endorsed the project of the British Raj to civilize its colonized subjects: "From the Indian natives, reluctantly and sparingly educated at Calcutta, under English superintendence, a fresh class is springing up, endowed with the requirements for government and imbued with European science" ("The Future Results of the British Rule in India" 320–21).

[23] As Edward Said argues, with Austen's *Mansfield Park* as his example, because empire is often taken for granted in the English novel and therefore requires no articulated representation "we can interpret Sir Thomas's power to come and go in Antigua as stemming from the muted national

In the waning days of empire, some hundred years after Macaulay's speech about the proper administration of India and not long before independence in 1947, the British Colonial Service still did not falter in its training of a professional class of administrators whose secular mission it was to civilize, and thus transform, the natives into compliant servants of empire. In the dark and early days of the Second World War, for example, men and women (mostly men) left bomb-cratered London with its rationing, its air-raid sirens, and its tube stations converted into bomb shelters, for jobs as district commissioners, education officers, and station magistrates in such places as Kenya, Tanganyika, Rangoon, and Bombay. In 1940, Lord Lloyd, the then colonial secretary, addressed such a group, composed of young officers about to assume appointments in various colonies: "You are not going to have a soft job. You will indeed have plenty of hard work and not too many of the comforts of life, and quite possibly no lack of danger, but I know you would not have it otherwise. . . . In what other task can you have so much power so early? You can at the age of twenty-five be the father of your people: you can drive the road, bridge the river, and water the desert; you can be the arm of justice and the hand of mercy to millions. You can, in fact, serve England" (Callaway 12).

Resonant with Kipling's evocation of the "White Man's Burden" and freighted with the close call of a Battle of and for Britain, the colonial secretary's remarks glorify a profession demanding considerable sacrifice in exchange for considerable power. Here, serving England means hard work, few comforts, some dangers; in return, young men become "fathers" of "their people," surrogates for George VI in the outposts of His Majesty's Empire. Moreover, this call for young men to take up Kipling's burden of being a "white man" in a dark place is characterized by a dominant Victorian figure: that of clearing the wilderness. The 1940 call to bridge rivers, water deserts, and dispense justice and mercy to millions brings to mind, most immediately, the noble ambitions of Tennyson's Arthur, who drives out the "heathen," fells the forest, and makes "Broad pathways for the hunter and the knight." Rather less comfortably, it reminds us of Carlyle's denigration in his "Occasional Discourse on the Nigger Question" (1849) of the black West Indi-

---

experience of individual identity, behavior, and 'ordination' enacted with such irony and taste at Mansfield Park. The task is to lose neither a true historical sense of the first, nor a full enjoyment or appreciation of the second, all the while seeing both" (*Culture and Imperialism* 97).

ans who allow their islands to produce "mere jungle, savagery, poison-reptiles and swamp-malaria," while "the noble elements of cinnamon, sugar, coffee, pepper black and gray" lie, as he puts it, "all asleep, waiting the white enchanter who should say to them, Awake!" (484).[24]

What we hear, then, in the 1940 rhetoric of the British colonial secretary is a language of self-effacement and dedication to service, of a subjectivity achieved through transformation of peoples unacquainted with "justice" and "mercy." It is also a language thoroughly male in its promise to young British men of becoming patriarchal rulers, and it resonates with Macaulay's call, in his androcentric rhetoric of empire, for superior minds to engage in the traditionally male-dominated activities of governing, trading, and guiding the expansion of the Indian mind to maturity. In Macaulay's extraordinary Charter speech of 1833, in the colonial secretary's exhortations of 1940, and in the prominent Victorian image of clearing the wilderness, the moral transformation of India, the assumption of political "fatherhood" of indigenous peoples, and the work of redeeming the waste land, are all, emphatically, male tasks and responsibilities. The letters of Emily Eden provide an excellent opportunity to hear a woman's voice speaking contrapuntally to Macaulay's master text of invasion.[25] To be sure, Eden's critique is voiced from a wry, ruling-class perspective, and this perspective may account, in part, for her criticism of a Whig obsession with bureaucratic order; for Eden, Macaulay's imperial world is one peopled by the dull middle class doing its dull Evangelical duty. More interesting, what she seems intuitively to understand, and he unselfconsciously does not, is a process defined and identified by Gayatri Spivak as "worlding."

---

[24] Suvendrini Perera has noted that Carlyle's essay is a document "so unreasoned and unrelenting in its invective that his twentieth-century adherents have conspired to exempt it from scholarly examination" (11). Despite my inclination to view conspiracy theories with some suspicion, it is certainly remarkable that "Occasional Discourse" has received virtually no attention from Carlyle's critics.

[25] Most scholars conducting research in the British archives of colonial and imperial writing discover little in the way of sustained opposition spoken by native figures in the first half of the nineteenth century. Gayatri Spivak, perhaps most notably in her attempt to locate the absence of a voice for a Rani of Sirmur who performed *sati* in the early days of the British Raj, has explored at some length this theoretical difficulty. See "The Rani of Sirmur: An Essay in Reading the Archives." In the reading that has produced this book, I have found a fair amount of criticism of imperialism spoken from within its political and textual structures, of which Emily Eden's skeptical assessment is but one example.

CONTRAPUNTAL VOICES

According to Spivak, so that the unnamed, uncontoured "other" may be rendered suitable and pliable material for Eurocentric cultural transformation, it must also be constituted as barbaric, anarchic, chaotic: in effect, "native." Spivak terms this discursive activity "worlding," a process whereby the economic nature of imperialism is mystified into an ideology of civilization of the barbaric peoples. Compelled by the internal workings of its own self-justifying ideology, imperialism must create the other as *human,* and, therefore, as capable of cultural and moral transformation ("Three Women's Texts" 267). Given Eden's social class and historical moment, it is understandable that in her letters we do not hear a voice speaking on behalf of indigenous peoples or in the absence of those peoples; nevertheless, we hear a voice unsettlingly aware of that group and also alert to the astonishing fact that a tiny group of Europeans controlled virtually half a subcontinent. In the complex "writing the nation" performed by Macaulay and Eden, her voice provides an alternative and adjacent narrative to his, ambivalent and disjunctive where his is assured and consistent. Moreover, her contrapuntal narrative opens up the possibility of other narratives, of other voices, of other eyes upon empire. This possibility arrives, I think, as a disruptive surprise in the letters of the sister of a governor-general of India.

On one level, Macaulay and Eden are similar in their strong criticism of the way the British were doing things in India in the early part of the nineteenth century. Both participate in the critique of a cash-nexus materialism that they, with others, perceived as the driving force of empire. But, as I have suggested, they are also very different from one another: one instructs from the Houses of Parliament, the other wonders about that instruction from a luxurious encampment in India. Without question, these differences stem from the forms of social and discursive power dictated by Victorian gender politics. Clearly, Victorian men were more likely than women to make speeches in the House of Commons since there *were* no women in Parliament; obviously Victorian men were far more likely to possess the astonishing familiarity with classical learning exhibited by Macaulay than were women since women were not given his kind of education; and House of Commons speeches were more likely than private letters to authorize the military and civil practices of imperialism. Macaulay's speech belongs to the indisputably male genre of public parliamentary performance. Eden's letters belong to the conventionally female genre of private confidence. Cooperative with the British Raj that promotes her privilege, yet caustic about the manner in which the British Raj exercises its immense authority, she implicitly questions Macaulay's speech and may be said to muddle the high seriousness with which he delivers it to the nation.

Published under the title *Up the Country* in 1866, Eden's letters were written to her sister between October 1837 when the governor general left Calcutta to tour the Upper Provinces and February 1840 when he returned two and a half years later. Vivid in their description of public places and private manners, they display a tart sensibility at variance with that prescribed for women at the height of the Victorian period. Eden is very much a clever Regency figure, a witty chronicler of the imperial scene, even when perpetuating a "worlded" sense of India: assessing Anglo-Indian society, she concludes, "A great many of the [British] men here have lived in the jungles for years, and their poor dear manners are utterly gone—jungled out of them" (70).

The Anglo-Indian experience that Macaulay regards as resolutely dedicated to "a reconstruction of a decomposed society" is viewed by Eden rather differently: "How some of these young men must detest their lives," she observes when describing the scene at a small station at the beginning of her journey. Her tone is uncharitable in describing those doing their improving duty to the empire: "There are three married residents: one lady has bad spirits . . . and she has never been seen; another has weak eyes, and wears a large shade the size of a common verandah; and the other has bad health, and has had her head shaved. [False hair] is not to be had here for love or money, so she wears a brown silk cushion with a cap pinned to the top of it. The Doctor . . . goes every morning to hear causes between natives about strips of land or a few rupees . . . rides about an uninhabited jungle until seven; dines, reads a magazine, or a new book when he can afford one, and then goes to bed" (7-8).

As Eden encounters situations less amenable to dry dismissal, her voice becomes more somber, less ironic. The starving districts of Cawnpore move her to evoke a wilderness of suffering and natural disaster immutable in the face of British will, scenes that are eerily suggestive of late-twentieth-century visual documentations of famine and genocide: "You cannot conceive the horrible sights we see, particularly children; perfect skeletons in many cases, their bones through their skin, without a rag of clothing, and utterly unlike human creatures" (65). Despite government-dispersed food for those unable to work, the natives continue to die, and she is moved to relate a bizarre fantasy that fractures Macaulay's supple transformations of imperial greed into imperial benevolence:

> Perhaps two thousand years hence, when the art of steam is forgotten, and nobody can exactly make out the meaning of the old English word "mail coach," some black Governor-General of England will be marching through its southern provinces, and will go and look at some ruins, and doubt whether London ever was a large town, and will feed some white-looking skeletons, and say what distress the poor creatures must be in; they will really eat rice and curry; and his sister will write to her Mary D. at New Delhi, and complain of the cold, and explain to her with great care what snow is, and how the natives wear bonnets, and then, of course, mention that she wants to go home. (66–67)

Victorian writing about the British Raj rarely advances the alarming possibility that racial roles could be reversed. To think of this possibility is to admit the root meaning of imperialism: the acquisition, subjugation, and exploitation by one racial or national group of the territory, people, and resources of another. To be sure, to picture a reversal of the master-slave relationship fails to address the moral meaning of such a relationship, regardless of who is slave and who is master. But to expect such interrogation is, I think, to make ahistorical and perhaps self-regarding demands; if one takes into consideration Eden's historical moment, her cultural situation, and her position as sister of the governor general, it is remarkable enough that she understands imperialism as power not as duty, that she unravels Macaulay's narrative of military intrusion and moral transformation, and unsettles powerful early nineteenth-century ideas about racial difference and superiority.

As the months of Eden's journey with her brother go by, her letters tend to become increasingly critical of Anglo-Indian snobbery and racialism. She explains to her sister that Anglo-Indians despise the racially mixed clerks, the babu figures who constitute the class of bureaucratic servants of empire, translators of British Raj language, literature, and ideology to the vernacular-speaking indigenous peoples: "Very well-educated, quiet men, and many of them very highly paid; but as many of them are half castes, we, with our pure Norman or Saxon blood, cannot really think contemptuously enough of them" (140). Eden, incidentally, was not the only woman to voice this kind of uneasiness. For example, Julia Maitland writing from Madras between 1836 and 1839, virtually at the same time as Eden, observes that the natives "are a cringing set, and behave to us English as if they were the dirt under our feet, and indeed we give them reason to suppose we consider them as such. Their civility is disagreeable, but the rudeness and contempt with which the English treat them are quite painful to witness" (40). And neither was it solely women who voiced a sociopolitical criticism, just as it was not solely men who discursively waved the union jack, as I shall show in my discussion of the Anglo-Indian novelist Maud Diver. As evidence of a kind of gender equality in social criticism, it is interesting to note that Bishop Heber, traveling in Northern India in 1825, was appalled by an "exclusive and intolerant spirit" displayed by the English. He finds them foolish, surly, bullying, and insolent in their dealings with Indians (249).

Toward the end of her letters, on 25 May 1839, Eden discloses a remarkable perception of the fragility and sheer implausibility of the British enterprise. She describes a ball held in Simla, the hill town that later became the cool center of Anglo-Indian summer life. It is held in celebration of the young queen's recent coronation. The English dine under magnificent tents, watching fireworks and illuminations of "Victoria" and "God Save the Queen."

> Twenty years ago no European had ever been here, and there we were, with the band playing the "Puritani" and "Masaniello," and eating salmon from Scotland and sardines from the Mediterranean, and observing that St. Cloup's potage à la Julienne was perhaps better than his other soups, and that some of the ladies' sleeves were too tight according to the overland fashions for March, etc.; and all this in the face of those high hills, some of which have remained untrodden since the creation, and we, 105 Europeans, being surrounded by at least 3,000 mountaineers, who, wrapped up in their hill blankets, looked on at what we call our polite amusements, and bowed to the ground if a European came near them. I sometimes wonder they do not cut all our heads off, and say nothing more about it (293–94).

In almost all ways, Eden's female understanding of the British presence in India is stunningly different from that of Macaulay's. Where he sees native talent ripe for education (of a certain sort), she sees alien figures wrapped in blankets; where his voice remains steadily somber in his role as moral and cultural leader for millions of natives, she speaks multiply—as social gossip, as novelistic recorder of domestic manners, and, lastly, as detached and politically alert observer of the institution she inhabits: the British Raj.[26] In Eden's consciousness, there seems little possibility of that transformation of the natives and their culture evoked by Macaulay in 1833 and by the British colonial secretary in 1940, although she does share Macaulay's belief in some kind of native agency that is the consequence of Spivak's "worlding" (the colonized native is transformed by the colonialist imagination into a figure capable of correct and incorrect choices). Where Macaulay believes the Indians skilled enough to cooperate with the British, she believes them rebellious enough to cut off some British heads. As the history of the British Raj in the next hundred years was to show, they were both correct. Eden's perception of 3,000 Indian mountaineers watching 105 Europeans have dinner presents something different from Macaulay's narrative of an uncultivated people.[27] Hers is a glimpse of something strange, of what perches on the hillside, lies beyond the pomp and circumstance of empire. I think, too, that Eden's perception of the dark side of the Simla celebrations suggests an affiliation between Victoria's initiation into sovereignty, into her reign as supreme emblem of Victorian womanhood, and the initiation of Victorian women into a lesser reign of sacrifice for the empire.

The important difference between the letters of a ruling-class Englishwoman (the St. Cloup, incidentally, who produced the potage à la Julienne was a black chef who came out from England with Eden and her brother) and the speech of a famous Whig politician rests finally, I think, in that unsettling glimpse Eden gives us of the gulf between gov-

[26] Catherine Stevenson argues that when faced by that "dangerous continent," Africa, Victorian women travel writers "develop strategies of accommodation, not confrontation or domination, and write richly eclectic, loosely structured narratives of their discoveries about the continent, its peoples, and their own psyches" (160). Eden's adoption of multiple narratives may be seen as somewhat similar to the strategy of accommodation identified by Stevenson.

[27] For something notably similar to Eden's emphasis upon a small vulnerable European community surrounded by potentially violent Indians, see Emma Roberts's *Scenes and Characteristics of Hindostan with Sketches of Anglo-Indian Society* for an extraordinary description of a British regimental march across country. Usually moving every three years, each regimental family was accompanied by at least one hundred native troops and servants: the native officers belonging to sepoy regiments brought along their own zenanas; two bazaars accompanied the march, one for the Europeans and the other for the native troops and servants (2:138). When judges or collectors traveled the country, they were accompanied by a large party of hunting, shooting, and golfing Europeans: according to Roberts, the entourage provided "the best display of the grandeur and magnificence of India which the Asiatic style of living can produce" (2:1:165).

ernor and governed. To be sure, some of the difference I have described may be attributed to the epistolary form itself and to the actual nature of Emily Eden's life—letters, after all, permit the political ambiguity, ambivalence, and questioning that is impermissible in public rhetoric. And that effacement in public rhetoric of the privileged "I/eye" ("unheroic, unparticularized, egoless"), which Mary Louise Pratt describes in her analyses of nineteenth-century travel narratives, requires no eradication in the epistolary form, authorizing as it does a sovereign, writing self ("Scratches on the Face of the Country" 60). Moreover, nineteenth-century letter writing from the outposts of empire is indelibly characterized by an unrestrained expression of personal observation and feeling. If you are Thomas Macaulay, travel to India means you are a privileged *man* writing a code of laws from a people whom God has entrusted to your care; you are, indeed, a father to your people. If you are Emily Eden, travel to India means you are a privileged *woman* writing letters to your sister and a journal for yourself—no need to silence a voice that might call into question the moral authority of imperial invasion, no need to squelch ridicule of British Raj pomposity. Macaulay's speech and Eden's letters suggest something of the differences and incongruities that characterize Victorian writing about empire, and also the gender politics that inflects such writing. For more detailed analysis of how Victorian gender politics assists in a negotiation of the brutal material facts of Britannic rule, I want now to turn to *The Old Curiosity Shop* and *Dombey and Son,* where we find that keeping British women in their private, suffering sphere helps keep millions of "natives" in their proper, governed place.

CHAPTER TWO

THE HEART OF THE EMPIRE:
LITTLE NELL AND
FLORENCE DOMBEY DO THEIR BIT

Getting and spending, we lay waste our powers:
Little we see in Nature that is ours;
We have given our hearts away, a sordid boon!
. . . for every thing, we are out of tune;
It moves us not.
— William Wordsworth,
"The World Is Too Much with Us," 1802

Wordsworth's image of a society out of tune, discordant, laying waste its "natural" powers in favor of worldly acquisition, nowhere evokes the wealth of empire. Given the fact
that the British empire in 1802 was a very small thing compared to
what it became at the end of the century, this is not surprising, yet the
"getting and spending" he laments was created, in part, by the early-
nineteenth-century possession of lucrative Indian provinces and by the
profitable management of colonies of white settlement.[1] Wordsworth
speaks at the beginning of what has long been recognized as a complex

[1] As Sally Mitchell and James D. Startt note in *Victorian Britain: An Encyclopedia,* in 1897,
the British empire included "India, Canada, New Zealand and the states of Australia; Ashanti,
Basutoland, Bechuanaland, British East Africa, Cape Province, Gambia, the Gold Coast, Natal,
Nigeria, Nyasaland, Rhodesia, Sierra Leone, Somaliland, Uganda, and Zanzibar in Africa; Aden,
Brunei, Ceylon, Hong Kong, Labuan, the Malay Federated States, North Borneo, Papua, Sarawak,
and Singapore in Asia; the Bahamas, Barbados, British Guinea, British Honduras, the Virgin
Islands, the Falkland Islands, Jamaica, the Leeward Islands, Newfoundland, Tobago, Trinidad,
Turks and Caicos Islands, and the Windward Islands in America; the Channel Islands, Gibraltar,
the Isle of Man, and Malta in Europe; and dozens of other islands scattered about the ocean of the
world, including Ascension, Bermuda, St. Helena, Tristan da Cunha, Mauritius, the Seychelles,
Ellice, Gilbert, Southern Solomon, Fiji, Pitcairn, and Tasmania" (264).

period of economic, social, and political change in which the development of industrialized power was accompanied by revisions in class, gender, and cultural attitudes.[2] In concert with these revisions, the possession of empire began both to define British national identity and to initiate in the metropolitan imagination an examination of the price of imperial glory. Wordsworth, in a sense, sounds the first chords of an orchestrated social critique, gathering volume in the Victorian period and fathoming ways for Britain not to give her metaphorical heart away as the price of economic and imperial supremacy. My interest in this chapter is in how early Victorian writing about empire appropriates significant ideas about gender in a negotiation of the advantageous but also disruptive "getting and spending" made possible by Britain's burgeoning colonial wealth. Two of Dickens's early novels, *The Old Curiosity Shop* (1841) and *Dombey and Son* (1848), in different and varying degrees, represent particularly well the complex embrace and interrogation of imperial glory I see as a constitutive mark of early Victorian writing about Britannic rule. I have aimed to show that these two novels, in order to shape some discursive insurance that Britain's heart continues to tick steadfastly, regularly, and in rhythm with the pulse of imperial expansion, appropriate culturally available images of women as suffering, salvational figures. Gender, in other words, conjoins with race in subordinating millions of indigenous peoples to Britannic rule and maintaining women in their private sphere.

The Old Curiosity Shop anticipates in oblique form the uneasiness with mercantile colonialism that becomes a much more explicit subject of political and moral criticism in *Dombey and Son*. The torment inflicted upon Little Nell by Daniel Quilp not only foreshadows the emotional and physical cruelty heaped upon Florence Dombey by her father, it also registers Dickens's participation in an emerging discourse about Africa at the beginning of the Victorian period. Even if, unlike *Dombey and Son* and Dickens's other novels more overtly attentive to the expanding empire, *The Old Curiosity Shop* depicts no native servants, blustery majors puffed up with imperial exploits, city merchants enriched by trading with the East India Company, or characters either

---

[2] The period from 1802 to 1804 is characterized by one late-nineteenth-century historian of empire as featuring military campaigns "perhaps the most glorious in the history of the British arms in India" (Hunter, 468). Armies led by Sir Arthur Wellesley (later duke of Wellington) engaged with local rajahs and emperors, and also the French, for possession of many rich provinces. Along the way, Wellesley secured the cities of Delhi and Agra for the British.

sailing to or returning from Australia, it intimates the growth of empire in the first quarter of the nineteenth century. *The Old Curiosity Shop* also demonstrates the distaste for foreign expansion which is comically registered by Mrs. Jellyby's program for cultivating coffee "conjointly with the natives" at the settlement of Boorioboola-Gha in *Bleak House.*

Of all Dickens's novels, *Dombey and Son* is the one most directly unhappy with domestic despotism purchased with imperial wealth, and it is also the only one that provides an angelic daughter of the mercantile city as savior of a father whose misused wealth is derived from empire. Dickens peppers *Dombey* with references to colonialism as thoroughly as Major Bagstock, his complexion like stilton cheese and his eyes like prawns, peppers his food. For instance, the Major, an explosive relic of nabob culture, has performed various military exploits in the East and West Indies; Mrs. Pipchin takes in sad little boys sent home from India, one of whom plaintively asks Florence Dombey if she can give him any idea of the way back to Bengal; and the House of Dombey, according to Major Bagstock (admittedly buttering up Paul Dombey but still grounding himself in plausible actuality) "is known and honoured, in the British possessions abroad" (126). In addition, the offices of Dombey and Son stand just around the corner from the East India House, not depicted gloomily as one might expect from the novel's brilliant representation of the House's mercantile delusion that winds blow "for or against their enterprises." Rather, East India House is invested with a kind of Arabian Nights glamour, a place "teeming with suggestions of precious stuffs and stones, tigers, elephants, howdahs, hookahs, umbrellas, palm trees, palanquins, and gorgeous princes of a brown complexion sitting on carpets, with their slippers very much turned up at the toes" (32). This is an exotic India of the popular imagination whose magical immunity to mercantile corruption suggests something of the negotiations I shall explore in this chapter between acceptance of national power invested in the East India Company and a distaste for the moral bankruptcy of Dombey himself.[3]

---

[3] In suggesting that an 1847 British novel of domestic life may be seen as a labor of accommodation to empire, I am influenced, in part, by the 1950s cultural materialism of Kathleen Tillotson and Raymond Williams. In *Novels of the 1840s*, Tillotson insisted that we examine the material conditions of literary production such as serial publication, the circulating libraries, the railway station bookstall, and so on. In *Culture and Society*, Raymond Williams showed that our understanding of nineteenth-century responses to industrialization must include reference to social-problem novels and that Victorian middle-class culture produced its own appropriate literary form, "bourgeois realism." In arguing for both literary and nonliterary works as participants in

As my earlier discussion of Macaulay's political plans for India suggested, the overseas administration of a developing empire and the incorporation of its effects into the domestic fabric posed a challenge to Victorian society: how to refashion the nation to fit the acquisition of overseas territory. Two political problems emerge from this work of ideological refashioning, addressed by the novels I shall discuss in this chapter. The first concerns a morally attentive desire on the part of the middle class that the late-eighteenth-century casual exploitation of indigenous peoples under British governance be replaced by their disciplined renovation; it is this social class to whom Macaulay, in his 1833 parliamentary speech, makes his appeal, and on whom he relies for the execution of his plans for administrative and legal reform. The second problem entails the need for more conservative groups in early Victorian society to find a compromise between contesting pressures: on the one hand, a desire to enjoy the material wealth of empire, and, on the other hand, a resistance to the political and social ascendancy of the social class responsible, in part, for the production of this wealth, and hence, for the rapidly growing geopolitical and economic power of the nation.

What one sees, then, in early Victorian colonialist discourse is the erasure of a narrative of corrupt exploitation of the native by a fable of his uplifting salvation; this fable gathers ideological force throughout the Victorian period and culminates in a British twentieth-century belief that its nineteenth-century sacrifices for the empire essentially saved millions of ignorant savages from the destructive anarchy feared by Macaulay in 1833. In 1924, for example, the catalogue of the British Empire Exhibition (held at Wembley) notes that many of the "Colonies" have "brought to this country for the Exhibition representatives of the native races which have survived and prospered under our rule" (43). Lacking benevolent British government, "native races," presumably, would have wiped each other out, a fantasy consistent, generally, with the extraordinary claims made by the catalogue, the most hyperbolic of which is the assertion that "the British Empire Exhibition is a revelation of history, power and purpose such as civilisation in recorded time has never before known" (39). Dickens never flaunts such an unembarrassed claim for British cultural superiority, and if he did,

---

the textual making of Victorian empire, I have also found John Bender's theoretical approach to the eighteenth-century novel suggestive and helpful. Bender views the novel and the penitentiary as parallel "social texts" (4).

analysis of how he writes the early Victorian nation would, I suspect, make for uninteresting critical work. What is engaging about the two novels I'm going to discuss in this chapter is a discursive management of contested, imbricated attitudes toward Britannic rule. As a way of preparing the critical ground for discussion of how *The Old Curiosity Shop* and *Dombey and Son* perform this management, I want to give a sense of what Dickens inherits, of how earlier texts negotiate the political and social difficulties that become more visible, more pressing, and in his case more brilliantly resolved, in early Victorian culture. First, then, I plan to talk about Aphra Behn's *Oroonoko* (1678) and Defoe's *Robinson Crusoe* (1719) as representative fictions that convey particularly well the complex nature of writing the early colonialist nation. Next, I shall discuss certain late-eighteenth-century and Regency interrogations of empire, together with three novels that are roughly contemporaneous with *The Old Curiosity Shop* and *Dombey and Son*.

COLONIAL FANTASIES

A pastiche of exotic travel literature, Eurocentric erotic fantasy, heroic romance, and late-seventeenth-century satire of "civilized" man engaging in the "savage" practice of slavery, *Oroonoko, or The Royal Slave* sentimentally contrasts two social orders: one associated with a time before colonialist merchants enslaved noble native princes and the other situated in the aftermath of these events, the time in which the story is told.[4] Narrated by the daughter of a lieutenant governor of Surinam, *Oroonoko* laments the unfortunate fact that only a "female pen" is available to "celebrate" the fame of heroic Oroonoko (169) and insists

---

[4] The critique of mercantile colonialism propounded by Behn's sensationalist romance can be heard in Swift's *Gulliver's Travels*. Gulliver expresses his "scruples" about such practices in a speculative digression about a group of pirates' discovery of land: "they go on shore to rob and plunder, they see an harmless people, are entertained with kindness, they give the country a new name, they take formal possession of it for the king, they set up a rotten plank or a stone for a memorial, they murder two or three dozen of the natives, bring away a couple more by force for a sample, return home, and get their pardon. Here commences a new dominion acquired with a title by *divine right*. Ships are sent with the first opportunity, the natives driven out or destroyed, their princes tortured to discover their gold, a free license given to all acts of inhumanity and lust, the earth reeking with the blood of its inhabitants: and this execrable crew of butchers employed in so pious an expedition is a modern colony sent to convert and civilize an idolatrous and barbarous people" (237). David Dabydeen observes, however, that "Swift was quite happy to invest hundreds of pounds, in 1720, in the South Sea Company whose sole business at the time was to ferry African slaves to the Spanish colonies" ("Eighteenth-Century English Literature on Commerce and Slavery" 44).

that he deserves "a more sublime Wit" than that of a woman to "write his Praise" (208). The self-deprecation of the female narrator contributes to the elegiac tone of *Oroonoko* in the sense that the historical time in which the narrative is produced is one not only degraded by the loss of Oroonoko's noble spirit, but also by the absence of vigorous male literary voices to tell his story. The gender politics exhibited by this female narrator contributes, as a consequence, to a fable of social and moral degeneration brought about by a number of factors, not least of which is a loss of male literary talent. Moreover, the lamentable current state of things is made even more lamentable when recorded in a woman's sad voice of moral reproof.

An enlightened preference for a more humane social order than that presented in the bulk of Behn's novella (and one similar to the nostalgic and wishful fantasies ventured by *Dombey and Son*) is established in the opening pages as the narrator describes her first encounter with the indigenous peoples of Surinam; these are Indian natives, who maintain an amicable trading relationship with Europeans. Rather than enslaving these people, the European colonists "caress 'em with all the brotherly and friendly Affection in the World; trading with them for their Fish, Venison, Buffaloes Skins, and little Rarities" (130). With *these* people, she declares, "we live in perfect Tranquillity, and Good Understanding" (132). Immediately on the heels of this evocation of affectionate trade undisturbed by mercantile colonialism, we learn of another social system existing adjacent to it: that of slavery. "Those then whom we make use of to work in our Plantations of Sugar, are *Negroes*, Black-Slaves altogether "(133). Heroic Oroonoko, however, is no ordinary "Black Slave." He is an African prince, produced entirely by Europe in at least two ways; in the late-seventeenth-century popular imagination, he emerges from British fantasies of exotic savage cultures, and in the plot itself he graduates, so to speak, from an astonishing education he has received from a French duke exiled to Africa for heresy. Captured by an English slave trader and brought to Surinam, he is sold to a Cornishman, renamed Caesar, takes to killing tigers and speaking Indian languages, and becomes beloved and admired by all who meet him, although he remains the property of the Cornishman. As the narrative works breathlessly to a conclusion, Oroonoko leads a rebellion against the cruelty of the European overseers, is tortured in the most explicit terms, and is finally dismembered, his bravery preserved in the sentimental prose of the female narrator.

The significant colonialist myth produced by this overheated tale is the establishment of a fabulous time when indigenous peoples and Europeans were able to live together sweetly, exchanging gifts and observing each other's quaint customs; Europeans voyaged to the West Indies not with profitable sugar plantations in mind, but with a desire to live peacefully alongside the natives. No slaves travel the Middle Passage and no Wordsworthian "heart" is given away.[5] No aggressive middle class, empowered by colonial wealth, invades the established social order. While I agree with Moira Ferguson's observation that *Oroonoko*'s "abolitionist and empancipationist" position is undermined by what she sees as Behn's inflammation of Eurocentric attitudes toward Africans (49), I want to make it clear that I am not arguing for a kind of infidelity on Behn's part to verifiable historical actuality. The sustained sheer implausibility of *Oronooko* suggests the inappropriateness of identifying one part of the text as more faithful than another to seventeenth-century Africa. Behn's steamy mix of violence and eroticism is designed, I think, to produce a fable of beneficent colonialism that in effect justifies that practice. In *Robinson Crusoe*, colonialism is implicitly justified through the prolonged suffering of the ideal colonialist, Crusoe himself, who long before critics began to read Defoe's novel as colonialist discourse was termed by Ian Watt to be in possession of the "calculating gaze of a colonial capitalist" (316).

As all of Defoe's readers will recollect, *Robinson Crusoe* begins in the "foundering" disaster upon an island near Trinidad and ends with the establishment of a colony. Just as Crusoe seeds his island with barley and rice, domesticates a flock of goats, and creates a forest, so finally, his pious frugality generates a small group of colonizers. In general, his punctilious self-awareness (the ledger of blessings and punishments, for example) and his superb self-reliance make him an ideal model for Victorian would-be colonists, an individual certain to flourish, say, in the Australia evoked by Charles Rowcroft's *Tales of the Colonies*. In addition, his experiences resolve an inherent political tension in colonialist practice, particularly as it develops in the Victorian period.[6] His work of building a colony and writing the British colonial nation originates in rebellion against the established patriarchal order: "a *Memento*

---

[5] In discussing the eighteenth-century slave trade, Peter Fryer notes that "To pay for slaves, Britain's manufacturing industries sent their products to the African coast . . . the yearly value of British manufactured goods exported to Africa soared from 83,000 pounds in 1710 to 401,000 pounds in 1787. These goods were bartered for human beings on what was then known as the Guinea Coast" (7).

[6] For a discussion of the popularity of *Robinson Crusoe* in the Victorian age, see Richard D. Altick, *The English Common Reader*, and William J. Palmer, "Dickens and Shipwreck."

to those who are touched with the general Plague of Mankind . . . that of not being satisfy'd with the Station wherein God and Nature has plac'd them" (152), he becomes, through being infected with this "Plague," extraordinarily rich. The wealth accumulated in an isolation that would have driven a less fabulously constructed individual entirely mad reconciles a familiar problematic of bourgeois individualism.[7] On the one hand, the individual is licensed to acquire competitively wealth and property, yet, on the other, is instructed according to Christian ethics to love his neighbor as himself. In the amazing world of *Robinson Crusoe*, bourgeois individualism does not lead to anarchy and violence, and Crusoe is both punished and rewarded for the competitive assertiveness that is a mainspring of invasive colonialism.

From the perspective of colonialist discourse, what is lamented in *Oroonoko* is omitted from *Robinson Crusoe:* the historical actuality of Britain's eighteenth-century Atlantic economy, wherein traders bought slaves in Africa, sold them in the West Indies, and returned to England with the sugar of the Caribbean slave plantations. Crusoe's fictive accumulation of wealth while suffering on his island occurs adjacently to the actual suffering of countless enslaved Africans. As David Dabydeen points out, a large proportion of eighteenth-century wealth "was derived from the traffic in human beings, the buying and selling of African peoples and the enforced labour of these peoples" (27). But if Defoe's novel omits this traffic, it does, of course, provide Crusoe with an affectionate slave in the form of Friday, and it is the arrival of Friday that shows colonial self-construction demands more than the bourgeois individualism to be found in Defoe's novel. Without the footprint that suggests the colonizer's invasion is inevitably accompanied by a symbolic counterinvasion of the colonized into the space and mind of the colonizer, colonizing Crusoe is incomplete.[8] Complete, then, as colonizer, he peoples his island with men, women, and children and ascends to full patriarchal sovereignty. In this process of circular accumulation of colonial/patriarchal power, Crusoe defies his father, is thrown into

[7] As John Richetti observes of Crusoe, "He has only innocently fought for his life but has been rewarded with great wealth he did not directly seek. That is a perfect and beautifully appropriate conclusion for a capitalist hero, combining freedom and innocence in a manner rather difficult to achieve in the real economic world" (61-62).

[8] J. M. Coetzee's *Foe* takes the historical and psychological realities necessarily evaded in Defoe's colonial fantasy and makes them its explicit subject. Essentially, *Foe* explores and revises the concept of a subjectivity achieved through telling one's story, and, by association, the concept of a nation writing itself in the solipsistic narratives of self-engenderment.

isolation on the island and intruded upon by Friday's footprint and then by Friday himself in the trope of invasion and counterinvasion; he "worlds" Friday in a manner similar to that described by Gayatri Spivak, so that he may construct him as savage "other" and thus name and enslave him (however benevolently), fights off cannibals, and finally returns home to England, accompanied by his pliable savage who has learned to mimic many of his gestures. Friday thus becomes a fictive ancestor of all the natives transported to the metropolitan center of empire, a group viewed with some dismay not only by the ladies' room attendant in Claridge's Hotel but by an upper-class Englishwoman writing in 1865. Traveling in the West Indies, Emelia Gurney marveled at the attractiveness of the black natives of St. Thomas; she finds them pleasingly "different from the dismal blacks about the streets of London" and attributes this to "their complete blackness and their projecting mouths" having been "mitigated by the mixture of another race."[9]

If, in the early eighteenth century, Britain's colonial practices are both appropriated for adventure fiction and made benevolent in the appropriation, then toward the end of the century, her more fully developed colonial power, particularly in India, becomes an object of satire. In Samuel Foote's 1778 comedy, *The Nabob*, for example, we find an early literary form of Victorian accommodation to mercantile colonialism.

The Nabob ridicules Sir Matthew Mite, freshly returned from India, a volatile and fiercely yellow complexioned man who berates his florist, Mrs. Crocus, for bringing him a bunch of jonquils. The apoplectic ancestor of Jos Sedley in *Vanity Fair* and Major Bagstock in *Dombey and Son*, and the comic butt of ruling-class society, Sir Matthew proposes marriage to one of the daughters of the Oldham family (promising to find husbands for her sisters in Madras and Calcutta). His wooing, and his attempt to buy his way into the upper crust by presenting valuable Eastern objects to the Antiquarian Society, are greeted with derision by Lady Oldham: "Preceded by all the pomp of Asia, Sir Matthew Mite, from the Indies, came thundering amongst us, and, profusely scattering the spoils of ruined provinces, corrupted the virtue and alienated

---

[9] Gurney journeyed to the West Indies as the wife of a member of the government commission investigating causes of the 1865 rebellions in Jamaica and their controversial repression by Governor Eyre. David Dabydeen cites various sources for estimates of the number of black people in Britain in the second half of the eighteenth century: in 1768, the figure was thought to be twenty thousand. Dabydeen quotes the *Daily Journal* of 5 April 1723 as reporting that "Tis said there is a great Number of Blacks come daily in this City, so that 'tis thought in a short Time, if they not be suppress'd, the City will swarm with them" (47).

the affections of all the old friends to the family" (Act I). In Foote's play, the ruling-class Oldham family is both hypocritical and deluded. Caring not a fig for "ruined provinces," they believe themselves untainted by colonial wealth. The comic irony of the play depends upon the fact that this family is in debt to Sir Matthew and must eventually, in their acceptance of him, also accept their dependence upon Britain's burgeoning empire for their social privilege, just as Dickens's socially conservative readers are assisted to an acceptance of a newly rich middle class that is bringing home the imperial wealth.[10] Both ridiculed and embraced, Sir Matthew Mite undergoes humiliation as an expression of the social difficulties presented to an established metropolitan culture by the developing wealth of empire.

At the beginning of the nineteenth century, Foote's comic accommodation becomes a bitter mockery of the materialism exhibited by Sir Matthew and his fellow Nabobs. The object of amusement in *The Nabob*, money making in India, becomes the object of biting satire in what is probably the most fully articulated and visually elaborate of attacks upon wealth derived from the British Raj. The Hudibrastic poem entitled *The Grand Master, Or Adventures of Qui Hi? in Hindostan*, with illustrations by Thomas Rowlandson, was published anonymously in 1816. *The Grand Master* narrates the miserable experiences of a cadet who goes to India, is named "Qui Hi?" by his companions who overhear a prostitute call this out to him (which means, roughly, "Who's Your Mother?"), is scorned by the English community, and is finally ruined by debt, dissipation, and venereal disease. Macaulay could well have derived his picture of an early-nineteenth-century dissolute Anglo/Indian society from *The Grand Master*, conceding as he does in the 1833 House of Commons speech that "there was too much foundation for the representations of those satirists and dramatists who held up the character of the English Nabob to the derision and hatred of a former generation" (704).[11] The poem mercilessly bombards the material foundation of Britain's colonial and imperial practices, with the East India Com-

---

[10] It is important to note, however, that not all nabobs were automatically the object of ridicule in eighteenth-century drama: Sir Oliver Surface, for example, in Sheridan's *School for Scandal*, is a benevolent and excellent figure who, for the fifteen years he was amassing his fortune in India, was also sending money back to London to support his ungrateful nephew, Joseph Surface.

[11] The wife of an army officer traveling in India in the late 1840s observes that "The extravagant profusion in which the British in India formerly lived, is now almost unknown. An officer told me, that when he entered the service, as cornet, he thought it necessary to have a set of silver dishes, covers, and wall shades!" (Mackenzie, *Life in the Mission, the Camp, and the Zenana* 2:266)

A NEW MAP OF INDIA FROM THE LATEST AUTHORITY.

From Thomas Rowlandson, *The Grand Master or Adventures of Qui Hi?* (1816). By permission of the British Library Oriental and India Office Collections, V2179.

pany as its principal comic target. In the text and Rowlandson's wonderful illustrations, an obscenely overloaded elephant symbolizes the Company:

> That elephant in all its pride,
> On which THE *Burea Sahib* does ride,
> Is by AMBITION's fetters tied.
> The *brute's o'erloaded,* and *they all*
> You'll *shortly see,* will get a fall.
>
> (Canto I)

This monstrous creature is laden with the paraphernalia of the Company, its body covered with the loot hoarded by grotesque versions of the worldly officials denounced by Macaulay:

> Casks of rupees, and debts, and charters,
> Cargoes of beer, and boots, and garters;
> Some hundred weight of cheese, just rotten

And bales of damag'd Indian cotton;
Two *barons,* coronets, and mitre,
Could make the burthen nothing lighter.
                                    (Canto I)

Some thirty years or so after the publication of this searing indictment
of the East India Company, Dickens's moral critique of Paul Dombey
depends for its political punch on his business affiliation with this institution. At Edith and Dombey's first dinner party, for instance, "sundry
eastern magnates" are in prominent attendance, and the first to arrive
is an "East India Director, of immense wealth." At the time Dickens
was writing *Dombey,* the East India Company, although no longer in
possession of its trading monopoly, was still a major force in spreading
commercial culture throughout the Indian subcontinent. Trading under
a charter granted by Elizabeth I on December 31, 1599, from its inception, the Company had maintained a militia and enlisted Indian troops
in protecting its trading ports. By the middle of the nineteenth century, the Company had created three separate native armies in India:
the Bengal, the Madras, and the Bombay, all officered by Europeans,
and in addition to the Queen's regiments and the Company's European
army. The presence of these armies accounts, in large part, for the fact
that the majority of early Victorian travel narratives about India were
produced by the wives of army officers.

According to Philip Curtin, it was the "rivalry between English and
French that set the English East India Company on the course that
led to a gradual transition from trading-post empire to real, territorial
control" (*Cross-Cultural Trade* 231). Defeating the French at Plassey in
1757, the British rapidly increased their acquisition of land and revenue.
In the early nineteenth century, banks, insurance companies, railways,
telegraphs, and new institutions such as the managing agency (it is to
the House of Dombey's managing agency in Barbados that Walter Gay
is dispatched to get him out of the way of Florence) flourished along
with the old trading order. In the 1840s, British officials dominated
India through mercantile alliances with local Indian rulers and administrative control by British Residents in the remote and less profitable
regions, those civil officials ridiculed and pitied by Emily Eden. Remarkably, in the period from 1840 to 1875, trade with India rose from
five million pounds annually to twenty-four million pounds annually;
Dombey's fictional power is derived from this economic actuality, and

his fictional wealth produces the solidifying hegemony of British rule in India and is produced by it.[12]

The bare thematic bones of what is complicated by Dickens's brilliant conjunction of domestic politics and wealth derived from affiliation with the East India Company in *Dombey* is apparent in three novels about the British Raj and the Company published in the 1840s and 1850s. They are *Peregrine Pultuney; Or, Life in India,* by John William Kaye (1844); *The Wetherbys, Father and Son; Or, Sundry Chapters of Indian Experience,* by John Lang (1853); and *Oakfield; or, Fellowship in the East* (1854), by William D. Arnold.

Peregrine Pultuney rather ploddingly relates the eponymous hero's romantic adventures and is far more engaging when it provides authoritative detail about taking up India as a career. (Kaye also wrote a fascinating work dealing with the Indian practice of thuggee whose suppression by the British will be discussed in Chapter Four.) The hero's father calls on "his friend the director" (1:23) to get him into the East India Company's "military seminary" and the plot thus evolves from a persistent middle-class preoccupation in the Victorian period: what to do with one's sons, or as is the case in *David Copperfield,* what to do with troublesome young men. In *Copperfield,* David recounts that Annie Strong's feckless cousin, Jack Maldon, is sent to India, just as at the end of *Hard Times* the sullen ingrate Tom Gradgrind is dispatched to the colonies, his banishment from so-called civilized society already figured in the disguise devised for him by Mr. Sleary—a comic servant in blackface, his "disgraceful grotesqueness" revealed in the partly worn-away blacking that gives him "the hands of a monkey" (284). Jack Maldon is waved off with these encouraging words, "The winds you are going to tempt, have wafted thousands upon thousands to fortune" (244). David, however, tends to see India less as a site of individual advancement and more as the gorgeous fantasy prompted by the words "East India House" in *Dombey and Son,* and he recalls that he saw Jack "as a modern Sinbad, and pictured him the bosom friend of all the Rajahs in the East, sitting under canopies, smoking curly golden pipes" (243-

---

[12] See Ramkrishna Mukherjee for a comprehensive history of the East India Company. R. J. Moore points out that from 1857 until 1914, "Britain managed India's finances so as to meet the needs of British trade, investment, employment, and imperial defence or expansion. . . . In essence, the *Raj* depended upon wringing a surplus from an overwhelmingly agricultural economy, and once the costs of empire were met there was very little left for India's development or to provide for the contingencies of famine and depression" (81).

44). Rather more prosaically, the hero of *Peregrine Pultuney* goes out
to Calcutta, undergoes romantic and military adventures (less devastat-
ing than those satirized in *The Grand Master*), and returns to England
bored by India. He sums up his Indian career as "desultory" but then
announces casually that "Life in India is always desultory" (3:330–31).
Kaye's novel seems most concerned (and most lively when it does so)
with offering precise instructions about how to get on in India and
in deflating the schoolboy glamour with which Dickens puffs up the
British Raj. Perhaps because Kaye's novel propounds no moralistic view
of empire and is therefore uninterested in any kind of ideological accommodation to it, *Peregrine Pultuney* can forthrightly represent the
practical benefits and tedious side effects of British life in India.

   The Wetherbys, initially serialized in *Fraser's Magazine*, is even more
didactic, offering practical ways to make money while building up the
empire. The narrator, the son of a captain in a Bengal regiment, relates
how his father amasses a small fortune for himself through controlling
supplies for the regiment, ordering books for the cantonment library,
directing the local bank, and snagging the local ice concession. He confides to his readers that the debts of "officers in the army of the East
India Company have so frequently formed a topic of discussion in the
English newspapers" that he resolved to provide some firsthand information. In *The Wetherbys*, young officers borrow from local banks to pay
off gambling, wine, and cigar debts, many die of drink, and army wives
are unfaithful in the hills. In general, in a manner that recalls Emily
Eden's skeptical if less dramatic assessment of life up the country, the
novel provides an unrelenting recital of the miseries of army careers
governed by corruption and lust. Part morality tale similar to the satiric
Grand Master of 1816 and part how-to-make-money-in-India manual,
The Wetherbys, implies, in effect, that if a young man acquires the sexual
and fiscal discipline lacking in the novel's feckless characters, private
fortunes may be made in concert with a public expansion of Britannic rule.

   William Arnold's *Oakfield* also indicts the materialistic marriage of
the British Raj and the East India Company that is satirized in *The
Grand Master*, but from the perspective of high moral superiority. In a
series of letters to his sister, the narrator describes a British India given
over to wholesale money making: "I came out here six months ago with
a vague hope of finding some great work going on. . . . It was a painful
thing to find oneself suddenly in the midst of a society, horrible, mon-

strous" (1:117). The East India Company is excoriated for its "beaver tendencies. . . . There is an utter want of nobleness in the government of India; it still retains the mark of its commercial origin; we see every year, in England, the evils of a merely commercial spirit, developing themselves in selfishness, in coarseness, in cowardly shrinking from brave endurance. . . . The evil is the money-getting earthly mind" (2:223). If the narrator of *The Wetherbys* aligns himself, in a sense, with Emily Eden's skeptical voice, then the narrator of *Oakfield* sounds somewhat like the Emily Eden who laments the demolition by commerce of traditional native values by writing to her sister in 1835 that Delhi had been ruined by the British: "I feel that we horrid English have just 'gone and done it,' merchandised it, revenued it, and spoiled it all" (98).[13]

In censuring the "pure professing secularism" (2:224) of the British Raj, *Oakfield* clearly and rather heavy-handedly contributes to the well-known Victorian critique of a cash-nexus ethos seen by Carlyle, Dickens, and others as a troubling symptom of a diseased society. Unlike Dickens, however, William Arnold produces writing about empire that seems to avoid acknowledgment of the power brought by empire.[14] *Oakfield*, while unhappy with the materialistic present, seems uninterested in providing adjustment to a national wealth founded, in large part, on mercantile colonialism.[15] In sum, the critique of empire to be found in *Oakfield, The Wetherbys,* and *Peregrine Pultuney* is either a somewhat priggish call for selfless dedication to the cause of civilizing India instead of turning it into the profitable economic heaven, which in historical actuality it already was, or an instructive guidebook about how to make money while expanding the British Raj, or a practical deflation of the putative glamour of military and civil service. Although drenched

---

[13] In the wake of the post-1857 reduction of the power of the East India Company, J. H. Stocqueler published one of numerous works designed to help the middle-class business get a firm financial footing in India. At a time when, he notes, "patronage must give way to competition," a young man of talent and energy "will find the road to preferment as open to him and to his children, as it has hitherto exclusively been to the offspring and connections of the Directors of the East India Company" (iii).

[14] *Oakfield* is saturated with the sentimentality identified by Fred Kaplan as a Victorian defense of "the vision of the ideal against the claim that the universe and human history are governed by mechanical, or rational, or deterministic, or pragmatic forces" (6).

[15] Criticism of the corrupt bond between materialism and empire continues throughout the nineteenth century. J. A. Hobson, in his 1902 elaboration of the distinctions between colonialist and imperialist practices, observes that Indian soldiers, civil servants, merchants, and planters are all "openly contemptuous of democracy; devoted to material luxury, social display, and the shallower arts of intellectual life" (159).

in sentimentality, *The Old Curiosity Shop* is neither priggish, instructive, nor practical. And the sustained satiric brilliance of *Dombey and Son* distances that novel far from the wooden, albeit politically interesting, literary imagination revealed in *Oakfield, The Wetherbys,* and *Peregrine Pultuney.* What's more, the formal and thematic difference of *The Old Curiosity Shop* and *Dombey and Son* from these three novels lies not only in Dickens's imaginative genius but also in the his deployment of established ideas about gender for negotiation of political tension. It is primarily through the suffering of Little Nell and Florence Dombey that Dickens manages acceptance and critique of empire.

WASTING NELL, CANNIBAL QUILP

One of the most pervasive images in Dickens's early novels is that of the child trudging along the road to his or her destiny. Fusing the literary tropes of the pilgrimage and the picaresque, Dickens sends his unhappy boy and girl characters out on the road to meet their fictional fates. Oliver Twist, in flight from his somber employment and physical abuse at Mr. Sowerberry's, is collared by the Dodger just outside London and thus positioned for his eventual discovery of family in the Maylies and Mr. Brownlow. David Copperfield, traveling in the opposite direction, flees the London bottle warehouse for the white cliffs of Dover, Betsey Trotwood, and the beginning of his career as a writer. And Little Nell, menaced by Quilp and frightened by her grandfather's helplessness, heads up to Wolverhampton and beyond. All three trudge along penniless, homeless, and without protection, on the road, respectively, to family, profession, and death. What is most notably different, of course, about the three characters is that the two boys, Oliver and David, live and are happy, and the girl, Nell, dies a lingering death, having made others happy in doing so. What is less noticeable about *The Old Curiosity Shop,* however, is that it is not only a quest novel about a secular pilgrim on the road to deadly rest, the sentimental story of Nell's suffering and apotheosis, but also a novel about the British empire. We find this aspect of the novel symbolized in the relationship between Little Nell and Daniel Quilp.[16]

---

[16] Steven Marcus points out that the pilgrimage "has always been one of the grand, universal subjects of literature" (*Dickens: From Pickwick to Dombey* 73). Alexander Welsh has perceptively

Quilp and Nell are customarily lined up as monster and angel; evil and good; grotesque and graceful; animal vitality and human frailty; inhuman lack of moral sentiment and human overload of pathos and suffering; demonic force surging from the underworld and spiritual power yearning for heavenly rest. At the risk of cementing this dualism, I would suggest that what we identify as moral/metaphysical difference in *The Old Curiosity Shop* may also be seen as racial. In some sense, this should come as no surprise, for the Other (whether race, class, or gender specific) is conventionally represented in European culture as dark and barbarian, and monstrous savages do not appear on the scene for the first time in the nineteenth century.[17] But they do have a historically specific meaning in *The Old Curiosity Shop*. Congruent with gender-specific tropes in early Victorian writing, Quilp represents the savage/dark/male and Nell the civilized/pale/female. Nell is doomed to death by her mission to replace heathen idolatry with Christian belief, by her enforced journey through the pagan wilderness suggested by the smoking inferno of the English Midlands, by her vulnerability, sacrifice, and passivity. All this is heightened by the fact that she is a thirteen-year-old girl. Quilp's savagery is derived from early Victorian myths about barbarism, and I want to place this colonial paradigm of British female suffering in the face of native male aggression in the context of Dickens's writings about Africa and the Noble Savage. To locate the affiliative presence of this model in *The Old Curiosity Shop*, we need to look at the physical Quilp, who is, as Mr. Podsnap would say, definitely "Not English!"

With a "head and face . . . large enough for the body of a giant" but possessing the body of a dwarf, Quilp is a dark, tough monster: he has black eyes, a complexion never "clean or wholesome," "discoloured fangs," and "grizzled black" hair (22). As "watchful as a lynx" (360), Quilp is also designated sharp as a ferret and cunning as a weasel. Panting like a dog, he is called demon, imp, goblin, ogre, and Chinese

---

interpreted Little Nell and her grandfather as "sojourners" from the "earthly city" (*The City of Dickens* 119). See also Barry Qualls for careful explication of the way Dickens deploys significant emblems in his description of Nell's death journey.

[17] For persuasive analysis of the presence of this figure in Renaissance writing, and in *The Tempest* in particular, see Paul Brown. See also Lamming and Retamar for debate of the contested question of how the once savage Caliban figure might deploy the colonizer Prospero's language in a postcolonial society.

idol, and, as many critics have observed, he bears some resemblance to Caliban, Richard III, and the generic dwarf of fairy tales.[18] But it is Dickens's likening of him to an "African Chief" squatting on a piece of matting as he devours vast quantities of bread, cheese, and beer (104) that is significant for my purposes here. The resonance of his animalism, his savage dexterity, and his "African" agility (despite his deformity) are enforced by a devouring, biting, engulfing performance throughout the novel. He is, seemingly, a symbolic cannibal, roaming the domestic spaces of early Victorian Britain in search of human food, a forerunner of the hungry Mr. Vholes in *Bleak House* who gazes at Richard Carstone "as if he were making a lingering meal of him with his eyes as well as with his professional appetite" (550). Quilp bites the air, "with a snarl" threatens to bite his wife (37), and leers at her—adding "Oh you nice creature!" and smacking his lips "as if this were no figure of speech, and she were actually a sweetmeat" (35). At his most antisocial and his most thoroughly cannibalistic, Quilp piles his stove high with coals and dines "off a beefsteak, which he cooked himself in somewhat of a savage and cannibal-like manner" (504).

As Patrick Brantlinger and others have noted, cannibalism becomes an important theme in British writing about Africa around the middle of the nineteenth century. Sensational treatments of anthropophagy abounded, and the more Europeans began to penetrate Africa, the more savage and cannibalistic the Africans came to seem; the myth of the Dark Continent, Brantlinger explains, developed during transition from the successful campaign against slavery in the early 1830s to the imperialist scramble for Africa in the final quarter of the nineteenth century (173–97). *The Old Curiosity Shop* was published at a time when Africa was becoming in British culture the dark locus of scientific exploration, mercantile adventuring and missionary conversion. Despite his affectionate description of the Nubbles family's preparation for Kit's journey across London to Finchley, "as if he had been about to penetrate into the interior of Africa" (166), Dickens did not look favorably on mercantile and missionary exploration.

Before Mrs. Jellyby and her dotty philanthropy make an appearance in *Bleak House* in the early 1850s, Dickens in 1848 made some choice re-

---

[18] Michael Hollington interprets Dickens's characterization of Quilp as expressing his critique of an industrial age: unnatural social systems produce unnatural monstrosities (91). For a complete guide to critical readings of Quilp from his first monstrous appearance in 1840 to recent interpretations, see Priscilla Schlicke and Paul Schlicke.

marks about the Niger expedition of 1841–42, a disastrous government-sponsored attempt led by Thomas Fowell Buxton. The Niger expedition aimed to establish Christianity and Free Trade in the Heart of Darkness, explore the Niger River, establish antislavery treaties with the Africans, and set up trading posts. Some of this was achieved, but a high mortality rate (approximately one-third of the 159-member group composed of members of the African Civilization Society and the Church Missionary Society) clouded any success. For Dickens, the Niger expedition was a tragic farce, a ludicrous failure to recognize that between "the civilized European and the barbarous African there is a great gulf set." To change the customs of "ignorant and savage races," he declared, "requires a stretch of years that dazzles in the looking at" (quoted in Brantlinger, 178). This is not to say, incidentally, that Dickens was indifferent to the slave trade; mounting his attack on "the upholders of slavery in America," he abominates "the atrocities" of the system, declaring, "I shall not write one word for which I have not ample proof and warrant." Scorning the hypocrisy that declaims "against the ignorant peasantry of Ireland" and keeps silent about those "who notch the ears of men and women, cut posies in the shrinking flesh, learn to write with pens of red-hot iron on the human face," he calls, romantically, for the restoration of "the forest and the Indian village" and the replacement of "streets and squares by wigwams" ("Slavery" 228; 242; 243). Just as fiercely, Dickens later demolished the myth of the Noble Savage, although his political aim seems opposed to that calling for a feather fluttering in the breeze in lieu of the stars and stripes.

Appearing in 1853 in *Household Words*, Dickens's essay on the legendary figure of the Noble Savage combines sympathetic condemnation of the exhibition in London of creatures such as the Hottenntot Venus (in 1810) and the Bushmen and Kaffir groups from Southern Africa (in the mid-to-late 1840s) with detestation of their sentimental distortion in the popular imagination.[19] What he detests most of all is "whimpering" over the loss of some putatively heroic existence:

> Think of the Bushmen . . . Are the majority of persons—who remember the horrid little leader of that party in his festering bundle of hides, with his filth and his antipathy to water, and his straddled legs, and his odious eyes shaded by his brutal hand . . . conscious of an affectionate yearning

---

[19] As Richard Altick has splendidly shown, in Victorian Britain, the exhibition of imperial curiosities (often human) accompanied imperial expansion (*The Shows of London* 269–87).

towards that noble savage, or is it idiosyncratic in me to abhor, detest, abominate, and abjure him?

"If we have anything to learn from the Noble Savage," he concludes, "it is what to avoid. His virtues are a fable; his happiness is a delusion; his nobility, nonsense" ("The Noble Savage" 337–39). Authentic savages, for Dickens, were more like Daniel Quilp than the sentimentally noble figures of romantic myth.[20]

In this essay, Dickens fixes his loathing of the exhibition of Bushmen on one figure, the abhorred, detested, abominated, and abjured "horrid little leader" repugnantly straddling his legs and shading his eyes with brutal hands. Descriptions of Daniel Quilp suggest that his repellency anticipates by some ten years that ascribed to the exhibited Bushman and, more importantly for the overall purpose of my argument, that Dickens's characterization of Quilp participates in the production of early Victorian writing about empire. With his festering, filthy neckerchief and his habits of smearing his "countenance with a damp towel of very unwholesome appearance" in lieu of washing, of straddling his legs to frighten his wife, of rolling his odious, inflamed eyes to intimidate Sampson Brass, and of using his brutal hands to batter a totemic representation of his enemy Kit "until the perspiration streamed down his face with the violence of the exercise" (461), Quilp behaves alarmingly like the exhibited Bushmen described by Dickens in 1853.

A sensational drawing card in the exhibition of savages in the 1830s and 1840s was a tableau vivant, usually given over to native war dances, ritualized chanting, and tribal cooking, which inevitably created for the horrified English viewer the prospect of cannibalism. Quilp's comically savage taste for doing "something fantastic and monkey-like" compels him to arrange his own tableaux vivants. For example, with no audience but a demented dog, he does a sort of ecstatic demon-dance, "arms a-kimbo"; he enacts for Sampson Brass a kind of rhythmic native ritual, a chanted "monotonous repetition of one sentence in a very rapid manner, with a long stress upon the last word, which he swelled into a dismal roar" (457); and for his wife's benefit, he plants his hands on his knees, straddles his legs out very wide, and stoops down and brings his head between them to ask, "Am I nice to look at?" Receiving a

[20] Jeff Nunokawa refers to Dickens's loathing of the exhibited Bushmen in arguing that *Dombey and Son* "exhibits" (primarily for Walter Gay's instruction) the different Victorian "bodies" of capitalism and sexuality.

less than enthusiastic response, he treats his wife and his mother-in-law to a nightlong performance of grimaces, leaps, and chilling glares, capped by the devouring of hard eggs, shells and all, gigantic prawns, watercresses, and boiling tea: he performs "so many horrifying and uncommon acts that the women were nearly frightened out of their wits and began to doubt if he were really a human creature" (40). Of course, Quilp is a human creature and not a savage African chief; he is more than and different from all the things suggested, comically monstrous, for one thing, sexually compelling for another. My concern is with a reading that supplements rather than negates others and that relies on rather than discards the core meaning of Quilp and Nell as emblems of leering evil and quivering purity. Quilp is a dark demonic force whose destruction allegorically requires the suffering and death of an English girl, "so small, so compact, so beautifully modelled, so fair, with such blue veins and such a transparent skin," as Quilp greedily describes her. In *The Old Curiosity Shop*, eradication of male barbarism is accompanied by the forfeiture of female life, or, to suggest how Victorian ideas of gender get affiliated with Victorian ideas of race, native savagery can be tamed only by the sacrifice of Englishwomen.

Hardly seeming to need nourishment, often "too tired to eat," always giving the "best fragments" from her basket to her grandfather, "so very calm and unresisting," Nell epitomizes the sentimental selflessness, the willingness to bear pain without complaint that is conventionally attributed to Victorian women. Just as Quilp's demonic performances symbolize his meaning as an uncivilized racial curiosity, so Nell's shy presence symbolizes her meaning as civilized racial curiosity. She is an immutable physical type whose genetic inheritance from her grandmother is perceived by her grandfather's brother, who regards her as the "same sweet girl . . . the Good Angel of the race" seen in generic English family portraits (524). In sum, she is an imperishable emblem of English sweetness, mildness, and angelic purity. She is, consequently, more mythological icon than living, breathing, female child. While Quilp takes up demoniacal vital residence in his counting-house, a performing savage grilling steaks and executing simian acrobatics from his hammock, Nell manages a wasting existence in the solemn, vaulted dwelling where she is to die, a performing angel exhausted by her journey through the wilderness. Attaining a kind of Clarissa-like transparency, she draws curious parties to the church. These people, seeing her, "speak to others of the child": eventually she has a throng of daily visitors (again like Clarissa) who praise her pale beauty and moral perfection and pity her decline (410).

Nell is the suffering female child whose flight from and symbolic death at the hands of the rapacious savage registers Dickens's discomfort with empire as it was developing in early Victorian culture. Appropriating Nell's home, invading her domestic space in much the same way that the "devilish Indian diamond" (symbol of the colonized) invades the English country house (home of the colonizer) in *The Moonstone*, Quilp sends her on the road. He drives her from the city in search of rest, a place "remote from towns or even other villages" where she might live in peace. To be sure, this is the ritualized flight from the infernally secular "City of Dickens" that Alexander Welsh has so fully articulated, but it is also a journey back in time to a place that existed before missionary interference, scientific exploration, mercantile colonialism. In that mythical place, there are no Quilps, no performing savages brought to the city and taught the tricks of a cash-nexus society, the ways in which to get and spend. Yet, paradoxically, Dickens also seems to be saying that it is too late to go back to that place, too late to escape Quilp and his symbolic companion, the savage: "A perpetual nightmare to the child," he is imaginatively present at Nell's death, even if his smoking rage has finally been quenched by the dark river. That Nell must die partially signifies Dickens's view that the changes wrought in early Victorian culture by empire building are inescapable, cannot be eradicated, must be problematically symbolized, and thereby are occluded. The attack upon empire metaphorically implied in *The Old Curiosity Shop* is more fully explicit and representational in *Dombey and Son*, Dickens's last novel of social criticism in the 1840s. Although the dark native in *Dombey* bears little resemblance to the savages of Dickens's essays (and certainly not to Quilp), Florence's injured female body affiliates her with the torment suffered by Little Nell.

BATTERING PATRIARCHY

In *Dombey*, two figures are beaten. Major Bagstock's "dark servant" is struck repeatedly by his master and Florence Dombey is struck once by her father. To put bluntly what in a moment I hope will emerge as a complex reciprocal constitution of ideologies of race and gender, the Native is struck because he is dark-skinned and Florence is struck because she is female. One of the many metaphorical native descendants of those "Fridays" brought to Britain in the eighteenth and nine-teenth centuries,[21] himself a fictive ancestor of the Indians, Pakistanis, and West Indians who settled in Britain after the Second World War, throughout the novel Major Bagstock's "dark servant" is heaped with verbal and physical abuse. He dodges a hurled footstool when the Major comes down with the gout, has no "particular name" but answers to "any vituperative epithet" (273), withstands a "pile of the Major's cloaks and great-coats . . . hurled upon him" as he accompanies Dombey and his master to the railway station (276), and on the trip to Leamington that Bagstock makes with Dombey, the "dark exile" endures a bat-tery of "violent assault," wearing earrings in his "dark-brown ears," and European clothes that sit on him "with an outlandish impossibility of adjustment" (284). Shrinking from his master's prodding cane, he is de-scribed as a "shrivelled nut . . . a cold monkey" (284). While the Major dresses for dinner, he undergoes the "pelting of a shower of miscella-neous objects, varying in size from a boot to a hairbrush, and includ-ing everything that came within his master's reach" (374). Occasionally comic but more often unsettling, the relationship between the Major and his servant is, at root, racialist and ugly. In sum, the "dark" servant is one of George Lamming's Caliban-figure whose purpose, he argues perceptively, is to be "appropriated and exploited for the purposes of another's development" (107). The physical blow dealt Florence by her father triggers a different, domestic story of exploitation.

At the same moment that Dombey and the firm begin a decline into isolation and bankruptcy, Walter Gay, Florence's devoted admirer, re-enters her life after having been banished by Mr. Dombey to one of his colonial outposts in Barbados. Shattered by her stepmother's dramatic bolt from the Dombey mansion, devastated by her father's cruelty, Florence has found refuge with Sol Gills. When she sees Walter, she is speechless, and all she can do is feel these words, "Oh Welcome home, dear Walter! Welcome to this stricken breast!" (693). This may sound like the language of a heroine who has been reading too many sentimen-tal novels, but it is also the language of a young woman who has been stricken literally upon her breast by her father, a desperate man per-forming the final scenes in his drama of surveillance and punishment.

---

[21] In *David Copperfield,* Julia Mills returns to England from India married to an "old Scotch Croesus, who is a sort of yellow bear with a tanned hide," and "a black man to carry cards and let-ters to her . . . and a copper-coloured woman in linen with a bright handkerchief round her head to serve her Tiffin in her dressing-room" (875).

On the morning that Dombey discovers he has been "dishonoured," Florence runs to embrace her father as she has embraced her dying mother and her dying brother, but "in his frenzy, he lifted up his cruel arm, and struck her, crosswise, with that heaviness, that she tottered on the marble floor; and as he dealt the blow, he told her what Edith was, and bade her follow her, since they had always been in league" (665). She runs through the London streets, propelled by her father from the private sphere into the public world, straight to Walter's uncle and the next morning discovers the literal mark of her father's blow: "on her breast was the darkening mark of an angry hand" (680), a "mark upon her bosom" that begins to make her afraid of herself "as if she bore about her something wicked" (688).

The ending of *Dombey,* in which a financially ruined and morally chastened grandfather pays tender attention to his family, may be said to forgive Dombey for striking his daughter, but the novel never forgives Major Bagstock for hitting his native servant, quite simply because it sees no moral need to do so. The configuration of race and gender politics in which it is explicitly not acceptable for a British father to hit his middle-class daughter but implicitly acceptable for a retired Indian army officer to beat his dark servant, speaks directly to Dickens's complex and unhappy view of empire. A significant moral imperative of *Dombey and Son* is to conjoin the worlds of domestic and public action; it is through Dickens's characterization of Dombey's behavior as tyrannical in both the domestic and the public spheres that we understand the mutually constitutive relationship between Dombey father and Dombey colonial capitalist. Consequently, we see that the blow dealt to Florence by her father in an act of family violence and the physical and verbal assaults launched by Bagstock upon the Native in acts of imperial tyranny are related. But the suffering of Florence and the misery of the Native clearly do not garner equal sympathy from the reader. It seems to me that the beating of Florence, the punishment delivered to her father, and the forgiveness he is granted, imaginatively overshadow but do not entirely erase Bagstock's brutalization of his servant, which is an instance of corrupt imperialism that Dickens admits into the novel as part of his political critique. Dickens punishes the colonial merchant because he is a bad father, not because he allows himself to be befriended by the native-bashing Bagstock, the symbolic representative of an East India Company criticized in the novels about India published contemporaneously with Dombey, or because he is responsible, by association, for the exploitation of millions of Indian peoples subjugated by the armies and economic tyranny of the East India Company. The blow delivered to an innocent Victorian daughter exposes her father's domestic wickedness so vividly that his wickedness in the public sphere is dimmed (by not entirely blotted out) by her suffering and forgiveness.[22]

Just as Bagstock walks in the "shadow" of his servant while at Leamington on a hot and sunny afternoon, the vivid shock of the blow that sends Florence tottering on the marble floor may be said, then, to shadow the sustained violence done to the servant and to his exploited brothers and sisters in the empire. In a resolution of political critique by establishment of domestic harmony (common to almost all of Dickens's novels), Dickens allows the Native into the novel as a symbolic victim of empire, ensuring that his suffering remains present but overshadowed by that of Florence and leaving unmolested the political institutions of empire that have, by association, created his suffering in the first place. In the words of Mr. Toots, at the end of the novel, Walter Gay is building an "edifice" from the wreck of Dombey's fortune. Given what we know of Walter's business experience, this is a work of money making that cannot fail to involve in one way or another an affiliated work of Victorian empire building.[23]

Dombey's domestic house of empire dominated by Florence offers a complicated conjunction of private and public and of gender and morality.[24] The blow delivered to Florence is preceded by a long narrative of patriarchal fear, control, and violence. Governed by his desire to

[22] None of this is to say that Dickens advocated regular bashing of natives. I should also emphasize that when I speak of Dickens's interrogations of colonial and imperial practices, I am not suggesting that he was opposed to the British governance of foreign territories: if nothing else, his support of Jamaica's Governor Eyre in 1865 after Eyre's suppression of local uprisings prohibits such a view. Dickens's unexamined racism takes a comic turn when he describes Mrs. Wilfer, at the end of *Our Mutual Friend*, walking through the Harmon mansion "with the bearing of a Savage Chief, who would feel himself compromised by manifesting the slightest token of surprise or admiration" (807).

[23] My argument here is different from that of Helen Carr as articulated in her essay "Woman/Indian: 'The American' and His Others." Carr argues that white male authority combines the images of female and native "others" and that "Woman is the European man's primary Other: using her as an image for the racial Other transfers the asymmetrical power relation embedded in her difference from the dominant patriarchal male" (49). My point, rather, is that Victorian androcentric imperial culture constructs woman as utterly different from the native and that such construction implicitly authorizes that culture to brutalize the native.

[24] My reading of *Dombey and Son* has much in common with that of Suvendrini Perera. Identifying Dombey as a premier imperial merchant prince, she argues that the novel reconciles "the old adventures of imperial trade with the stability of the mid-Victorian family" (72).

control the female body on which he is dependent for his own patriarchal reproduction, and hence for his projected importance in the world
of business and empire, Dombey is also driven to keep his son Paul's wet
nurse under surveillance, to discipline Edith Dombey's bitter resistance
to his will, and to punish Florence for, in fact, having a female body.

After the irresponsible refusal of baby Paul's mother to make an
"effort" and rally round to exalted life as Mrs. Dombey, Dombey and
Son finds itself in an embarrassing situation. "Tottering for a nurse"
(15), the House must engage the services of Polly Toodle, jolly wife
of a stoker on the railways and mother of five apple-cheeked children.
Dombey's fear of female power, his appalled awareness that the survival of Dombey and *Son* depends upon a working-class woman, and
his perception of the world in terms of commodities are all expressed
in his dealings with Paul's nurse. Dombey orders Polly to call herself Richards, an ordinary, convenient name that strips her of female
identity as *Mrs.* Toodle and mother of non-Dombey children, to have
nothing to do with her natural family when she is nursing Paul, and to
remember that when she leaves the Dombey household she will have
concluded "what is a mere matter of bargain and sale, hiring and let-
ting." In transforming the natural function of breast-feeding into a
commercial transaction, Dombey anticipates the stern strictures contained in Mrs. Beeton's chapter on "The Wet Nurse" in her *Book of
Household Management,* published in 1861. Articulating the middle-
class distrust of all servants that accompanies Dombey's fear of dependency on female power, Mrs. Beeton declares that those who are "driven
to the occupation from the laudable motive of feeding their own children . . . are too often both selfish, and sensual . . . many nurses, rather
than forego the enjoyment of a favourite dish, though morally certain
of the effect it will have on the child, will, on the first opportunity,
feed with avidity on fried meats, cabbage, cucumbers, pickles, or other
crude and injurious ailments, in defiance of all orders given" (1022–23).
In a manner that anticipates Mrs. Beeton's stern warnings, Mrs. Chick
(Dombey's domineering sister) and Miss Tox, her sycophantic friend,
instruct Polly to exercise "abstinence" regarding vegetables and pickles
and to remember that she will have "a little cherub connected with
the superior classes, gradually unfolding itself from day to day at one
common fountain" (20). Polly becomes, for Dombey, a stereotype: the
lower-class, coarse, slothful wet nurse, a woman whose transformation
into a cunning commodity helps to obscure (for him, and in the ideo-

logical economy of the novel) her essential function in his field of commercial "getting and spending."[25]

As a means of controlling Polly/Richards, Dombey commands her to engage in a twice-daily ceremony suggestive of Foucault's theories of social surveillance in which, Foucault argues, "it is the subjects who have to be seen. Their visibility assures the hold of the power that is exercised over them. It is the fact of being constantly seen, of being able always to be seen, that maintains the disciplined individual in subjection" (187). Dombey's house is "on the shady side of a tall, dark dreadfully genteel street," his own apartments at the back of the house consisting of a sitting room, a library, and "a kind of conservatory or little glass break-fast room beyond." These three rooms connect with one another and are accessible from the hall, which means the conservatory may be entered without first passing through the sitting room and the library; in effect, it is possible to enter the conservatory as if one were making a stage entrance from the side, the audience, of course, constituted by whoever is in the sitting room and library. The conservatory resembles a lighted stage and the sitting room and library a darkened auditorium. Obsessed with time, constantly jiggling his great gold watch chain and speeding up Paul's young life so that he may become *Son* in the firm, Dombey orders Polly to repair punctually to this "glass chamber" while he is at breakfast and in the afternoon when he comes home to dinner. There, she is ordered to walk backward and forward with baby Paul in her arms. To be sure, as she walks she does not literally breast-feed Paul, but the ritual is sufficiently resonant with Dombey's compulsion to watch and to control through watching that it may be associated with his humiliating knowledge that Dombey and Son has been restored to vitality from its "tottering" state by a woman's natural function.[26]

In placing Polly in this conservatory flooded with light and watching

[25] In his important essay on colonialist, racialist stereotyping, Paul Brown observes that colonialist discourse is "always producing a disruptive other in order to assert the superiority of the coloniser" (58). Dombey must always produce stereotypes of deficient women and rebellious servants in order to produce his own domestic authority.

[26] Alexander Welsh was the first critic to explore ideological opposition between the city and the female sex in Dickens. Welsh argues that Florence Dombey is but one of Dickens's suffering daughters who possess the redemptive powers necessary to meet the perversity of their fathers. Welsh also points to the image of Little Dorrit comforting her father in the Marshalsea, which reads as follows: "her father's wasted heart upon her innocent breast, and turning to it a fountain of love and fidelity that never ran dry or waned" (179). My argument about Florence Dombey seeks to unite Welsh's perception of Little Dorrit's nurturing breast and what I see as Dombey's need to injure that part of the female body.

from the "dark distance," Dombey literally incarcerates the feared and needed female body. Privileged in his own shadowy patriarchal space, he becomes jailer to his brightly lit female servant, and his enactment of this twice-daily ceremony suggests some of the meanings ascribed by Foucault to Bentham's Panopticon. As Foucault observes, the prisoners are confined to windowed, lighted spaces like "so many small theaters," and the panoptic mechanism makes it possible "to see constantly, to recognize immediately," which Foucault declares is essential to a perfection of the regulation of potentially disruptive forces by those holding political and social power. Dombey is the governing jailer in a household of women: his first wife, Fanny, his daughter, Florence, his servants Polly/Richards and Susan Nipper, and his second wife, Edith. In one way or another, Dombey's authority is threatened by dependence on these women, who form an alliance of what Foucault terms "horizontal conjunctions" (219).[27]

In the context of Victorian writing about empire, Dickens's novel, in the domestic and psychological sphere, imaginatively discloses the rule of power we see in the public and political sphere of colonialist politics, just as the novel also links a once-beaten Florence with a regularly beaten dark-skinned servant. What's more, Dombey's unraveling of the self as ruler involves repetition in the Polly/Richards episodes of what he has already witnessed at the deathbed of his first wife. It is as if he must reinvent in his mind those moments of exclusion from scenes of female love so that he may rewrite them with himself as the lord of female humankind.

He cannot forget that he had "no part" (29) in his wife's death and he remains tormented by the memory of two figures clasped in each other's arms (Florence and her dying mother); his dying son asks not for his father, but for his old nurse, who takes his wasted hand and puts

[27] In terms of affiliations between domestic and imperial power to be found in *Dombey,* one of the significant aspects of Dombey's behavior is its meaning as an anglicized version of a despotism often ascribed to oriental rulers in Victorian writing about empire. In *The Private Life of an Eastern King* (1865), for example, written by an English "member of the Household" (William Knighton), we find a "savage Hindu rajah" declaring that if his wife does not make him "the father of a *son,* I will whip her to death with my hunting whip" (70). Fanny Dombey eventually manages to end Dombey's ten-year condition of "hope deferred" by producing a son, and dies, exhausted, one suspects, by Dombey's enactment of the male obsession with male inheritance displayed by the brutal rajahs who stalk the pages of Victorian popular writing about India. In addition, Susan Nipper's remark that "girls are thrown away in this house" (79) suggests how metropolitan narratives of domestic tyranny are influenced by the sensationalist oriental stories brought back to Victorian Britain of discarded daughters, enslaved women, whip-wielding Eastern despots.

it to her breast "as one who had some right to fondle it (224)," perhaps because of the "sharp weaning" (90) he suffered when Dombey discharges Polly for having taken the Dombey children to Camden Town. Dying, Paul embraces not his father but his sister, excluding Dombey a second time from a scene of death: brother and sister wind their arms around each other as the golden light comes streaming in, locking them together and suggesting an illumination different from that which shines upon the incarcerated Polly. Excluded from the embrace of mother and daughter and of brother and sister, condemned to patriarchal observation, Dombey therefore attempts to transform through repetition these scenes into a drama of omnipotent male surveillance. The melodramatic final scene of this one-man drama features the climactic blow dealt to Florence.

If the life-giving, dangerous Polly must be monitored, then the rebellious Edith must be curbed. Hawked here and there by her mother and eventually sold to Dombey, with Major Bagstock as bombastic middleman, Edith cannot be brought to heel in the imperial way that Dombey controls his firm and his household. Once more, he finds himself exiled to a dark space from where he witnesses a scene of female affection. Shortly after the return from a "cold" honeymoon trip to Paris (500), Dombey withdraws into a shadowy corner of the drawing room, a handkerchief over his head so that he may more easily watch his daughter sewing, as he has watched Polly in the "glass chamber" from the darkness of his private apartments. He is about to speak tenderly to Florence when Edith enters the room, an unknown Edith, softened by Florence's desire for maternal affection. When the two women leave the room "like sisters" (504), he remains in his chair for three hours, contemplating his powerful yet powerless condition, master in his own house but an exile from its female center of affection.[28] It is this knowledge of himself that precipitates, I think, his eventual understanding of the reciprocal constitution of private and public spheres. Initially contemplating the world with the "calculating gaze" of the colonial capitalist attributed to Crusoe by Ian Watt, Dombey's vision begins with surveillance of his mercantile empire, proceeds through visual monitoring of the women in his household, and ends with his horrified, conscious contemplation of a decomposing image of "A spectral, haggard, wasted

---

[28] For exploration of the Edith and Florence relationship in the context of 1840s gender politics, see Louise Yelin.

likeness of himself" (842). As we know, the patriarchal world of discipline and darkness is eventually overwhelmed by the female world of freedom and light, just as, I have been arguing, the beaten dark-skinned servant is overshadowed by the stricken Florence. Dombey moves from his patriarchal theater of panoptic watching to the final scenes of the novel, where, rather than monitoring the women in his household, he "attends upon" his grandchildren, "the object of his life" (878). The new Dombey family is constituted by a morally superior middle class well equipped to reform the corruption satirized and lamented in *The Grand Master* and in the novels about India I have discussed in this chapter. And if that family were to employ a "dark" servant, one may be sure he or she would be the object of kindness not a target for verbal and physical abuse. Also, the renovated domestic world of *Dombey* can continue to enjoy the wealth brought by empire, Dombey's cruel colonialist practices rehabilitated through instructive punishment for his domestic violence. The dark servant, however, remains in painful bondage to the Major. His suffering precipitated by the economic exploitation of native peoples caused indirectly by Dombey's business dealings, his narrative almost eclipsed by Florence's story of pain and paternal renovation, he is a visible product of empire that Victorian writing such as *Dombey and Son* cannot erase but must represent, either in the formal cause of social realism or in the thematic cause of political critique, as shadowed, dimmed, discomfiting.

In the public sphere, the novel's political critique of empire building is brilliantly conveyed in this well-known description of Dombey's distorted perception of the universe: "The earth was made for Dombey and Son to trade in, and the sun and the moon were made to give them light. Rivers and seas were formed to float their ships; rainbows gave them promise of fair weather; winds blew for or against their enterprises; stars and planets circled in their orbits, to preserve inviolate a system of which they were the centre" (2).[29] Floating ships with cargo for the East India Company is what keeps Dombey in power, the lord

[29] Dombey's imperialistic imagination is echoed in President William McKinley's remarks about the acquisition by the United States of the Philippines: "I have been criticized a good deal about the Philippines, but I don't deserve it. The truth is, I didn't want the Philippines, and when they came to us, as a gift from the gods, I did not know what to do with them. . . . Late one night it came to me this way. . . . There was nothing left for us to do but to take them all, and to educate the Philippinos, and uplift and civilize and Christianize them. . . . Next morning I sent for the chief engineer of the War Department (our map-maker) and told him to put the Philippines on the map of the United States" (Malcolm and Kalaw, *Philippine Government* 65–66).

of a counting-house "much abstracted in appearance, from the world
without" (169). This image of a business so obsessed with record keeping that actual life becomes subordinate to the calculations of profit
made from empire imaginatively suggests mystification of colonial exploitation of the colonized into abstract financial calculation. In a sentimental preference for long-lost modes of trading that recalls *Oroonoko*'s
celebration of "brotherly and friendly" exchanges between Europeans
and the Surinam Indians, *Dombey and Son* declines, however, to attack directly the financial institutions with which Dombey is affiliated,
favoring instead a kind of jolly free trading.

Dombey and Son values economic practices rendered obsolete in the
early Victorian period. For example, Walter Gay's uncle, Solomon Gills
possesses a "secret attraction towards the marvellous and the adventurous" (40), not a useful quality in a competitive industrial society, and
finds himself and his business redundant. That Walter must work for
the House of Dombey rather than for his uncle also registers changing times. At the beginning of the novel, Sol's shop is empty, devoid of
customers and most recently entered by a woman who inquires the way
to Mile-End Turnpike. In a rueful observation imbued with the Victorian obsession with cannibalism that we see ferociously embodied in
Daniel Quilp, Sol remarks that "not being like the Savages who came
on Robinson Crusoe's Island" (38) such customers cannot provide sustenance for himself and his nephew.[30] Sol is an elegiac emblem of human
values vanquished by abstract calculations of profit, by modern modes of
thought indifferent to a love of careful craftsmanship and a fondness for
shipwreck narratives. On the evening of Walter's first day at the House
of Dombey, Sol brings out a bottle of his "ancient Madeira" and he and
Walter entertain each other telling familiar stories: the *Charming Sally*
that went down in the Baltic Sea on February 14, 1749, with five hundred casks of Madeira on board; the *George the Second* driven ashore on
the coast of Cornwall on March 14, 1771, with two hundred horses on
board; the *Polyphemus,* a private West India trader, that went down with

[30] As Dorothy Hammond and Alta Jablow note, "in the imperial period writers were far more
addicted to tales of cannibalism than . . . Africans ever were to cannibalism" (94). It is interesting
to see that the British believed cannibalism to be present not only in Africa: in Rowcroft's *Tales
of the Colonies,* an aboriginal servant, Black Tom, confides to his master that "bad black fellow eat
man sometimes" (3:156), and a government dispatch to the first governor of New Zealand dated
14 August 1839 advised that although the maoris may be allowed to observe their own customs,
"the savage practices of human sacrifice, and of cannibalism, must be promptly and decisively
interdicted" (Bell and Morrell, *Select Documents on British Colonial Policy* 558).

a fair wind out of Jamaica harbor. What neither of them say (or could be expected to have thought to say) is that floating alongside these vessels filled with the mentionable cargo of wine and horses were ships filled with the unmentionable freight of African slaves being transported across the Middle Passage. Sol and Walter are enmeshed in an ideological ambiguity in the novel that may be said to precipitate a wishful rewriting of eighteenth-century shipping history. If one considers the novel's accommodation to the railway, however, it becomes clear that it may be easier to erase Britain's slave-trading past than it is to ignore her industrialized present. Imaginatively adjusting a resistance and an accommodation to empire, *Dombey and Son,* through offering critique of one social transformation, suggests critique of another. Bearing in mind that British development of the railway both at home and in the empire became an essential Victorian means of economic expansion, one can see that in *Dombey,* ambivalent accommodation to the railway suggests an adjacent accommodation to empire. R. J. Moore observes that in the mid-Victorian period, British control of India benefitted British investors to the extent that by 1869, seventy million pounds "had been invested in Indian railways and some 50,000 Britons held shares or debentures in them, at government guaranteed rates of interest" (80). In a pattern of adjunct relationship, Carker's death by means of the railway may be read, I think, as the symbolic death of Dombey's brand of heartless money making and empire building.

In chapter six of *Dombey,* Polly Toodles with baby Paul in her arms and Susan Nipper with a curious Florence in tow arrive in "Camberling Town," smack in the process of excavations for the railway. Home for Polly is that curiously named street, Staggs's Gardens, a place "regarded by its population as a sacred grove not to be withered by Railroads" (64). As things turn out, it is more than withered: it is totally wiped out, and some seven years later when the Nipper and Walter go in search of Polly to come to Paul's deathbed, there is no Staggs's Gardens. All is swallowed up, to be replaced by Dickens's taxonomic culture of the railway, to which we remain captive, whether we share Kathleen Tillotson's view that it is full of "dread" or agree with Steven Marcus that the novel embraces social change. We return to Staggs's Gardens, to the brilliant juxtaposition of Dombey's thoughts as he takes the train from Euston to Birmingham, to the novel's exulting, shrieking, devouring personification of the railway as Death, that fiery monster that dismembers Carker, Dombey's "Grand Vizier." How, though, does one critique of social change become an imaginative critique of another? How does the transformation of Staggs's Gardens from squalid but vital street of row houses in Camden Town to being the London end of the London-Birmingham railway connect with the novel's accommodation to Britain's colonial wealth?

Dickens's superb imagination finds a symbolic resolution to a problem that was, of course, in historical and political actuality, far less tractable to redressive negotiation. The novel deploys the railway death of Carker (he is run over by a train) not just to put a dramatic end to the teeth-baring villain of the novel, but also to symbolize the desired termination of heartless, despotic empire building that is embodied in Dombey. Taken apart like Edith Dombey's mother, Carker, who was Dombey's mercantile surrogate in life, becomes his surrogate in death. Walking along "the lines of iron," Carker feels the earth tremble, sees the "red eyes bleared and dim" close in upon him: the engine beats him down and whirls him away, striking him limb from limb, and "licks his stream of life up with its fiery heat" (779). He seems killed, however, as much by an improbable heat—a kind of grilling alive not in Calcutta but somewhere near the south coast of England—as he is by the train. The cold light of the morning is marked by a "red suffusion of the coming sun," he feels hot even though the air is chill and comfortless, and he beholds the sun in all its dreadful glory before he is smashed to pieces. By virtue of a burning, explosive imagery that suggests the geography and population of colonized peoples whose labor has produced Dombey's wealth, the colonized destroy the grand vizier of a soon to be deposed mercantile potentate.[31] In his reconstitution of the Dombey family as a symbolic moral center of Macaulay's morally impeccable colonialism, Dickens sentimentally allows Dombey to live, the ideological negotiation of empire assisted by Florence Dombey's willingness to suffer in the cause of Britannic rule.

The misery of Little Nell and the pain of Florence Dombey symbolize, in part, the actual suffering demanded of women in the work of creating Britannic rule. Although protected by military and civil forces and pampered by more servants than she could ever expect to command at home, the British woman of empire was deified into an emblem of

[31] Carker's death may be said to anticipate, in part, the anxieties about empire that Judith Wilt argues are present in the gothic and science fiction published some thirty years after *Dombey and Son*: the terrors of this fiction, she argues, are about "punishment for past actions, sin coming home to roost" (620).

sacrifice, a figure whose misery is heard in the cry of a character in one of Flora Annie Steel's Anglo-Indian novels: "India is an ogre, eating us up body and soul; ruining our health, our tempers, our morals, our manners, our babies" (*Miss Stuart's Legacy* 4). In chapter 3 I have documented more fully this ideology of female suffering for empire through a reading of *Jane Eyre*. Jane is disposed to suffer like Little Nell and Florence Dombey, but she is also capable of managing (in ways they never could) Rochester and St. John Rivers, the male figures of mercantile colonialism and missionary renovation who created Britain's mid-nineteenth-century imperial power.

CHAPTER THREE

THE GOVERNESS OF EMPIRE:
JANE EYRE TAKES CARE OF
INDIA AND JAMAICA

Our possession of the West Indies, like that of India . . . gave us the strength, the support, but especially the capital, the wealth, at a time when no other European nation possessed such a reserve, which enabled us to come through the great struggle of the Napoleonic wars, the keen competition of the eighteenth and nineteenth centuries, and enabled us . . . to make our great position in the world.
—Winston Churchill, address to
West Indies sugar planters, 20 July 1939

The grammatical mode in which Jane Eyre reveals her marriage to Rochester provides an apt finish to the commanding manner in which she has conducted her life and told her story. Rather than confiding "Reader, we were married," which would consolidate the novel's rhetoric of equality in defiance of class and gender difference, she announces "Reader, I married him." With Rochester as her grammatical and erotic object, Jane places herself in the subject position. In what follows, I will elaborate the familiar readings of *Jane Eyre* as a resonant text in the making of Victorian female subjectivity, arguing that the novel also imagines the ideal Victorian woman of empire, a figure who combines the selflessness of Little Nell and Florence Dombey with the complicated authority of the young Queen Victoria. If not quite the battered daughter of Victorian patriarchy—and certainly no death-wishing female child, as her response to Mr. Brocklehurst's enquiry about how she will avoid hell affirms, "I must keep in good health, and not die" (64)—Jane suffers much pain, beginning with John Reed's verbal and physical assaults and ending with three days of homelessness and hunger after she leaves Thornfield. Despite her inability, as she puts it, to "comprehend" the "doctrine of endurance" articulated by Helen Burns, she actually endures a great deal. On the other hand, her imperishable sense of a powerful identity distinguishes her dramatically from Florence and Little Nell, the former steadfastly loyal to another self (her father) and the latter resigned to having no self at all. Yet the political meaning of Jane Eyre's misery is similar to that associated with the tribulations of Florence Dombey and Little Nell. Jane suffers on the road to achieving a Victorian female subjectivity that is defined, in part, by a gendered service to empire. In addition, she possesses the moral authority required of Britain's newly fashioned colonial governance, from the moment she defiantly shouts that the Reed children are "not fit to associate" with her (59) to her final confident announcement that *she* has married Rochester, and thus reclaimed him from the gloom, sterility, and isolation of Ferndean.

Armed with the physical toughness, moral high-mindedness, and innate bossiness of the Victorian governess, Jane Eyre may be seen as a female assistant in the androcentric work of empire building envisaged by Macaulay in his 1833 House of Commons speech. Different from Emily Eden by virtue of her middle-class prudery, her willingness to get down to gritty work, and her unrelenting gravity, Jane Eyre is the symbolic governess of empire.[1] Always in her life and in her narrative the subject on which she predicates Gateshead, Lowood, Thornfield, Rochester, Bertha, St. John Rivers, the lower classes, and, by extension, the colonized objects found in Rochester's West Indies and St. John's India, Jane is an adept discursive participant in Victorian justification of the British control, education, and reformation of subjugated peoples. But as much as she is the subject of her own narrative (the disciplinary governess), she is also necessarily an object in that narrative (the disciplined governess). As object, she is constructed by the political enterprise to which she contributes, that of defining British national identity through possession of empire, and by the patriarchal undertaking in which she is necessarily an accomplice, that of constituting

[1] Mary Poovey usefully points out that the economic and political turmoil of the 1840s caused the British middle class to "demand some barrier against erosion of middle-class assumptions and values. . . . Women, and the governess in particular, were invoked as the bulwarks against this erosion" (127). My argument about Jane Eyre relies upon the affiliation identified by Poovey between middle-class values and the figure of the governess. M. Jeanne Peterson's essay on the Victorian governess remains essential reading in any exploration of political links between this figure and Victorian values. See "The Victorian Governess: Status Incongruence in Family and Society."

Victorian womanhood. Seen from this perspective, the magnetic inconsistency of Brontë's novel that has long attracted critics emerges also as an expression of the contested nature of female service to British imperial expansion. Granted and denied agency in her gendered labor for empire, Jane Eyre may be said to fit Althusser's category of the "interpellated" individual (Althusser, 170), or to situate Brontë's novel within my primary frame in this study—women, empire, and Victorian writing—Jane Eyre enacts what Homi Bhabha has termed a "pedagogical" and "performative" writing of the colonial and imperial nation.

For Bhabha, "writing the nation" constitutes individuals as the " 'objects' of a nationalist pedagogy, giving the discourse an authority that is based on the pregiven or constituted historical origin or event; the people are also the 'subjects' of a process of signification . . . by which the national life is redeemed and signified as a repeating and reproductive process. . . . In the production of the nation as narration there is a split between the continuist, accumulative temporality of the pedagogical, and the repetitious, recursive strategy of the performative" ("DissemiNation" 297). From the position of Bhabha's complication of Althusserian principles of subjectivity by colonial discourse theory, one can see that Jane Eyre is an "object" in a "nationalist pedagogy" that securely identifies her as created by Britain's evolving history of colonial acquisition and racist ideology.

An assured self-alliance with a national authority is to be found everywhere in Jane's thinking. For example, the historical circumstances that sanction her question to herself—whether it is better "to be a slave in a fool's paradise at Marseilles . . . or to be a village schoolmistress, free and honest, in a breezy mountain nook in the healthy heart of England" (386)—reside exactly in her sense of being British, of being able rationally to resist Rochester's sexuality (unlike his French, Italian, and German mistresses), of working steadily in the "healthy heart of England" rather than lounging around in a stifling villa in Marseilles. Jane's values coincide with those prescribed for British imperial womanhood: first, a belief in her own social and cultural superiority to the native; second, recognition that she must sacrifice her physical comfort in the cause of civilizing the native; and third, an acceptance of her ancillary status in the male-dominated business of running the empire. We know, for example, that a colonizing Jane would never lapse into the languorous manners of the colonized, as some Anglo-Indian women were said to do when away from the "breezy mountain nooks" of Britain. A late Victorian chronicler of the British Raj sadly noted that it is "only a really energetic character, in fact, that does not become demoralized into flabbiness and inertia under the combined influences of heat, laziness, and servants at command. The first sign of deterioration is when a woman omits her corsets from her toilette, and begins lolling about in a sloppy and tumbled tea-gown in the mornings. Then the downward course is rapid" (Billington, 291). Jane Eyre's extraordinary physical buoyancy, alone, would prevent such a slide. "I will not be your English Celine Varens," she indignantly announces to Rochester when he attempts to buy her expensive clothing and jewelry; that is to say, I will not become your sexual plaything, will not, so to speak, relinquish my moral corsets for a "tumbled tea-gown."

But just as the national and gender identities of Jane Eyre have been created by her condition as an "object" in the enterprises of writing the nation, constructing Victorian womanhood, and establishing class relationships, she is also actively producing and reproducing herself, as Bhabha puts it, in "the repetitious, recursive strategy of the performative." Her performative enactment of herself as a British and as a female "subject" happens simultaneously with the construction of Jane Eyre as "object" so that the adamantine authority derived from a knowledge that British women do not swoon into loss of nation and self enables her to resist Rochester; yet this unyielding authority is purchased at the price of having it, in fact, created for her by the ideologies of gender and race that dictate the terms of her agency. As a symbolic governess of empire, Jane Eyre is the medium of Rochester's punishment for sexual corruption licensed by dissolute colonialism and the spur to St. John Rivers's missionary ambition. Everywhere she enacts her authority, and everywhere she implicitly accepts her unhappiness, subordination, and restriction as the price of its construction. "Because you delight in sacrifice," Rochester teasingly gives as the reason she would marry a blind, crippled, and deeply depressed man twice her age (470). However much she is sexually attracted to Rochester, or perhaps because of the sadomasochism that in part defines their sexual bond, Jane does delight in sacrifice: for the attainment of her own social power, for the gratification of her erotic desire, and, on the symbolic political terrain I shall explore in this chapter, for the rehabilitation of corrupt colonial practices and establishment of morally correct Britannic rule.

If one sees Jane Eyre as a figure who draws Conrad's red spaces on the Victorian map of empire, then the nagging questions that recur in

T. Jones Barker, Queen Victoria Presenting a Bible in the Audience Chamber at Windsor (1861). By courtesy of the National Portrait Gallery, London.

criticism of Brontë's novel become evidence of, rather than a problem about, Jane's complex position in writing the nation, and, of course, of her position as object and subject in Victorian class, gender, and race relationships. Whether a ruling-class man must be maimed in order to marry a governess, whether Bertha Mason Rochester symbolizes Jane's angry self or whether she represents the West Indian natives oppressed by Rochester and his social class, whether Jane ultimately embodies British genderless initiative or whether she signifies feminist rebellion against patriarchy, whether Jane's bourgeois individualism is vitiated by the novel's exclusion of the voice of a native female—the very possibility of asking these questions indicates the often contradictory nature of Victorian writing about class, gender, and race. Jane Eyre is many things, and some of them are not always consistent with one another. She is battered by John Reed, humiliated by Mr. Brocklehurst, deceived by Rochester, and made homeless by her refusal to become his mistress. She is also the fierce "discord" (47) in the Reed family, the fiery rebel at

Lowood, the stern governess of Adele, the prudish sexual conqueror of world-weary Rochester, a prissy middle-class snob, and an impassioned voice for feminist freedom.

As a sign of her perfected identity as pedagogical object and performative subject in the writing of Victorian empire, Jane is a coherent, direct, and considerate storyteller. Her narrative of incremental acquisition of esteem, money, family, and a husband to whom she is "ever more absolutely bone of his bone and flesh of his flesh" (476) is delivered to the reader in the clean terms one expects from a woman who is a symbolic emblem of impeccable colonial practices. That colonized peoples lack Jane's talent for constructing a coherent frame for events not always rationally explicable (her paintings, her dreams, Rochester's voice) is suggested, for example, in the observations of J. H. Stocqueler, writing in the aftermath of the Indian uprising in 1857. Scorning the fact that the natives employ no "dates, or clues to dates, in their temples and monuments," he argues that they furnish "to posterity no starting point in their story upon which a rational mind can place the smallest reliance" (2). With great care, Jane Eyre scrupulously provides a "starting point" to her story (a day on which there is no possibility of a walk) and that she trusts her own British "rational mind" is made evident in her approach to escaping Lowood after eight years of servitude. Casting around for ideas, she orders her "brain" to find a way, which comes in the plan to advertise: "This scheme I went over twice, thrice; and it was then digested in my mind: I had it in a clear practical form: I felt satisfied, and fell asleep" (118). Rochester's bemused explanation of his attraction to Jane affirms the unusually mature nature of Jane's "mind." He has been drawn to a mind "not liable to take infection: it is a peculiar mind: it is a unique one" (174).

As someone who enunciates and embodies middle-class racist ideologies of individualism, Jane Eyre achieves what Harriet Martineau in her "Essays on the art of thinking" (1836) terms the British triumph of "right reason" over "superstition and authority" (*Miscellanies* I:57). In her influential reading of *Jane Eyre*, however, Gayatri Spivak argues that the construction of "feminist individualism in the age of imperialism" entails the exclusion of the " 'native female' as such (*within* discourse, *as* a signifier)" and that one needs to "wrench oneself away from the mesmerizing focus of the 'subject constitution' of the female individualist" ("Three Women's Texts" 263–64). Rather than finding the "native female," my interest has been in tracing the way Brontë's novel and affiliated nonliterary texts construct the idea of a "native female" and how British metropolitan culture "worlds" the West Indies and thus imagines Bertha as such a figure ("Three Women's Texts" 262). In tracing this invention, I have tried to avoid what Spivak terms, in another essay, "subject restoration." In her critique of the work of the Indian Subaltern Studies group, whose aim is to recover native voices eradicated by British and Indian historiography, she argues that the group falls "back upon notions of consciousness-as-agent, totality, and upon a culturalism, that are discontinuous with the critique of humanism" (*In Other Worlds* 202). Jane's vivid creation of her own subjectivity, enacted with the ideological prop of Spivak's consciousness-as-agent, is always vexed by her status as object in the labor of writing the British colonial nation. Any attempt, in fact, to restore Jane Eyre as a "subject" would inevitably confront the race, class, and gender terms under which she is granted her subjectivity.

Looking back, for a moment, to the argument of my previous chapter, it seems to me that *Jane Eyre* navigates some of the rocky political terrain traversed in *The Old Curiosity Shop* and in *Dombey and Son*. For readers uneasy about the expanding empire (as a costly burden, an avenue to class advancement), Brontë's novel enables an acceptance of colonial and imperial power through punishment of Rochester for his association with immoral political practices. Jane Eyre vanquishes the figure of counterinvasion from the colonies, suffers magnificently in the process, and erases the economic exploitation and sexual debauchery represented by Rochester and his inheritance. In the reunion of Jane and Rochester at Ferndean, he brokenly declares that he is "no better than the old lightning-struck chestnut-tree in Thornfield orchard" and asks "what right would that ruin have to bid a budding woodbine cover its decay with freshness?" Jane's response that he is no ruin, that "plants will grow about your roots . . . and as they grow they will lean towards you, and wind around you, because your strength offers them so safe a prop" (469) figuratively anticipates, to be sure, their marriage and their children. In the context, however, of Rochester's Jamaican experience, his ten years of roving Europe, and his vow, after Jane agrees to marry him, "to lead henceforth a purer life than I have done hitherto!" (473), it is also possible to see the "ruin" of Rochester as the "ruin" of colonialist practices that conspire with the greed of Rochester's father and brother Rowland for the thirty thousand pounds that comes with Bertha. Undoubtedly, Rochester is the sacrificial son, but what is more to the point in reading *Jane Eyre* as a novel whose romantic plot is imbricated by empire is the fact that the Mason money is derived from a Jamaican plantation. It is the money produced from slave labor that finances Rochester's "roving" around Europe, the maintenance of Thornfield, and, eventually, his impeccable life with Jane.[2] When Jane is set to watch over Richard Mason after he has been bitten by his sister, she wonders what is hidden at Thornfield: "What crime as this, that lived incarnate in this sequestered mansion, and could neither be expelled nor subdued by the owner?" (239).[3] The "crime" is invasion into West Indian society by a greedy gentry class in search of profitable marriage; it is committed by Rochester's father, his brother, and himself, and its victim is Bertha, "incarnate" in her prowling counterinvasion into the life and domestic space of the invader.

Putting aside the formal inheritance that dictates Brontë's romantic plot must end in marriage between tormented hero and steadfast heroine, or, rather, placing alongside this inheritance the political presence of Victorian national identity founded upon developing empire, one sees that *Jane Eyre* devises a fantasy of rehabilitated wealth. In the orderly domestic sphere, symbolized by the union of reformed Rochester and reformer Jane, and supported by his colonial wealth and her much smaller inheritance, will be bred the corps of high-minded imperial administrators the British believed it was sending out to the reaches of empire in the second half of the nineteenth century. Brontë's novel suggests that although wealth from the colonies may have been acquired corruptly, it may still serve to fashion a chastened colonial governance. Jane Eyre's choice between Dionysian and Apollonian lovers may be seen also as a choice between two forms of female work for the empire. Both are essential, and although Victorian colonialism did not value one more than the other, of two historical imperatives in the colo-

---

[2] What I have in mind in reading *Jane Eyre* as a novel whose romantic plot is imbricated by empire is similar to Edward Said's view that nineteenth-century "literature itself makes constant references to itself as somehow participating in Europe's overseas expansion" (*Culture and Imperialism* 14).

[3] Susan L. Meyer argues that the third floor of Thornfield incarnates "the history of the English ruling class as represented by the Rochesters" (255). She also claims that the primary aim of Brontë's political critique in *Jane Eyre* is "gender oppression and the economic oppression of the lower-middle class" (266). One cannot fail to agree that *Jane Eyre* attacks these two forms of oppression, but my reading tends to place greater emphasis than does Meyer's upon the oppression of the colonized native as serving to constitute European subjectivity, especially female subjectivity.

nial politics of the 1830s and 1840s, rehabilitating the colonizer seems to have come first, and converting the colonized second. Jane Eyre's affiliation with the symbolic renovation of colonial governance suggests her more likely presence in Macaulay's still anarchic India (and therefore with St. John Rivers), but early Victorian events in the West Indies conjoin with Brontë's romantic plot to grant Jane Eyre subjectivity in marriage to a romantic hero and in reformation of the colonizer rather than the colonized. The feminist urgency of Brontë's novel dictates, I think, that Jane be given the most powerful form of agency available to a woman of her social class and experience in the 1840s: in the complex ensemble of Jane Eyre's gendered existence as pedagogical object and performative subject, marriage to Rochester constitutes her as less of the former and more of the latter.

For Jane, marriage to Rochester means a symbolic transformation of metropolitan culture and to him, after a life passed "half in unutterable misery and half in dreary solitude," she is his "better self," his "good angel" (342). Marriage to St. John would have meant a literal dedication to the transformation of native superstition into Christian faith, demanding from her a cold vow to become his "invaluable" assistant in the missionary project. To explain how Jane Eyre's destiny is not to be "grilled alive in Calcutta" on the altar of St. John's misogynistic narcissism, I want to explore more fully the gender, race, and class politics of the novel. First I shall discuss St. John Rivers, missionary activity for Victorian women, and the much-debated meaning of the imagery of suttee in Brontë's novel, then the bond between Rochester and the West Indies in conjunction with examining nonliterary texts whose race politics are similar to those in *Jane Eyre*, in particular Carlyle's "Occasional Discourse on the Nigger Question," originally published anonymously in *Fraser's Magazine* in December 1849, and a parliamentary report prepared in January 1847 on how to educate the "Coloured Races of the British Colonies." Later, the ideology of female sacrifice for empire discovered in various travel narratives and memoirs of British women in India will be considered in an elaboration of the meaning of Jane Eyre's suffering and eventual marriage to Rochester. My aim throughout the chapter is to argue that the ideal Victorian woman of empire (Jane Eyre) is always and simultaneously an object constructed by powerful ideas of racial superiority and class difference as well as a subject enacting her own agency through the very ideas that constitute her as an object. But these two forms of self-constitution achieved through a female writing óf the Victorian nation do not exist in a perfect balance. The process is dynamic, shifting, and contested.

EASTERN ALLUSIONS

Beginning his stern wooing of Jane Eyre, St. John Rivers describes how he arrived at his decision to go to India. He admits that under his "curate's surplice" has beat "the heart of a politician, of a soldier, of a votary of glory, a lover of renown, a luster after power" (388). Deploying an image that suggests the unmapped spaces of uncolonized territory (Marlow's worrisome "blank" spaces on a map), St. John suddenly sees his missionary existence "all at once spread out to a plain without bounds," and he articulates his imagined life in the East as one of aggressive and transformative public action: he will carry knowledge "into the realms of ignorance," will substitute "peace for war," "freedom for bondage," "religion for superstition" (400). His ambition, he announces, is "unlimited," and it is interesting to discover in actual missionary literature many warnings against the pride with which Brontë invests St. John Rivers. The remarks of Hannah Kilham, for example, who wrote letters to London from Sierra Leone in the early 1830s (the probable historical time in which Brontë arranges Jane's fictive stay with the Rivers family), could very well be derived from observing a man with the steely aggressiveness of St. John: "To such minds there is something very inviting in the idea of crossing seas, travelling to a great distance, seeing new countries and new people." But too often, Kilham goes on to say, the missionary begins to indulge "feelings of pride concerning himself" (Biller, 430). Brontë's characterization of St. John Rivers astutely identifies the desire for power that drives the career of a politician or soldier, which St. John, of course, is the first to admit. Consequently, he is a missionary who could very well be a colonial administrator; Macaulay's disciplined colonial administrator emerges from St. John's characterization of himself as a man who has channeled secular ambition into conversion of the heathen.

Assuming that the latest date by which Jane and Rochester could have married would be 1836,[4] St. John speaks at a time when the hege-

---

[4] Meyer speculates that Rochester and Bertha might have married in 1821, which would set the Rochester/Jane marriage in the mid-1830s.

mony of British military and commercial rule enabled the proliferation of missionary societies (in 1813, the East India Company lifted its ban on their entry into India).[5] Allotting Jane the common function of women in Indian missionary activity (come and be a "conductress of Indian schools"), which was to infiltrate the zenanas (women's quarters) as well as work as teachers, St. John sounds remarkably like an official of the Church Missionary Society who observed in the late 1840s that "the missionary is too often forced into a position of controversy and antagonism, while the attitude of the female evangelist is free from even the appearance of aggression" (quoted in Pollock, 47).[6] It seems to me that St. John's plans for Jane's social isolation through missionary work among native women suggest something similar to the Indian woman's seclusion in the zenana, just as Diana Rivers's remarks about British women getting "grilled alive" in the Calcutta sun evoke the British obsession with suttee.[7]

[5] As Philip Curtin observes in his examination of links between early Victorian Evangelicalism and missionary involvement in the Niger expedition of 1841–42 (the Church Missionary Society was the missionary group of choice for this ill-fated venture), "The spread of British mission stations inevitably involved the British government (*The Image of Africa* 314)."

[6] Had Jane traveled to India with St. John, she would probably have taught in a school founded by the Society for Promoting Female Education in the East, which came into being in 1834. In 1852, the first Calcutta Normal School opened, which trained teachers, to be followed in 1857 by the foundation of the first public high school for native Indian girls. See Pollock for a comprehensive history of the roles of female teachers and medical missionaries in India up until the mid-nineteenth century. For a recent account of women working in the public sphere in India, see Barbara N. Ramusack, "Cultural Missionaries, Maternal Imperialists, Feminist Allies: British Women Activists in India, 1865–1945."

[7] Early in the nineteenth century, the allure of the exotic zenana had entered sensationalist literature. A representative text of what one might call the Orientalist-zenana-harem genre is *The Bengalee* (1829), written by a retired officer in the Bengal Civil Service (H. B. Henderson). The British officer, and narrator, becomes the savior of a native princess of a high caste by somehow getting her out of the zenana: "here he had found a young creature, loveliness itself, with a soul of enterprise and energy beyond the common stamp, and yet more gentle and timid even than our forest poets had delighted to pourtray [sic] in their glowing pages of Eastern imagery" (37). In these adventure tales featuring the British rescue of lovely young creatures incarcerated by oriental despots, the native woman becomes a victim of her own barbarous culture, and her liberation depends upon the chivalrous intervention of the British raj. Toward the end of the nineteenth century, the zenana became much in demand as a tourist site for British women. Usually recorded in terms of Western regret that the lives of native women were being wasted, these visits were flavored with a Jane Eyre–like distaste for physical and mental indolence. A Mrs. Aynsley, for example, describing her meeting with a widowed rani in 1879, recalled that it made her "very sad to think of the life of perpetual seclusion to which such an intelligent young lady is condemned by Hindu prejudices as, from what I saw of her, I could well imagine she might become a useful and happy member of society if only it were possible to emancipate her" (264). Throughout this book, incidentally, I have deployed the anglicized term, *suttee*, rather than the Hindu term, *sati*.

From their inception in the middle of the eighteenth century, British missionary societies had been organized and controlled by men; but female missionaries were always deemed necessary for what St. John had in mind for Jane. In 1784, for example, a tract directed "To the Members of the Church of the Brethren, who minister in the Gospel among the Heathen" noted that the male missionaries "could not be of effectual service, without the assistance of some Sisters among the heathen women. For when people are truly awakened, they are very desirous to open all their circumstances, in confidence to some person, and to seek good advice" ("Instructions for the Members of the Unitas Fratrum" v). However, as is often the case in male-dominated social, cultural, and political organizations, women discovered some benefits in their ancillary status. Despite St. John's chilling obsession with what Jane will do for him, rather than how, together, they might serve the missionary cause, in the 1830s, missionary work was beginning to offer women a liberty and employment often denied them at home. And some thirty years after the publication of *Jane Eyre*, women's missionary labor in India possessed little of the selfless dedication to the male missionary demanded by St. John Rivers, as the founding in 1880 of the Church of England Zenana Missionary Society on explicitly feminist principles demonstrates (Buckland, 13). It is possible to imagine that a woman with Jane Eyre's intelligence and energy might well have gone to Calcutta at the end of the Victorian period—and that she would have gone alone, perhaps as a medical missionary. When unmarried female medical missionaries started going out to India in the 1870s, they were often recruited by the promise of employment unavailable to them in the British androcentric medical establishment: for instance, the *Madras Times* on 3 December 1881 promised that a female doctor "would have a magnificent practice, and would soon win fame and fortune."[8] By this time, there were nearly two hundred Western women working as medical missionaries in the zenanas, who had arrived in India ready to deliver native women from ignorance and oppression. To be sure, the oppression of Indian women was perceived in Eurocentric terms; the seclusion of women in the zenanas, for example, which was seen as barbaric superstition by no-nonsense New Women, was not necessarily regarded as such by the native women secluded behind their veils and in their women's quarters. Anchored as they may be

[8] Quoted in *India's Women* 2:80.

in myths of Western industry and Eastern sloth, however, the stories of Victorian women in India setting up schools for the blind and the deaf, working as medical doctors, and training Indian women to work in small factories, seem preferable to St. John's misogynistic dream of Jane's exclusive allegiance to himself.[9]

Addressing Jane, then, more in terms of colonial command than romantic persuasion, as she sits translating Schiller, St. John tells her imperiously "I want you to give up German and learn Hindustani" (422). Admitting that he has been observing her character and also revealing that he, together with Rochester, has understood that character very well, he announces that he recognizes in her a soul that revels "in the flame and excitement of sacrifice" (an echo of the imagery of suttee deployed by Brontë in the parry and thrust of Jane and Rochester's courtship). He proposes marriage in these terms: "Jane, you are docile, diligent, disinterested, faithful, constant, and courageous; very gentle, and very heroic: cease to mistrust yourself—I can trust you unreservedly. As a conductress of Indian schools, and a helper amongst Indian women, your assistance will be to me invaluable" (429). In language that nearly repeats that used by the missionary widower of a young woman who died in Jamaica in 1836—to her husband she was an "invaluable assistant"—St. John gets it almost right.[10] Jane possesses virtually all the qualities with which he endows her, except docility. Moreover, if we read Jane from the double perspective of her performance as symbolic governess of empire and as pedagogical object in the novel's negotiation of early Victorian sexual and race politics, then we see that her missionary task is not to be trusted by St. John Rivers; her vocation is to rescue Rochester from his career of materialism and debauchery in a manner that grants her agency in the service of patriarchal rehabilitation. In terms of historical actuality, at the time Jane marries Rochester, Macaulay's plan for the moral renovation of India, spurred by Evangelical beliefs, is just getting under way. As a consequence, it seems safe to say that some twenty years later, the British empire having more securely

[9] A late-Victorian writer about women in missionary work notes that in the Church Missionary Society in 1873 there were 11 female missionaries and that by 1893 there were 134. (See Buckland, 13).

[10] Mary Ann Hutchins was eulogized by her husband in this way: "Her lively disposition, her quickness at discerning countenances and remembering them, and the extraordinary manner in which she would listen to, and converse with the Negroes so as to understand them, soon caused her to become a great favourite with them, and to me an invaluable assistant" (Middleditch, *The Youthful Female Missionary* 139).

matched its moral authority to its territorial conquests, there would have been less political need for women like the fictional Jane Eyre to rehabilitate men like the fictional Rochester.

St. John's warning to Jane that if she refuses to be his wife and work with him "amidst savage tribes," she will limit herself to a "track of selfish ease and barren obscurity" reveals his deep distrust of women. With Jane he is an emotional sadist. Jane, knowing she can deal better with the physical abuse dished out by John Reed than with St. John's punitive detachment, admits, after he has sentenced her to frivolity and sterility if she fails to marry him, that she would "much rather he had knocked me down" (435). As victim and agent in writing the Victorian nation, Jane is always prepared to suffer in the cause of that discursive enterprise, but it is her own lucid awareness of having chosen sacrifice or of having no control over the misery that is imposed upon her that secures her survival. As pedagogical object, Jane is instructed to play whatever role is scripted for her by the history of Britannic rule, but at the same time, as performative subject, she is provided with some degree of her own agency, her own subjectivity, her own discursive stage. Jane Eyre chooses to leave Thornfield, and she does not choose to be intimidated by St. John Rivers; she knows she must suffer at Lowood, but it is essential for her to gain some control of the situation, a feeling she fervently expresses to Helen Burns, "I must resist those who punish me unjustly. It is as natural as that I should love those who show me affection, or submit to punishment when I feel it is deserved" (90). What enables a frail, friendless, and virtually destitute young woman to endure emotional and physical abuse at Gateshead and Lowood, and absolute isolation and sorrow for three days on the tramp after leaving Thornfield, is the powerful sense of self expressed in her conviction that she must not give in to Rochester: "'Who in the world cares for *you?* or who will be injured by what you do?' Still indomitable was the reply: '*I* care for myself!'" (344) Jane's disinclination to be "grilled alive in Calcutta" emerges from this sense of self, as does as her refusal to commit a symbolic act of suttee in subjugation by Rochester.

Jane Eyre's spry announcement that she will not be "hurried away in a suttee" (301) should Rochester die before she does has engaged almost all recent critical readings of *Jane Eyre,* whether undertaken from the perspective of feminist analysis or colonial studies.[11] Suvendrini Perera

---

[11] See Mary Ellis Gibson, Suvendrini Perera, Jenny Sharpe, and Laura Donaldson. Gibson, Perera, and Sharpe each offer cogent interpretations of *Jane Eyre,* but Donaldson's infatuation

argues, for instance, that "Jane must reject 'the Eastern allusion' in the text of Western feminism she is inscribing with her life. At the same time . . . only this allusion makes possible the telling of Jane's story, supplying the vocabulary for the sexual risks faced by the unattached Englishwoman" (81).[12] In general, Perera's analysis of links between the English novel and empire is astute, but her belief that it is only through reference to the seraglio and to suttee that Jane can tell her story requires expansion and complication. Perera claims that "Having become a widely accessible European symbol sati could function simultaneously as an emblem of female oppression through which Western women represented their own struggles" (91). It seems to me, however, that metaphors of empire in Brontë's novel seem more to express the fact that Jane Eyre is not controlled by native superstition (as are women who commit suttee) and that she is not a slave in an "Eastern" harem (as are the eroticized figures in Rochester's sexual imagination). Some readers of the novel may be tempted to see Thornfield as a kind of Yorkshire harem, what with Bertha in the attic and Rochester's female servants waiting breathlessly for the sound of his horse in the driveway, but this simplifies the complex (and racist) meanings of *Jane Eyre*. *Jane Eyre* is about the way Thornfield is not the West Indies and is not India; and it also about the way that what is in the West Indies and what is in India comes back to invade the metropolitan spaces of empire. Who would have imagined, asks an amazed Gabriel Betteredge in *The Moonstone*, that a "quiet English house" could be "invaded by a devilish Indian Diamond"? Who would have imagined, Jane Eyre could very well ask her reader, that the third floor of Thornfield Hall could contain something brought back from the colonies, something that may be

---

with theoretical jargon hobbles the intelligence of her insights. She declares, for example, that in the "Eastern-allusion" conversations with Rochester, "The knifelike edges of Jane's discourse cut the chimerical threads sutering the wound of the subject together, and it is precisely this heterogeneous sharpness that Althusserian interpellation blunts" (27). Donaldson also asserts that Brocklehurst "textually installs a phallic Personhood over the castrated womanhood of Jane" (24). In my view, Gayatri Spivak has provided, to date, the most politically sensible reading of the meaning of suttee in the British colonial imagination. Searching through the archives for a Rani of Sirmur who committed suttee in the nineteenth century, Spivak argues that both the British Raj and "the Brahminical discourse of widow-sacrifice" deny the rani any subjectivity: "Between patriarchal subject-formation and imperialist object-constitution, it is the dubious place of the free will of the sexed subject as female that is successfully effaced" ("The Rani of Sirmur" 268).

[12] Mary Ellis Gibson makes a similar point in her article on the meaning of the seraglio and suttee in *Jane Eyre:* the metaphors associated with empire in Brontë's novel "create a subversive, if covert and ambiguous, criticism of domination in domestic relationships, a criticism that extends to British imperialist impulses themselves" (1).

said to invade the bleak countryside just as much as the Indian rogues of Collins's novel (67) invade Betteredge's beloved country house? Certainly, Jane advances her pursuit of female and feminist independence through appropriation of Eastern images of oppression, but it seems to me that Brontë's references to suttee are meant to show a female oppression imagined in Victorian popular thinking as much worse than Jane's governess confinement in England. These images distinguish the Victorian values that Jane evokes in her preference for healthy England rather than steamy Marseilles. That "wogs" are thought to begin at Calais is the thinking behind Jane's disdain of the "Eastern allusion" (297), her crisp references to the harem, her ironic evocation of suttee.

As she and Rochester return from an uncomfortable shopping expedition that Jane has determined to turn into a one of her severe moral lessons, she recalls, "He smiled; and I thought his smile was such as a sultan might, in a blissful and fond moment, bestow on a slave his gold and gems had enriched" (297). In this episode, Jane is determined to show Rochester that they live in the healthy heart of England not in the besotted sultan culture of the East: for her, there can be no alignment of the Eastern confinement of women in harems and her own acquiescence in confinement as an English governess. When Rochester delightedly declares that he would exchange her for an entire seraglio, she promptly retorts that if this is what he wants, then he should head in the direction of Istanbul. And if he does so, she vows, "I'll be preparing myself to go out as a missionary to preach liberty to them that are enslaved" (297). Note that in this fantasy, she will be the one doing the preaching, not serving as helper. That Jane is not "grilled alive in Calcutta," suggests, as I have argued, that her destined sacrifice is on the domestic fire of resisting and rehabilitating Rochester's passionate temperament. If one hears in this resonant phrase the moans of Indian widow-sacrifice and remembers that Jane's values station her in direct opposition to what was seen as barbaric superstition in British culture, then one sees that the sacrifice of Indian widows is very different from the rational sacrifices demanded from British women in a gendered labor for empire. This important difference is apparent in the many myths of suttee embellished by the Victorians. For example, in Fanny Parks's travel narrative, *The Wanderings of a Pilgrim in Search of the Picturesque* (1850), she rejoices that "no more widows are to be grilled, to ensure the whole of the property passing to the sons of the deceased" (1:162). In Tennyson's "Akbar's Dream," the enlightened seventeenth-century Islamic king envisions a time when neither the "Fires of Suttee, nor wail of baby-wife, / Or Indian widow" are heard. In a poem by the travel writer Emma Roberts, the speaker contrasts what she believes to be a Brahmin reverence for life with "those impure, unhallowed fires, / Where by a living corse's side, / In fierce and torturing pangs expires, / Untimely doomed, the shrinking bride" (*Oriental Scenes* 24).

In less sensationalist language, in October 1852 the *London Quarterly Review* provided the story of a Major Ludlow who in Rajpootana in 1844 almost singlehandedly (it is claimed) eliminated the last vestiges of suttee. Presiding over the council of regency in Jypore, Ludlow first deals with the problem of female infanticide, practiced primarily because parents could not afford the dowries demanded in the region. Ludlow brings some rational economic thinking to bear upon the problem and persuades the various Rajpootana provinces to agree to a common scale of marriage portions "apportioned to the revenue of the bride's parents, with uniform penalties for all demands in excess" (137). The issue then confronting Ludlow (a kind of real-life counterpart to the hero of the 1825 oriental tale, *The Bengalee*) is phrased by the *Quarterly Review* in this way: "He had rescued her child for the mother. Could he rescue the mother for the child?" (138). A fervent representative of the high-minded British Raj, Ludlow persuades the priests that suttee is a perversion of religious teaching, and he succeeds.[13] The Indians are filled with "wonder and awe" at the British "veracity, justice, and energy" exemplified in Major Ludlow's arguments. But this, in fact, becomes another problem. Rather than attempting to remedy "the defects of their own system," the Indians spend all their time admiring the British way of doing things. The fresh challenge facing Major Ludlow, and by extension the British Raj, is how to deal with a native culture acknowledged by the British as not savage, but more problematically as having degenerated from a once admirable condition. The *Quarterly Review* essay concludes that no religious instruction should

[13] Vina Mazumdar questions the distortions of Indian history involved in the British persuasion of ruling-class Hindus that suttee was contrary to traditional teaching: "The social reformers of the nineteenth century, in their efforts to improve the lot of high-caste Hindu women, particularly widows, fell back on the ancient scriptures, arguing convincingly that women did enjoy far higher status in the Vedic period, which had permitted them free access to education, ritual sacraments, divorce under special circumstances, and remarriage" (271). What is left out of the Victorian arguments, for Mazmudar, is the fact (proved, she claims, in historical scholarship) that in the Vedic period, Hindu women provided the main productive labor force at a time when men were preoccupied with military or political conquests.

be attempted because although Christianity may be written "on the tablula rasa of a savage mind," people "not in the infancy of barbarism, but in the decrepitude of a precocious civilization" must be untaught before they can be instructed.[14] The distinguishing marks of what the *Quarterly Review* regards as Major Ludlow's noble fight against native superstition characterize much of the Victorian discourse on suttee.[15]

The Adventures of Naufragus. Written by Himself, published anonymously in 1827 by James Moffat Horne, provides what purports to be a firsthand description of the practice that so fascinated and repelled the British in the early part of the nineteenth century. The scene begins with a procession headed by a forty-five-year-old widow, loaded down with gold ornaments, accompanied by many female attendants and priests, who mounts the funeral pyre of her dead husband, after which "a quantity of straw, rosin, butter, and oil, was strewed over her and the corpse" (203). The widow then empties a pot of oil over her head, ignites herself and the corpse, prompting this assessment from the British observer: "Such was the end of a woman, who, instead of living to serve and adorn society, thus became the victim of a cruel and barbarous superstition" (207), a sentiment that encapsulates the British view of suttee as a barbaric ritual calling upon women to suffer without useful purpose. In contrast, according to almost all Victorian writing about empire, the purpose of British female suffering is rational, useful, sensible: to produce moral transformation in the uncivilized peoples who engage in barbarous rituals such as suttee. Jane's instruction of Rochester in a culture of female sacrifice and discipline, which begins on the shopping expedition, proceeds through her insistence on spending their courtship evenings in conversation rather than

[14] Ram Mohun Roy, an Indian educated in Oriental and European literature who supported the 1835 decision by the British Raj that Indians would be educated in English, expressed something similar to the admiring sentiments that prove difficult for Major Ludlow. He declares that Indians are hopeful the 1835 decision will mean that British funds will be "laid out in employing European talents and education to instruct the natives of India in mathematics, natural philosophy, chemistry, anatomy, and other useful sciences, which the nations of Europe have carried to a degree of perfection that has raised them above the inhabitants of other parts of the world" (quoted in Trevelyan, *On the Education of the People of India* 66).

[15] I use the term "discourse" here quite deliberately, rather than the phrase, say, "ideology of suttee." As Lata Mani aptly observes, the term "discourse" is a more useful analytical tool "for it retains the dialogical processes implied by speech and requires at least two parties. I believe it is useful to speak of a 'colonial discourse' on *sati* rather than a colonial ideology, precisely because knowledge about colonial society was produced through interaction between colonialists — officials, scholars, missionaries — and select natives" (108).

in hand-holding, and concludes with her assumption of her final role as his wife/nurse/moral teacher/authoritative mother at Ferndean, is affiliated with the moral teachings of empire. The language of seraglio, suttee, and sacrifice in *Jane Eyre* certainly suggests the reciprocal constitution of ideologies of empire and gender in the Victorian period, but this language always elaborates British female superiority over the women of the seraglio.[16]

Several critics have argued that Jane's sexual desire for Rochester can only be satisfied through the metaphorical suttee performed by Bertha Mason Rochester as she flings herself from the burning roof of Thornfield Hall.[17] But Bertha Mason Rochester is also an insane, creole white woman from the West Indies figuratively described as having the obscene propensities of a black woman, and at the end of *Jane Eyre*, she flings herself to the ground as her lunatic asylum goes up in flames. If she may be said to commit suttee, then she does so not in order to be with Rochester, or to perform superstitious homage to Rochester; she burns down Thornfield out of her hatred of him, just as she has attempted to set him on fire and later kindled Jane Eyre's bed after she leaves Thornfield. What is to be found, though, in the image of Bertha flinging herself to the ground from a burning building is a trope of extreme female suffering, and it is here that Bertha may be aligned most fully with her physical and moral opposite, Jane Eyre. Bertha is a woman "grilled" by flames sparked by Rochester's corrupt colonialist practices, and it is through her own and characteristically British form of female suffering

---

[16] Overall, the most sensible commentary on British ideas about suttee is that of Vina Mazumdar. Seeking to locate the practice historically, Mazumdar observes that "the subjugation and seclusion of Hindu women, denying them the rights of divorce, remarriage, and property and other basic rights, was a practice confined to the higher castes.... For peasant women, whether Hindu or Muslim, *purdah* was an impossible luxury, and remarriage of widows was a fully accepted practice" (271). Mazumdar's argument is grounded in a rejection of the British attacks on suttee from the perspective of personal freedom, a concept, she claims, that was foreign to upper-class Hindu women.

[17] See Susan Meyer's essay and also that of Mary Ellis Gibson, which anticipates many of the points made by Meyer. Gibson argues that "the metaphors associated with empire in *Jane Eyre* create a subversive, if covert and ambiguous, criticism of domination in domestic relationships, a criticism that extends to British imperialist impulses themselves" (1). Gibson also claims (plausibly) that Brontë read the missionary reports of the *Methodist Magazine*, and, of course, the travel accounts that regularly appeared in the quarterly magazines, both of which featured accounts of barbaric "Eastern" practices. Winifred Gerin provides detailed description of how the Brontë children were strongly influenced by the religious training of their aunt; she also notes the "potent" effect of the "children's readings in her complete set of the *Methodist Magazine*, which was sent after Mrs. Brontë from Penzance, salvaged from shipwreck on the way to Liverpool, and stained with salt waves of 1812" (35).

that Jane must rescue and reform Bertha's colonial creator and destroyer.

Acting always as an "I" that cares for itself, during the period of Rochester's ardent wooing, Jane refuses the expensive dresses he picks out for her, although she carefully tells the reader that one was of a "rich silk of the most brilliant amethyst dye" and the other "a superb pink satin" (296). In this way, we are led to know the strength of her renunciation, just as we recognize the moral strength of Dorothea Brooke in *Middlemarch* when the narrator confides that Dorothea has given up riding, in part, because it affords her so much pleasure. With "infinite difficulty," Jane says, she persuades him to exchange the dresses she clearly admires but chooses not to have, for "a sober black satin and pearl-gray silk" (296). Filled with the moral rectitude of a British woman of her social class and education, she rejects the bright clothing, just as she refuses to sink into what she terms "a bathos of sentiment" in her month-long engagement, preferring instead to devise for her husband-to-be a "season of probation." To be sure, Rochester's dominating masculine personality is associated with the imagery of oriental despotism, and Jane's notions of what he may and may not do during their courtship, her construction of a probationary period as prelude to the rehabilitation of a past tainted by tropical lasciviousness, are flavored with imagery of the harem.[18] But as a symbolic woman of Victorian empire, Jane forcefully objects to the "Eastern allusion." It is she, enacting her gender, class, and race agency, who evokes this allusion, not Rochester; it is she who introduces into the novel fantasies of Eastern enslavement of women in order to negate them.[19] Described as "that midge of a governess" (452) by the innkeeper who reveals what has happened to Rochester after Jane leaves Thornfield, she powerfully controls the imagery of her narrative and the life of her supposed enslaver, Rochester.

To restrict the aim of Brontë's political critique in *Jane Eyre* to the oppression of middle-class women and to limit the function of her imagery of oriental despotism to evocation of tyrannical Victorian patriarchy seem to me to play things critically safe, boxing the novel into

---

[18] See Meyer, 162.

[19] The images of oriental despotism set forth in Knighton's *The Private Life of an Eastern King* (1856) present a king retiring "into the female apartments at an unusually early hour," a move that occasions this horrified response on the part of the narrator: "Heaven help the poor woman who has the misfortune at such a moment to displease or disgust an irritated despot! an accidental sneeze, a louder cough than usual, nay, even an ungraceful movement, may bring down punishment terrible to think of" (67–70).

gender without race, gender without social class. If one broadens the historical context of *Jane Eyre* to the distinction made in early Victorian writing about empire between its own colonial practices and those that have gone before, then Rochester becomes an antiquated patriarch whose imaginative affiliation with Eastern sultans places him in the morally tainted stages of colonial governance. The political critique in *Jane Eyre* has to do with 1830s patriarchy, to be sure, but it is more than that: its race and gender politics evoke the proper role of women in the empire and the need for high moral standards in the governance of that empire. The political aims of Brontë's novel thus become wide-ranging and about more than the indictment of the miserable life of a midge of a governess. They are directed to how Britain should refashion itself as a nation at a time of social change occasioned, in part, by colonial expansion. Moreover, the qualities thought to constitute a good Victorian governess—self-discipline, immense patience, willingness to endure physical and emotional deprivation—are the qualities that also were thought to constitute a good woman for ancillary assistance in colonial governance.

Jane Eyre, then, does not merely evoke the "Eastern allusion" to dramatize the leering wickedness of Victorian patriarchy or give Rochester his West Indian experience so that Jane may be his salvational angel or merely introduce St. John Rivers's cold fanaticism as contrast to Rochester's warm vulnerability. *Jane Eyre* is about a specific historical moment when women were called upon to be agents in the labor of both renovating and expanding Britannic rule. Let me turn now from St. John Rivers, missionary India, and the imagery of suttee to the colonial world of Rochester, the West Indies, and a female agency achieved through moral renovation. I would like to begin by demonstrating similarities in ideas about race and the West Indies between Carlyle's notorious exploration of what he terms the Nigger Question, the parliamentary report of 1847, and *Jane Eyre*. This discussion will serve to disclose the historical actuality of the Jamaica evoked by Rochester in his narrative of tropical desire.

TROPICAL DESIRES

Carlyle's essay has become a whipping post for postcolonial critics, and given the appalling racism of his thinking, it is easy to see why. But it seems to me that the central ideas propounded in this essay are, in essence, not so different from those advanced in *Jane Eyre*. Jane's fervent observation at the end of the novel, after all, that St. John is in India clearing "the painful way to improvement" by lopping down "the prejudices of creed and caste that encumber it" (477) is not too different from Carlyle's fantasy of a reeking jungle in desperate need of literal and metaphorical cleansing. Cast in Carlyle's familiar narrative device of an editor or witness reconstituting a text or reporting an event, and framed by perceived threats to the social order posed by the 1848 European revolutions, lingering Chartist activity, and the Irish economic disasters of the 1840s, the "Nigger Question" essay purports to render a speech given on the "Rights of Negroes." Although Carlyle suggests little danger of revolution in the West Indies (his "Quashee"s are far too lazy to agitate for political change), his evocation of Ireland in talking about Demerera indicates the pervasive geopolitical popping up, as it were, of one subjugated group in the colonialist discourse of another. Some twenty years later, James Anthony Froude observes that "the keener-witted Trinidadians·are watching as eagerly as we do the development of the Irish problem. . . . They see that if the Radical view prevails, and in every country the majority are to rule, Trinidad will be theirs and the government of the English will be at an end" (98). Equally worried about the radical view, Carlyle warns against the indulgence of West Indian blacks in idleness while "British Whites" are hanging on the edge of famine and British society on the edge of possible revolution. He proclaims a remedy in his well-known "Gospel of Work" and in affirmation that man is but God's vice-regent on earth in execution of the hierarchical order of things.[20] For Carlyle, it is sacrilege to mess with the natural supremacy of European civilization over all others, within and outside the empire.

Written with the wild energy and linguistic abandon that so often characterizes Carlyle's prose, the "Nigger Question" argues that black West Indians are destined "to be servants to those that are born *wiser* than you, that are born lords of you; servants to the Whites, if they *are* (as what mortal can doubt they are) born wiser than you" (488). Sharing

---

[20] The prescription of work as salvation for many Victorian ills is, of course, not restricted to Carlyle. Harriet Martineau, for example, when criticizing in 1838 the American practice of placing criminals in solitary confinement without labor, hard or otherwise, announces, "Work is, in prison as out of it, the grand equaliser, stimulus, composer and rectifier; the prime obligation, and the prime privilege" (*Retrospect of Western Travel* 1:208).

none of his contemporaries' belief in mid-Victorian moral superiority to late-eighteenth-century moral laxity, Carlyle finds mid-Victorian Britain sunk "in deep froth-oceans" of rubbish about benevolence, fraternity, emancipation, and philanthropy (465), its citizens deaf to what is, for him, their "everlasting duty": to work. In Demerera (not technically in the West Indies, but grouped by Britain with the Caribbean plantations), one may find "an idle Black gentleman with his rum-bottle in his hand, (for a little additional pumpkin you can have red-herrings and rum, in Demerera), – rum-bottle in his hand, no breeches on his body, pumpkin at discretion, and the fruitfulest region of the earth going back to jungle round him" (470).[21] This is the core of Carlyle's fable of tropical sloth in the absence of correct "regulation" (471). An enduring Victorian fable, it is worth noting: a *Macmillan's Magazine* article published in 1885 terms the "Barbadian negro" "a treacherous, idle, lying, thieving, sensual creature" (19).[22] Britain is awash in sentimental nonsense about equality, according to Carlyle, abandoning itself to the worship of money as "the real symbol of wisdom" rather than developing a proper disciplinary order for its empire. Although different in almost every way, say, from William Arnold's *Oakfield* (1854), the "Nigger Question" shares the novel's critique of what Arnold terms the "beaver" tendencies (2:223) of the East India Company, city finance, and colonial politics.

Seeming intuitively to understand the complex process of "worlding" identified by Gayatri Spivak, Carlyle describes the changes brought by Europeans to the "West India Islands" in a manner that demands lengthy quotation:

> For countless ages, since they first mounted oozy, on the back of earthquakes, from their dark bed in the Ocean deeps, and reeking saluted the tropical Sun, and ever onwards till the European white man first saw them some three short centuries ago, those Islands had produced mere jungle, savagery, poison-reptiles and swamp malaria: till the white Euro-

---

[21] Peter Fryer notes that in 1823, "about 12,000 slaves rose in revolt on the east coast of Demerera, one of the three Guyana colonies the British had finally taken from the Dutch 20 years before. There was in the Guyana colonies a long tradition of slave rebellions, suppressed with utmost ferocity, and in 1763 slaves led by Africans had controlled the entire colony of Berbice for over a year" (*Black People in the British Empire* 91).

[22] The article also dwells upon the "idleness of the negro"; where Carlyle's Demereran native need do no work, with "pumpkin at discretion," in Barbados "the idleness of the negro is not so unnatural . . . the sugar cane, of which he is particularly fond, lies open to his hand" (20).

pean first saw them, they were as if not yet created, — their noble elements of cinnamon, sugar, coffee, pepper black and grey, lying all asleep, waiting the white enchanter who should say to them, Awake! (484)

What one notices first about this passage is the proposition that the islands were, and were not, created before the invasion of Europeans: in Carlyle's narrative, before that advent, the islands mount "oozy," "reeking" salute the sun, and are "mere jungle." "Worlded" as jungle so that the British colonial mind may then construct the lazy, drunken inhabitant of that jungle (pumpkin-loving Quashee), the islands, however, are also "as if not yet created" until the Europeans arrive. Somewhat inconsistently, Carlyle's argument constructs a native jungle going to ruin, which suggests the existence of something before the presence of empire. But the jungle is also described as a void awaiting form, "as if not yet created." In one part of the "Nigger Question" essay, the speaker laments the fact that the "fruitfulest region of the earth [is] going back to jungle" but at another point observes that "Swamps, fever-jungles, man-eating Caribs, rattlesnakes, and reeking waste and putrefaction" are what the Europeans find upon their arrival, thus suggesting that natives are unable to clear their own wilderness, cultivate their own land, produce their own commodities. In sum, what we find in Carlyle's text is a multiple set of images of a native place: "mere jungle" before the Europeans arrive — fetid, rotting, and dangerous, awakened by the "white enchanter in a kind of colonialist rewriting of the Sleeping Beauty myth, "worlded," so that it may be cleansed by the colonizer, and made a place of profitable work for colonizer and colonized. The one thing needful in Carlyle's West Indies is the moral medicine that works wonders for Rochester, and, on another and associated level, the economic management that wipes out a native reliance upon pumpkin and brings that fruit, along with other tropical specimens, to Brixton market after World War II.[23]

[23] Carlyle's recitation of Jamaican history also discloses an island that imaginatively exists and yet does not exist before the European invasion. Before the "white enchanter" arrives in the shape of Saxon heroes who leave their "bones" in the West Indian soil, Jamaica seems to have had no history. In Carlyle's ideological "worlding," British heroes give their bones to the willfully neglected soil, but this is wasted life and effort because nothing has come of it but black idleness: "Any poor idle Black man, any idle White man, rich or poor, is a mere eye-sorrow to the State: a perpetual blister on the skin of the State" (486). Carlyle's medicine for this festering condition is, as we know, work — a dedication on the part of the empire to a strict disciplinary project that will prune, shape, and cultivate tropical exuberance. As Jean D'Costa and Barbara Lalla note in the

Carlyle's myth of native jungle tangled with fecund vegetation is elaborated in Emma Roberts's *Scenes and Characteristics of Hindostan with Sketches of Anglo-Indian Society*. Published in 1835, the work displays neither scenes nor sketches as appealing: the former paints a picture of careless neglect that affirms British cultural superiority and the latter unveils a picture of paralyzing discomfort that works, in part, to minimize, and consequently authorize the British colonial presence.[24]

Nothing can be more "melancholy," Roberts observes, "than the aspect of a building in India which has been suffered to fall into a dilapidated state" (2:3).[25] In a manner that makes us suspect she has been reading Tennyson's "Marianna," Roberts dwells upon cement falling from the wall, weather stains on the brickwork, rusted iron hinges of venetian blinds, and "gigantic lattices" creaking and groaning with every breeze. She sums up this Eastern equivalent to Tennyson's "lonely moated grange" by saying that "there is an air of squalor spread over the whole establishment which disgusts the eye" (2:3). Her evocation of Indian squalor understandably depends upon the visual.

Conjuring scenes of Indian indifference to maintaining valuable buildings, of a "barbaric grandeur" (2:96) revealed in the arrangement of expensive china on garishly patterned cotton cloths, Roberts implicitly frames, and thus orders, the threat of an anarchic society (or at least one so utterly different from British life as to appear anarchic), and causes her British reader to recoil from a lack of propriety and social order, shudder at the vulgar juxtaposition of what is expensive with what is cheap. (All of Roberts's female readers would know that

---

introduction to their chilling selection of Jamaican texts of the eighteenth and nineteenth centuries, *Voices in Exile*, "By the middle of the eighteenth century they [the British] had transformed Jamaica into one of their most prosperous colonies and were producing coffee, dyeing woods, hard woods, and ginger as well as rum, molasses, and sugar" (2–3). D'Costa and Lalla also note that during the second half of the eighteenth century, the white population was overshadowed by the influx of African slaves so that by the time Rochester would have arrived in Jamaica (probably around 1820), the small settlements under white labor would have been replaced by large plantations owned by whites and worked by black slaves.

[24] The *Asiatic Journal* in 1835 took note of the publication of Roberts's volume by praising "its value as the means of familiarizing the people of England with India and Indian topics, which . . . is a necessary preliminary step to bringing public opinion to bear upon the government of our vast Eastern dependency" (32).

[25] This sentiment was anticipated by Bishop Heber writing from India in 1825. After having visited the palace of the king of Delhi, Heber deplored what he termed "dirty, desolate, and forlorn"—defaced marble, old furniture piled in corners, faded tapestry hanging from the walls. He attributes this neglect to the Indians having "no idea of cleaning or mending any thing" (233).

Wedgewood belongs on Nottingham lace, not on the fabric worn by female factory workers.) In these scenes, Roberts justifies the British colonial presence by sketching a disregard of the marks of civilization taken for granted in metropolitan, colonizing culture. A native mingling of magnificence and neglect, grandeur and barbarism, and delicacy and brutality implicitly justifies the classifying presence of British military and civil officials, just as, analogously, Macaulay justifies the British development of a code of laws for India on the grounds that "Hindoo law, Mahometan law, Parsee law, English law" are "perpetually mingling with each other and disturbing each other" ("Government of India" 713). Moreover, the emphasis in Roberts of Indian life as a mess of mingled objects, mismatched fragments, and ruined remnants creates a sense of decayed and decaying culture. Yet, in contradictory images similar to those found in Carlyle's "Nigger Question," India lacks anything resembling proper culture—that is until the arrival of British women upon the scene. These are women who possess the colonial power to reclaim and renovate the wilderness, a talent that finds domestic expression in Jane Eyre's busy reformation of Rochester.

The transformation of Indian life by Western women is celebrated in a terrible poem by Roberts. An "Address, Spoken at the Opening of the Cawnpore Theatre" in October 1829 presents a kind of late-Romantic scene of exotic animals, fantastic vegetation, and ruined temples:

> Where late a jungle spread its tangled dells,
> And panthers lurked within the forest's cells;
> Where still in troops the famished jackalls prowl,
> And the wolf bays the moon with dismal howl . . .
> Mid reliques and remains of tall Kiosks
> Pagodas, minarets, and dome-crowned mosques;
> Where towering palms and spreading banians rise,
> A Doric structure meets the spell-bound eyes—
> Its fair proportions formed in every part
> Just to the classic rules of Roman art . . .
> (*Oriental Scenes* 202–4)

This extraordinary building, the Cawnpore Theatre, was erected through the power of a woman's smile, through the refined and refining presence of British women, who, arriving in India, work alongside their husbands, fathers, and brothers to provide decent monuments to proper civilization. As male civil and military officials set about transforming the laws and customs of British India, so their women begin to establish libraries, country clubs, theaters—the essential pieces of colonial culture designed to comfort the colonizers and inspire, through example, the colonized. Having blessed the wilderness, Roberts's poem concludes, the Victorian woman of empire transforms it into a temple of art so that "lone exiles from a distant coast / No longer mourn for all that they have lost." This clearing of a place in the native wilderness in order to build literal monuments of British civilization is remarkably similar to the work called for by Carlyle in the "Nigger Question" and recalls the renovative labor of Arthur and his knights in Tennyson's *Idylls of the King.*

The transformation of slothful West Indian native ways into disciplined behavior is the aim of a report entitled "Brief Practical Suggestions on the Mode of Organizing and Conducting Day-Schools of Industry, Model Farm-Schools, and Normal Schools, as Part of a System of Education for the Coloured Races of the British Colonies" that was brought before a House of Commons committee in January 1847. The emancipation of the slaves in 1838 occasioned an urgent need to reorganize British plantations so that they could become economically feasible under a new system of hired labor rather then indentured slavery.[26] In addition, the British government began to consider the most effective manner in which to educate the children of former slaves, a group said to have agitated loudly for such educational opportunities. As Joseph Sturge and Thomas Harvey, two Baptist travelers in Jamaica in 1837 observed, "The world has seen no example of so general and intense a desire for education and religious instruction, as has been shewn by the apprentices on behalf of themselves and their children within the last few years" (374).

Driven by the myth of races made excitable by a tropical climate, the report argues for education of the natives so that the British may develop an underclass of workers for the empire, a group capable of protecting property, cultivating the land, and keeping accounts.[27] The purpose of

[26] When slavery was proclaimed at an end on 3 July 1838 in Jamaica, Mary Ann Hutchins, the wife of a Baptist missionary in Savanna-la-Mar, wrote home to her father that "Before this reaches you, you will doubtless have heard that the vile demon *slavery* in Jamaica is *no more!*" (Middleditch, 142).

[27] According to Raymond T. Smith, in the years immediately following the emancipation of the slaves in Jamaica (1838), there was a major effort on the part of the plantation class, the missionaries, and colonial administrators to transform the ex-slaves "into a stable, obedient, docile and hard-working class of wage-labourers; that is, to try to preserve the basic structure of relations

"creating a native middle class among the negro population, and thus, ultimately, of completing the institutions of freedom" is to produce men "interested in the protection of property, and with intelligence enough to take part in that humbler machinery of local affairs which administers to social order" (Curtin, *Imperialism*, 193–4). The purpose of teaching geography to the "coloured races," for example, the report argues, is to enable them "better to understand the Scriptures, and the connection of the colony with the mother country" (200). Whatever civilization one may find in the colonies is vitiated, the report implies, by "the peculiarities of a race which readily abandons itself to excitement, and perhaps needs amusements which would seem unsuitable for the peasantry of a civilized community" (192). The climate, as always for the British, is a real problem, making for torpor and sloth among the "coloured races," and the report argues that European agricultural technology must be deployed "to replace the system of exhausting the virgin soils, and then leaving to natural influences alone the work of reparation" (194). In the "Nigger Question" essay, the native West Indians live in a perilous state of having too much and too little. They enjoy an abundance of natural vegetation in desperate need of Carlyle's "white enchanter" to bring it all to productive life, a condition thought to have been remedied, as Jamaica Kincaid has recently observed, in the prevalent colonialist fantasy that it was the "ingenuity of small shopkeepers in Sheffield and Yorkshire and Lancashire" that enriched the colonies, not the appropriated labor of her Antiguan ancestors (*A Small Place* 10).

In the turbulent postemancipation Caribbean economic and political situation, some mid-nineteenth-century writers about empire nostalgically evoked a time when paternalistic slave masters were efficient and faithful slaves were hardworking. Rather than articulating Carlyle's fantasy of riotous vegetation, the report's program for rational education, or Emma Roberts's myth of the British woman's power to transform the wilderness, these writers create a world of economic production so harmonious that it discounts the benefits of emancipation to the former slaves. For example, a novel by Mrs. Henry Lynch, *Years Ago: A Tale of West Indian Domestic Life of the Eighteenth Century*, published in 1865, describes serene life on a late-eighteenth-century plantation.

Constructed in the form of a journal kept by a fifteen-year-old girl

---

of production by deploying ideological, rather than physical, means of coercion" (93). Peter Fryer also notes that the establishment of the postemancipation apprenticeship system and the institution of the Trespass and Vagrant acts proved almost as brutally punitive for black West Indians as slavery itself. (See *Black People in the British Empire* 28) in the 1790s and given the fictional frame of an editor, Mrs. Lynch's novel is a fascinating text, interlarded with poems by William Cowper, commentaries on Burke's views of the French revolution, and engrossing domestic details of plantation privilege. Mahogany floors are polished every day by eight maids; four little black boys fan the family with orange boughs while at breakfast; an exemplary sugar mill encompasses the curing house, the molasses cistern, the distilling house, and a large hospital for "sick negroes" (32); the provision store is full of "good things" newly arrived from Bristol such as herrings, salted cod, tongues, hams, soap, candles, flour, peas, and groats. The sugar mill is an efficient and economical self-contained unit. Run by white officials and black overseers, dotted with the "rough houses" of "newly-arrived African negroes" who, happily for all, "soon become more civilized, and learn how to satisfy their increasing requirements" (34), this is a world of consensual slavery in which "negroes" labor regularly in watches at crop time, cultivate the land around their cottages, trade poultry, vegetables, clothes, and salt pork, and have their own market day. *Years Ago* also discloses the recurrent tendency in Victorian writing about empire to displace responsibility for restlessness and rebellion on the part of subordinated groups (whether they be the British working classes, colonized natives, or enslaved laborers) on to foreign influences. Mrs. Lynch's novel suggests that Britain's enslaved population is not inherently rebellious but may become so through inflammatory French rhetoric and example. The fault lies not in British slave practices but in the French Revolution: "The whole white population of our Island was in a state of turmoil about this revolution. They seemed very much afraid of the negroes comprehending in any way these insurrectionary feelings, lest it should incite them to rebellion; and certainly there is something very alarming in being in the midst of a wild people, who, if they were to act with energy, and skill, and courage, could soon make themselves masters of the whole Island" (27).

Published eight years after the Indian uprising and precisely at the moment of the 1864–65 rebellions brutally suppressed by Governor Eyre, *Years Ago* offers to the curious British reader details of the early days of empire and provides warnings and reassurances about contemporary events and possibilities. Rebellion on the part of the colonized, the invasion, say, of the enslaved from their picturesque thatched huts into the polished splendor of the slave owner's mansion is, in effect, always already present in order to be denied. In Lynch's novel *The Cotton Tree; or, Emily, the Little West Indian*, published in the same year as

Jane Eyre, the heroine recalls that "I was born in Jamaica, and my first recollections are those of a large shadowy house, and wide piazza, and kind black faces . ... there were smiles from these sable nurses that filled my infant heart with happiness" (1). Kind black faces, sable smiles: these are the images that erase the possibility of black revolution, that blot out the dismayed reaction by Lady Nugent, wife of Jamaica's lieutenant governor, of her visit to a sugar mill: "I asked the overseer how often his people were relieved. He said every twelve hours; but how dreadful to think of their standing twelve hours over a boiling cauldron . . . and he owned to me that sometimes they did fall asleep, and got their poor fingers into the mill; and he shewed me a hatchet, that was always ready to sever the whole limb, as the only means of saving the poor sufferer's life!"[28]

After the Jamaican uprisings of 1864-65, more temperate and less fantastic views than those of Carlyle and Mrs. Lynch emerge in writing about West Indian colonial politics. The letters of Emelia Gurney, wife of one of the members of the commission charged to investigate the causes of the rebellions, reveal a colonial sensibility far different from Emma Roberts's feverish fear of the natives and Mrs. Lynch's recollections of smiling "sable nurses." In Emelia Gurney's letters (to which I have referred in discussing the presence of black people in Victorian London), we hear a woman thinking about empire who struggles to support the political views and ambitions of her husband but who also, in a manner that recalls Emily Eden's frankness, insists on recording the brutality of plantation life. Gurney's intelligent impressions of Jamaica aim at fairness, even if they are inevitably derived from her position as wife of a ruling-class colonial official. Participating in a civil discourse about race relations in the colonies clearly shaped by the Jamaica events of the mid-1860s, the letters urge more than one perspective: the whites are shown to be threatened by the emancipated blacks and worried by their diminished incomes caused by the loss of slave labor; the blacks are painfully shown as the brutalized victims of years of abuse.[29]

[28] Quoted in Fryer, *Black People in the British Empire* 14. In a manner similar to that of Lady Nugent, in 1837 Joseph Sturge and Thomas Harvey described their reaction to the use of the treadmill in this way: "There were two gangs of men and women, who, we were told, worked alternate spells of fifteen minutes each; an almost incredible amount of punishment. . . . No regard was paid to decency in providing [women] with a suitable dress to work on the mill" (169).

[29] Gurney also argues that the different missionary factions must be held responsible for stirring up trouble. As Philip Curtin observes, missionary groups in Jamaica tended to ally themselves either with agitators or with planters, depending on their affiliation: the dissenters were inclined

Gurney also records in scrupulous detail her husband's view that "the whole system has been utterly rotten" (297). Visiting plantations that once worked ten thousand slaves and whose owners prided themselves on being able to distinguish the African ancestry of their former slaves (usually either Mandingo or Ebo), Emelia Gurney sees Jamaica as occasionally the awesome wilderness of Carlyle's turbulently racist imagination but never the rank home of black sloth and tropical exuberance. Perhaps as a way not to confront more fully the brutality she documents so painfully, Jamaica, for her, becomes an anglicized Eden: "We are now in the district of St. Thomas in the East, which looks like a rich exotic garden, the ground swelling in soft hills, cut through by numbers of streams, hastening to the sea—such a garden of Eden!" (312).[30] Carlyle's West Indies is an Eden gone to rack and ruin; Roberts's India will be made Edenic through the female cultivation of Western culture; Mrs. Lynch's Jamaica is a paternalistic paradise of benevolent masters and smiling slaves; for Emelia Gurney, writing in the mid-1860s in a place long colonized by the British (and some forty fictional years after Rochester languished in Spanish Town) Jamaica is, finally, a British garden paradise—richly exotic, nicely swelling hills, nothing too frightening, everything under control, and utterly different from the Jamaica that Rochester evokes for Jane Eyre.

We learn from Rochester's narrative that his father married him off to the daughter of a West Indian planter and merchant, not an unusual arrangement for impoverished gentry sons.[31] "Ignorant, raw, and inexperienced" (that is to say, sexually naive), he goes out to Jamaica

---

to support the agitators and the Anglicans tended to support the planters. Curtin provides an excellent survey of the volatile mixture of emancipation and church politics in Jamaica in the 1820s and 1830s: "The missionary had a peculiar place in Jamaican society: he was simultaneously a member of the white caste and an ally of the slaves. In this dual capacity, he was only partly accepted by the Negroes and he was rejected by the white caste as a deserter and an enemy of white society" (*Two Jamaicas* 35). Curtin gives the historical background for the native rebellions of the 1830s in which white planters, having blamed the unrest on radical missionary activity, formed the Colonial Church Union, a planters' organization operating behind the facade of the Church of England and calling for the expulsion of dissenting missionary organizations.

[30] Images of Eden are fairly common in nineteenth-century travel writing. For example, Bishop Heber in 1825 described the Botanic Garden in Delhi as "a very beautiful and well-managed institution, . . . a picturesque and most beautiful scene, and more perfectly answers Milton's idea of Paradise, except that it is on a dead flat instead of a hill, than any thing which I ever saw" (48).

[31] In Mrs. Henry Lynch's novel *Years Ago,* the Rochester and Mason family arrangement is viewed from the Jamaican side: the narrator of Mrs. Lynch's novel recalls that "a West Indian planter's daughter was too noble forsooth to be the wife of an English merchant's son" (255).

and marries a woman who initially proves to be sexually exciting. In a manner similar to that of one of the important male characters in Wilkie Collins's *Armadale* who confesses he has lived "in idleness and self-indulgence" in the West Indies where passions were left "entirely without control of any kind" (20), Rochester, by his account, lapses into gratification of his desires. But he begins to find Bertha's nature "wholly alien" to his, her "cast of mind common, low, narrow," her char- · acter ripening after four years, as he puts it, into one of "rank" vices and "giant propensities." Revealing his Victorian terror of the sexual intemperance that he has himself practiced (the memory of being her husband is "odious" to him), Rochester declares that Bertha's excess "had prematurely developed the germs of insanity" (334). On a fiery West Indian night as the mosquitoes buzz, the moon sets like a hot cannonball, and the world "quivers with tempest," Rochester decides to shoot himself. Then, however, the famous "fresh wind from Europe" blows through his window, the storm breaks, and the air grows "pure" (335). The Atlantic now thunders in "glorious liberty," and Rochester returns to England with his "filthy burden," a sexually rank woman from an invaded colony who becomes a counterinvasive figure transported to the metropolitan center of empire.

Rochester's description of his wife is saturated with racist attitudes, and what it means for Brontë to have termed Bertha the daughter of a creole mother has become a matter of critical speculation. According to the *OED*, the term "creole" is derived from the Spanish for country and indicates "native to the locality"; also, the definition continues, in the West Indies and other parts of America, a creole is "a person born and naturalized into the country, but of European or of African Negro race: the name having no connotation of colour." On the basis of this definition, it is certainly possible to argue that Bertha is either of European or African origin—the novel never specifies whether she is black or whether she is not.[32] But it seems to me that Brontë does something

---

[32] In Mrs. Henry Lynch's *The Cotton-Tree; or, Emily, the Little West Indian* (published in the same year as *Jane Eyre*), the heroine is sent from Jamaica to an English boarding school where the girls and teachers laugh at her Creole accent, ask her if her father is a "negro" and express surprise at her fair complexion since they believe that "one born in the West Indies must necessarily wear the shadow of Africa's sable daughters" (44). The didactic purpose of Lynch's story is to explain that there are such things as white West Indians and that they are also religious. Winifred Gerin suggests that the prototype of Richard Mason in *Jane Eyre* is to be found in the brother of one of Brontë's fellow pupils at Cowan Bridge School: "a sallow man doubtless suffering from the English cold" (333). I believe that Brontë means Richard Mason to be a white West Indian.

more subtly racist in *Jane Eyre* than merely allow us to think that filthy, crazed Bertha is a black woman. *Jane Eyre* provides images of Bertha that associate her with Victorian fantasies of African Negro behavior, even with Dickens's loathing of what he calls the straddling Bushmen on display in London, which makes her thus doubly horrible (and fascinating) to the Victorian sexual imagination. For example, the vision of Bertha trying on Jane's wedding veil is described as a figure of "a woman, tall and large, with thick and dark hair. . . . It was a discoloured face—it was a savage face. I wish I could forget the roll of the red eyes and the fearful blackened inflation of the lineaments . . . the lips were swelled and dark; the brow furrowed; the black eyebrows widely raised over the bloodshot eyes" (311). In my view, a literal interpretation of Brontë's language diminishes her brilliant imagination and excuses her racist politics because the Bertha of Rochester's narrative is made even more dreadful, even more obscene, even more monstrous, by virtue of the fact that she is a white creole who behaves like a demented black person. In other words, if one sees that Brontë intensifies the horror of Bertha by incarnating in her all the Victorian myths of demonic black behavior—a white woman engorged with the rage and sexuality attributed to West Indian black women—then *Jane Eyre* becomes an even more racist text than if Bertha were merely a mad half-caste Rochester had carted back to England.

The fear of excitable dark races is a connecting thread throughout *Jane Eyre,* Carlyle's essay, and the 1847 House of Commons report. The report, for example, argues strongly in favor of disciplinary education for "a race emerging from barbarism" (196). Among the aims of such education should be accustoming "the children of these races" to habits of self-control and moral discipline, teaching them "how health may be preserved by proper diet, cleanliness, ventilation, and clothing." It hardly needs saying that Bertha Mason Rochester is described as drunken, corpulent, and filthy, an "it" rising like a "clothed hyena" before Jane's horrified English eyes. Grounding its strategies for control of the fearsome colonized in transformation of coercion to consent (a tactic coherent with the decision of the British Raj in 1835 to educate its Indian subjects in the English language), the report states that the "most important agent of civilization for the coloured population" is the acquisition of grammatical knowledge of English (194). Through learning English grammar, the emancipated slave will be disciplined in two ways: first, the rote learning of grammar constitutes a means of instilling orderly methods of thought, and second, the acquisition of English will produce the desired "thriving, loyal, and religious middle class among the agricultural population" (201), desired, that is, for the maintenance and administration of a colonial government.[33]

Arguing that a knowledge of writing and arithmetic, for example, "may enable a peasant to economize his means, and give the small farmer the power to enter into calculations and agreements" (194), the report promises that education will liberate the children of emancipated slaves from ignorance and provide Britain with trained servants of empire. Older students, for example, should be taught "Mensuration, land-surveying and levelling, and plan-drawing"—the skills of measuring the red spaces of empire that prove so important, one recalls, in the initiation of Kipling's Kim into the Great Game of preserving and expanding British control on the Northwest Frontier.

In *Jane Eyre*, Jane is both disciplined pupil (at Lowood) and disciplinary teacher (at Thornfield and Morton). She reforms the French manners of Adele Varens into the genteel behavior of English young ladies, and she refines the "heavy-looking, gaping rustics" at her Morton school, who turn out to be, as she puts it, "sharp-witted enough" (392). That these rustic girls become "obliging," "amiable," and acquire "quiet and orderly manners" (392) is due to Jane's perfected pedagogy. From her, they learn grammar, geography, history, and acceptance of their class and gender subordination. Since she is so strong an influence upon them—their parents, she confides in an Esther Summerson moment, load her "with attentions" and she becomes "a favourite in the neighbourhood" (392)—it is likely that they also learn to share Jane's belief that it is preferable to be a "free and honest" village schoolmistress in England than a slave of love in France. However subjugated they may be by virtue of their class position in English society, these working-class girls will learn to understand their own superiority to the colonized, just as Jane knows her superiority to a Creole woman polluted by the sexual passion and uncontrolled rage associated with black West Indians. From Jane, they will learn to share and propagate the

---

[33] It is notable that most missionary education in all parts of the empire was based upon a curriculum devised for the British working class; as Philip Curtin observes in contrasting the educational methods of the Methodists and the Church of England, "In either case, the missions transferred to Africa a curriculum and method designed specifically to meet the needs of the British working class. Since the goals of both systems was to teach the virtue of hard work and the principles of Evangelical Christianity, the choice was natural" (*Image of Africa* 264).

ideology of racial superiority expressed, for example, by a woman missionary toward the end of the Victorian period. Writing from India, she declares: "Probably only those who have practical acquaintance with heathen lands can estimate the extreme ignorance of the masses of the people, the difficulty of conveying any definite ideas to their vacant minds. However degraded and ignorant a person may be in England, there is at least something to work upon" (*India's Women* 1:141). As Britannic rule trains the West Indies and India to become compliant and lucrative colonies, so Jane trains the farmers' daughters to become, in their own small way, British women of empire. But the strongest form of discipline enacted by Jane Eyre is upon herself so that she may, I think, fulfill her political destiny as Rochester's moral instructress. Throughout the novel, she brings the power of her rational mind, her brain, to bear upon her emotional pain and physical distress.

JANE'S FORTITUDE

Having painfully witnessed the erotic attractions of Blanche Ingram, looked at her plain self in the mirror, and realized that she loves Rochester, Jane Eyre examines her emotional state in this way: "When once more alone, I reviewed the information I had got; looked into my heart, examined its thoughts and feelings, and endeavoured to bring back with a strict hand such as had been straying through imagination's boundless and trackless waste, into the safe fold of common sense" (190). Just as the colonialist will bring the "boundless and trackless waste" of foreign territory and barbaric native practices into the safe fold of benevolent British colonialism, so Jane curbs her wandering, anarchic imagination with the reins of her identity as citizen of a powerful imperial nation. She concludes her painful narrative of self-restraint by saying that "the course of wholesome discipline to which I had thus forced my feelings to submit" enabled her to meet what follows with "a decent calm": so, too, the British colonization of native wilderness and savage culture is beneficial not only to the colonized but also to the colonizer. The colonizer must possess the resilience to meet native resistance (one thinks of the English immigrants in Van Diemen's Land in Rowcroft's *Tales of the Colonies*). Jane Eyre must possess the fortitude to handle tumultuous emotional events. Explicitly in the life of the individual woman and implicitly in the political relationship between colonizer and colonized, *Jane Eyre* discloses a pattern of disruptive disorder brought under control by stern measures. The physical suffering of Jane Eyre is essential in her training as discipliner of herself and others and suggestive of the physical suffering demanded of actual women of empire in their participation in creating the Victorian imperial nation. Although both British men and British women abroad suffered from enervating climates, strange foods, and social isolation, dominant Victorian ideas about the allotment by gender of cultural labor tend to prescribe more for women than for men sacrifice for the moral good of society, the nation, and the empire. This cultural prescription may be seen both in Jane's metropolitan existence and in the lives of women stationed in the red spaces of empire.

In Emma Roberts's *Scenes and Characteristics of Hindostan with Sketches of Anglo-Indian Society,* there is an ideologically complex justification of the British colonial presence. Life is so dreadful for British women in "grilling" India that they can only be there for the good of the "native." They suffer in order that the colonizer may tame the jungles of social life and landscape, which are evoked everywhere in Victorian writing about empire and specifically in Carlyle's essay and the House of Commons report. Aiming to deflate the myths of Anglo-Indian nabobs—figures such as Samuel Foote's Sir Matthew Mite—waiting at dockside in Calcutta to woo the latest female arrivals with cashmere shawls and diamonds, Roberts shows that British men in India were more devoted to the interests of Leadenhall Street (headquarters of the East India Company) than to romance. Roberts discloses that British marriages in India were sad affairs, far from the pretty comfort of the village church; yellowed muslin dresses kept in trunks for months did for wedding gowns, and young officers desperate for "companionship" married young women desperate for economic support: "Many young women in India may be considered almost homeless; their parents or friends have no means of providing for them except by a matrimonial establishment" (3:32). Roberts catalogs what she calls the spinsterhood of India into three groups: daughters of civil and military servants and merchants, who return to India after education in Britain between the ages of sixteen and twenty; sisters of brides of Indian officers who travel to India with the newly married couple; and orphan daughters of Indian residents who are housed at the Female Orphan School in Kidderpore, just outside Calcutta. If a young woman is unable to snare a husband, she will endure a miserable existence while living with her married sister. She cannot venture beyond the garden without a chaperon, she cannot tend flowers because the heat will wilt her before she gets to the flower beds, she can have no music because "the hot winds have split her piano and her guitar" and "white ants have demolished her music books" (3:35), and she can do no embroidery because the punkahs send everything flying from the worktable. The female servants surrounding the Anglo-Indian women, according to Roberts, are dissipated slatterns with no knowledge of a European toilette and no desire but to parade around the bungalows in "crushed flounces, broken feathers, and gauzes eaten through and through by cock-roaches" (3:93). "Female listlessness" for British women is the result of this dramatically dreadful life. The principal message of Roberts's "Sketches" is that Anglo-Indians are inevitably damaged by their experience—a situation suggested by her image of a British family confined in its bungalow with open doors, while countless servants clad in flowing white garments ceaselessly "glide with noiseless feet in all directions" watching their masters who seem imprisoned by their own privilege and authority (3:8).

If the Englishwoman in India lacks Jane Eyre's physical and moral fortitude, she runs the risk of loosening her literal and moral corsets and wearing tea gowns in the morning. If she has sent her children back to England for an education—or as Maud Diver puts it rather more bluntly later in the century, away from a place where it is not easy "to keep the eager, all-observant little minds fearlessly upright and untainted in an atmosphere of petty thefts and lies, such as natives look upon as mere common-sense and good policy" (*The Englishwoman in India* 43)—the British woman in India may end up spending her days in malicious gossip and cosseted by "the handings, and shawlings, and fannings, of male attendants" (3:79). But if British women were fated to endure paralyzing heat, loss of children, the tedium of regimental marches across the wilderness, and the risk of moral lassitude, then they also possessed, as we know from Roberts's poem about the Cawnpore Theatre in the wilderness, the magical ability to transform the jungle into something resembling English culture. In her colorful "Scenes" of native life and in her dismal "Sketches" of Anglo-Indian domesticity, in her enthusiastic verse about the transformation of heathen barbarism into Christian civilization, Emma Roberts creates a congruent, peculiarly circular, discourse of race and gender. Native disorder authorizes colonial control, which in turn authorizes women's sacrifice; and women's sacrifice transforms native disorder into English civilization. Thus, one discovers a self-authorizing pattern of influential Victorian ideas about gender and race.

The memoirs of Harriet Tytler (1828–1907), whose husband was an infantry captain at Delhi, also provide a graphic record of the hard life in India for British women, which is not so much the drama of stark misery evoked by Emma Roberts but the tedium of daily doings in the cantonment and the horror of the uprising in 1857.[34] Married at seventeen, the mother of eight children, Harriet Tytler spent her days before the uprising riding around the station before breakfast, never mixing with the wives of the "other ranks," sleeping through the afternoon, taking an evening drive, and attending an occasional evening party in the mess or dining in someone else's bungalow. This sedate and rather boring life (one hears echoes of Kaye's Peregrine Pultuney who finds life in India "desultory") is violently interrupted by the uprising, and what had been in Tytler's memoirs until this point a dutiful recitation of tedious, privileged activity suddenly becomes graphic, gory, and vivid.

The events begin with her French maid's response to the question about what is causing the station servants to run out into the street: "Madame, this is a *revolution*, I know what revolution is" (116). Rehearsing the common British nineteenth-century association of any kind of rumblings from below with the French, Tytler memorably evokes the siege of Delhi. She spends three months huddled with her children in the ammunitions building, gives birth on a wagon to a boy she names Stanley Delhi-Force (thereby linking him with the Bagnet children in *Bleak House*, even if they are of "other ranks"), and listens to tales of violence enacted upon British women. The story of a Mrs. Leeson who staggers into the besieged camp dressed as an Afghan boy is particularly gruesome. She has seen her three children shot in front of

---

[34] Tytler's memoirs were actually written between 1903 and 1906, so one needs to bear in mind that she is looking back over a perspective of some fifty years, a fact curiously unacknowledged by Sara Suleri who argues that the "complete narrative calm" of Tytler's recollections "bespeaks a disequilibrium" (82). Suleri's view tends to perpetuate an essentialist notion about women travel writers: that they suffer psychic malformations because they are accomplices in colonialism; that they possess inherently finer feelings than their colonialist husbands, fathers, and brothers. In general, although I admire Suleri's discussion of the problem of "alterity," I find her interpretations of British women travel writers in contradiction to what she claims to want to avoid: critical reproduction of the binary opposition of colonizer and colonized. Suleri's readings reproduce a binary opposition of knowing critic (herself) who can decode what is really going on in the text—a "colonial panic" felt by women such as Fanny Parks and Harriet Tytler.

her by Sepoy troops: "the baby boy, who was shot by the same bullet, was thrown out of her arms and lay, some distance, moaning. After those soldiers of the King had butchered the rest of the family they came up to her little boy and cut his throat. . . . They then took the poor little girl and cut her from ear to ear through her mouth" (156).[35] To be sure, Jane Eyre experiences no such horror, yet her gendered physical pain may be linked to a powerful Victorian ideology in which women suffer in the cause of male action in the public sphere, whether the violent events in India in 1857, the fictional reformation of a capitalist father in *Dombey and Son,* or the salvation of Rochester from his corrupt colonialist past in *Jane Eyre.*[36]

I have referred many times in this chapter to the actual suffering of Jane Eyre, the price, I would argue, she pays for her agency as performative subject. As a child, she is attacked by John Reed and she feels "a drop or two of blood from my head trickle down my neck, and was sensible of somewhat pungent suffering: these sensations for the time predominated over fear, and I received him in frantic sort" (43). At Lowood, she is fed a diet of burnt porridge, strange stews "redolent of rancid fat," and many glasses of water. In the cold weather, the pitchers of water are frozen, the girls march to church without boots and without gloves, and many are felled by typhus brought on by semistarvation and neglected colds. When Jane has revealed before her horrified eyes Rochester's "filthy burden," and determines she must leave Thornfield, she finds that being homeless makes her as hungry as she was when back at Lowood: feeling "much exhausted, and suffering greatly now for want of food" (353), she knocks on the door of a farmhouse and asks, simply, "Will you give me a piece of bread? for I am very hungry" (355). What I am trying to get at here is Brontë's emphasis upon Jane Eyre's physical suffering, the three nights spent "wretched" on damp ground and "intruders" passing near her "more than once" (355). Seeing a child

---

[35] Postmutiny literature features many such incidents and fears of rebellion by natives in other parts of the empire: Dickens, for example, in *The Perils of Certain English Prisoners,* his Christmas story for 1857, creates a horrifying picture of menacing pirates who are a grab bag of nations led by a "hideous little Portugese monkey," and including Malays, Maltese, Greeks, Negroes, and convict Englishmen from the West Indies. The pirates brutalize the English colony on an island off Honduras where silver mined on the mainland is stored and shipped once a year to Jamaica (an interesting detail of contemporary colonial trading practices).

[36] Nancy Paxton points out that British novels written after 1857 "shored up traditional gender roles by assigning to British women the role of victim, countering British feminist demands for women's greater political and social equality" (6).

about to throw a mess of cold porridge into the pig trough, she asks that it be given to her: "The girl emptied the stiffened mould into my hand, and I devoured it ravenously" (356). At this miserable point in her narrative, it is as if Jane's life at Lowood seems to be repeating itself, as if Brontë wants to show that the life that concludes in the happy rehabilitation of Rochester must be punctuated by moments of physical and psychological pain. Friendless, homeless, penniless, the governess who has scorned the luxuries offered by Rochester is thankful for vile, cold porridge. In this experience of physical deprivation, she is similar to Emma Roberts's unhappy British women in India, and, less extremely, to Harriet Tytler at the siege of Delhi. Jane Eyre's physical misery and remarkable resilience reveal how she is formed by the Victorian gender codes of female sacrifice, and they also qualify her as a fit woman for the empire—more precisely, for her redemptive erasure of Rochester's colonialist past.

In their influential feminist reading of *Jane Eyre*, Sandra Gilbert and Susan Gubar argue that Brontë is unable "to envision viable solutions" (*The Madwoman in the Attic* 369) to the problem of social inequality between a thirty-eight-year-old, upper-middle-class, sexually experienced man and an eighteen-year-old déclassé impecunious virgin. Consequently, they claim, Brontë must symbolically castrate Rochester, magically elevate Jane through acquisition of money and family, and situate them both far from the public sphere in Ferndean. My claim for Jane Eyre as an ideal Victorian woman of empire has attempted to complicate this argument through giving it a particular form of historical specificity. I have tried to show that in the magical forest world of Ferndean, Jane and Rochester become a symbolic couple, produced by and also producing Britain's culture of empire, and defined by their complete difference from native tropical sexuality, corpulent and sweating bodies, Blanche Ingram's sterile snobbery, and a languid gentry indifferent to the colonial sources of its wealth.

That Jane Eyre, as Gilbert and Gubar claim, must be made Rochester's social equal signalizes the contested nature of her identity in writing the Victorian nation. In confronting Rochester in the midsummer's eve scene in which he sadistically teases her with sly references to his promised "bride," she passionately declares, "I am not talking to you now through the medium of custom, conventionalities, nor even of mortal flesh: it is my spirit that addresses your spirit; just as if both has passed through the grave, and we stood at God's feet, equal—as we are!" (281). For Jane to achieve agency in the rehabilitation of Rochester's past, she must be licensed to effect this transformation, must be given the authority associated, on the grandest level, with Victoria, the disciplinary colonial mother of her domestic subjects and subjugated native children. But Jane is also the pedagogical object produced by Victorian gender and class politics, the middle-class former governess with a small inheritance, the midgelike figure obedient to social and moral convention. Clearly, then, as Gilbert and Gubar point out, Brontë must remove Jane Eyre and Rochester from the historical determinants of social being. As one might expect, Jane is the bossy agent of this removal. Claiming that she is equal to Rochester in a fashion that transcends custom and conventionalities, Jane creates for them an essentialist social being that paradoxically erases class and gender difference and situates them in a precise historical moment of Britannic rule. *Jane Eyre* is a novel deeply influenced by that rule and also one that richly contributes to its constitution.

CHAPTER FOUR

BABU KALICHARAN BANERJEE PUTS HIS ARM AROUND MISS MARY PIGOT

"There is no escape from the prison of Prospero's gift."
"How in the name of Heavens could a colonial native taught by an
English native within a strict curriculum diligently guarded by yet
another English native who functioned as a reliable watch-dog, the
favourite clerk of a foreign administration: how could he ever get out
from under this ancient mausoleum of historic achievement?"
—George Lamming, *The Pleasures of Exile*

I f Jane Eyre's governess sensibility may be said to symbolize ideal
female service to empire, then in the actual world of Victorian
colonial and imperial politics, women often failed to match her impeccable moral performance. To be sure, the tedium of Anglo-Indian
existence related by Emma Roberts and the violence of 1857 recorded
by Harriet Tytler suggest that women's lives in India exacted physical
and emotional sacrifices similar to the sort demanded of Jane Eyre. In
part, my argument has been grounded in this resemblance, but it has
also been necessarily attentive to the slippery differences between Jane
Eyre as a character in a novel and the actual women who produced
Victorian travel narratives and memoirs. Yet the lives of these women
and of Brontë's fictional character merge in a gendered image of ideal
labor for Britannic rule, and as is often the case in the Victorian novel,
ideological tension and social desire resistant to management and gratification in historical reality find their symbolic resolution in fiction.
In India, for instance, the restless wives of army officers were often
deemed by guardians of Victorian female propriety such as the Anglo-
Indian novelist Maud Diver to be in serious need of the moral medi-

cine dispensed by Jane Eyre. Toward the end of the Victorian period, women teachers and missionaries, deputizing, as it were, for Victoria in her colonial possessions, were rarely the obedient figures of St. John Rivers's misogynistic imagination. Moreover, these women sometimes found allies in English-educated native subaltern figures with whom they often worked and formed professional friendships—figures who were, in essence, created by the empire to administer and maintain its bureaucratic structures, and who were, as the epigraphs to this chapter suggest, bound by the language and customs of their colonial educators. That a strong-minded British woman and an educated native could pose a threat to late Victorian patriarchal imperialism is revealed in an incident and its aftermath said to have taken place at a church picnic in Barrackpore Park in Calcutta in 1882.[1] During the grilling Victorian days of the British Raj, the Anglo-Indians stationed in Calcutta found some relief from the climate to which they never became accustomed by making day trips to Barrackpore, sixteen miles from the center of the city. With glades and coppices arranged in the style of Capability Brown and strawberry beds flourishing from plants brought out from England in 1836, Barrackpore was a resonantly Anglicized place in Victorian imperial culture. Writing to Queen Victoria in 1856, Charlotte Canning, wife of the governor-general, noted that the "Park is carefully planted with round headed trees to look as English as possible. . . . The luxuriant growth in the jungly ground outside, of dazzling green during the Rains, is more beautiful than I can describe and I always think of the Palm House at Kew."[2] Charlotte Canning's admiration of Barrackpore echoes that of James Moffat Horne, who wrote in 1827 that the grounds "are laid out with infinite taste, in imitation of our parks in England, and produce a splendid effect on the eye" (135), and it was repeated by another ruling-class Englishwoman in India, the Marchioness of Dufferin and Ava, who recorded in the journal she kept from 1884 to 1888 that the landscaped beauties of Barrackpore happily reminded her of

[1] I am deploying the term "patriarchy" to indicate the male domination of women, children, and other men. In this book, I have taken patriarchal control to mean that men hold power in all the important areas of culture and society, and that women, children, and other subordinated men are less enabled to possess such power. See Gerda Lerner's *The Creation of Patriarchy* for a comprehensive history of patriarchal practices.

[2] Quoted in Charles Allen, *A Glimpse of the Burning Plain: Leaves from the Indian Journals of Charlotte Canning* 41.

Samuel Bourne, Oakover, Simla (1867). By permission of the Royal Photographic Society Collection, Bath, England.

"the Duke of Westminster's place on the Thames, Cliveden" (Blackwood, 1:23).

As the rich example of Kew Gardens indicates, beginning in the eighteenth century, the British technology of empire literally uprooted vegetation from the colonies, replanted it in the moist earth of Surrey, and created a horticultural monument to colonial appropriation.[3] And when not bringing home chunks of colonized land, the British were busily planting literal and symbolic emblems of their own culture

[3] Kew Gardens was founded by the dowager princess of Wales in 1761 and was presented to the nation as a royal gift in 1841. The Gardens now cover some 288 acres and in addition to the famous Palm House mentioned by Charlotte Canning, contain a Chinese pagoda. In another example of the far-ranging cultural effects of empire, Joseph Sturge and Thomas Harvey, on their visit to Jamaica in 1837, observed that the Botanic Gardens were formed in the late eighteenth century "to receive part of the collection of trees from the East Indies and South Sea Islands, brought hither by Captain Bligh" (168).

and horticulture in subjugated territory: witness the strawberry plants at Barrackpore and also some roses in the Castleton Botanical Gardens in Jamaica, admired by James Anthony Froude on his visit in the 1860s as the "newest importations . . . called after the great ladies of the day" (98). The actual palm trees of Barrackpore make Charlotte Canning think of their replication in Kew Gardens, and Kew Gardens, of course, prompted (and continues to prompt) in the imagination of the British visitor fantasies of exotic places, cultures, and peoples whose fascination remains safely enclosed within the technological wonder of the great glass Palm House built between 1844 and 1848. With the aid of the conservatory, Indian palm trees become an exotic colonial specimen, and just as the Anglo-Indians of Calcutta visited Barrackpore Park in search of leafy England, so Victorian inhabitants of the metropolitan center of empire spent a day at Kew Gardens admiring vegetation that was both product and reproduction of India. This is an imperially managed process of such perfected hybridity that seeing the real thing reminds Charlotte Canning of its replication. In the grilling heat of Calcutta, the British look at an Anglicized India, and in the gray damp of London, the British look at an Orientalized England. Whichever way you look at it, however, the British do the looking and the colonies provide the spectacle.

In the early 1880s in Barrackpore, this piece of India made over to look like England, the Church of Scotland Missionary Society held a picnic for the teachers and inhabitants of its orphanage in Calcutta. During the picnic, the behavior of Babu Kalicharan Banerjee, a Christian teacher at the orphanage, was regarded with alarmed suspicion by the Calcutta directors of the Missionary Society; he was thought to be sitting too close to Miss Mary Pigot, the principal of the church's zenana mission. Mary Pigot, a representative of the independent, unmarried women who went to India in the second half of the nineteenth century to work as teachers and medical missionaries, was suspected of having invited his improprieties. In the ugly legal battle that followed this dynamic moment at a church picnic, Banerjee and Pigot were accused of other indiscretions: they were said to have shared a reclining chair on her verandah, and, even worse, to have stood together at a window of the orphanage, his arm around her waist. A "babu," the Anglo-Indian term for an educated native usually performing bureaucratic functions, may have touched a "memsahib," the Anglo-Indian term for an Englishwoman, although Mary Pigot was charged (incorrectly) by her detractors with being a "hybrid" Eurasian and therefore not quite the real thing.[4] In a native place disguised to appear English, a native male who has been transformed by an English education to appear Anglicized was said to have made advances (perhaps encouraged) to a female representative of the empire. In what follows, I plan to explore this historical moment from the governing critical perspective of *Rule Britannia:* the part played by Victorian writing and Victorian women in the discursive business of getting the tropical fruit to Brixton, and, one might add, the palm trees to Kew Gardens. If Jane Eyre symbolizes ideal gendered assistance in rehabilitation of the colonizer and civilization of the colonized, then Mary Pigot's friendship with an Indian male teacher suggests some of the difficulties confronted by patriarchal imperialism that, when forced by the need to maintain the political power symbolically perfected in Rochester's moral makeover by Jane Eyre, must license the education of women and of natives. To state a complex problem in simple terms, the recurrent difficulty in all Victorian colonialist practice was to maintain effective civil governance of the colonized after its military subjugation. In this chapter, I plan to discuss four related discursive events, what one might call "social texts,"[5] that disclose challenges posed to patriarchal and imperial authority in Victorian India. I am interested in exploring the different ways a political debate, a military campaign, a detective novel, and a legal case may be said to respond to these challenges. This exploration will be focused by the constitutive relationship between gender and race politics that has, to this point, governed my analyses of the intersection between women, empire, and Victorian writing.

It was in India, through the development of a social class of English-educated native civil servants and teachers, that Britannic rule fashioned its own hybrid means of substituting consensus for coercion in retaining its grip on Victoria's imperial subjects. The origin of this social class is to be found in the well-known debate between Orientalists and Anglicists in the 1830s about whether to educate Indians in English or in vernacular languages. I want first to illuminate the agonistic positions of the Orientalists and the Anglicists in order to suggest that Banerjee's presence in Barrackpore Park may be traced almost directly to the

---

[4] For detailed description of this legal case, see Kenneth Ballhatchet, *Race, Sex, and Class under the Raj* 112–116. I first learned of the Mary Pigot episode from Ballhatchet's book, to which I am indebted.

[5] I am using this term in the sense that John Bender deploys it in *Imagining the Penitentiary.*

passing of the English Education Act in 1835. The debate in Britain and India leading up to the passing of the act was, at root, a discussion of ways to negotiate the bond between intellectual knowledge and political power: The questions of what constituted appropriate intellectual knowledge for a colonized people and what degree of political power they might acquire through possession of such knowledge underlie this discussion. After 1857, the British administration of India became more widespread, detailed, and demanding, and as a consequence, English-educated Indian male clerks, teachers, and lawyers became more visible in the running of empire.[6] Second, I shall explore the theatrically vigorous campaign conducted by the British in the 1830s against the Indian thuggee gangs, whose guerilla activities hampered British plans for developing consensus in place of coercion. Raj records of this victory constitute a quasi-detective narrative of surveillance and dramatic disclosure of thuggee secrets. Next, I shall discuss Wilkie Collins's complex interrogation of high Victorian imperialism in *The Moonstone*, which I see as concentrated in the subaltern functions performed by Ezra Jennings, a feminized and babulike figure. To conclude, I shall return to the case of Banerjee and Pigot to examine the violations of race and gender codes enacted by an uppity babu and an independent woman — to my mind, acts of resistance that necessarily accompanied the Victorian development of imperial and patriarchal power. The measured essays of the Orientalists and the Anglicists, the lurid narratives of wiping out the thuggee gangs, the calculated suspense of *The Moonstone*, and the sensationalist newspaper reports of the Mary Pigot case all constitute a British "writing the nation" predicated upon the obedience of Indian men and British women to patriarchal imperialism.[7] In

---

[6] As R. J. Moore notes, "By the 1880s these Western-educated 'collaborators' were demanding larger opportunities for advancement, by entry to the higher levels of administration and access to the counsels of government. They demanded, too, a lightening of the land tax in the interests of agricultural improvement and the division of expenditure from imperial to national ends: to education, irrigation and industrial development" (82). For more extended discussion of these important issues, see Anil Seal, *The Emergence of Indian Nationalism: Competition and Collaboration in the Later Nineteenth Century*.

[7] In her analysis of the effect on Anglo-Indian society in 1883 of the proposed Ilbert Bill, which aimed to remove a clause in the Indian Penal Code barring native civil servants from exercising jurisdiction over British subjects living outside the chief presidency towns, Mrinalini Sinha observes, "Even the hint of any liaison between a white woman and a native man was shocking to the Anglo-Indian community. The Pigot versus Hastie Defamation Case, which came for trial during the Ilbert Bill agitation, highlighted some of the sexual taboos necessary in maintaining the racial division of colonial society" (105).

many ways, these two subaltern groups may be said to share a fused and feminized subordination to white male British power.

GENERATION OF THE BABU

Macaulay's "Minute" of 2 February 1835, which contains his assertion that he has never found anyone who could deny "that a single shelf of a good European library was worth the whole native literature of India and Arabia" (722), a judgment based on his own deep and astonishing command of Western classical literature and a total ignorance of anything written in Sanskrit or Arabic, is undoubtedly the best-known document in the debate between Orientalists and Anglicists.[8] Gauri Viswanathan has demonstrated, however, that there were equally blunt assertions in the dispute whose resolution profoundly influenced India's cultural history in the Victorian period and beyond. In her admirable examination of the establishment and development of English literary study in India, Viswanathan shows that although Orientalist and Anglicist positions seem opposed, they are not. Viswanathan claims that Orientalist scholarship provided Anglicists with evidence for making "comparative evaluations in which one culture could be set off and measured against the other" and that the two positions are "points along a continuum of attitudes toward the manner and form of native governance" (30). The rhetorical combat of the two groups betrays the shared sense of British superiority to Indian culture that Viswanathan identifies in her analysis of how English literary texts become "a mask for economic exploitation" (20). Their exchanges also reveal tangibly opposed views about the purpose of educating the governed.

Horace Wilson, a well-known early Victorian nineteenth-century scholar, is probably the most deft elaborator of the Orientalist position. Arriving in Calcutta in 1808 as a member of the medical service of the East India Company, he served as secretary of the Asiatic Society of Bengal and secretary to the Committee on Public Instruction (of which Macaulay was president). His article in the *Asiatic Journal* dated 5 December 1835 (almost exactly nine months after the governor gen-

[8] Eric Stokes writes of the Education Minute that "Never was the doctrine of assimilation so baldly and crudely stated" (46). Stokes's study of the Evangelical and Utilitarian influences upon Britain's India policies is indispensable for any examination of Victorian social and political thought in regard to India.

eral, Lord William Bentinck, authorized the English Education Act) laments the formal establishment of English as the language of instruction and the attendant cessation of financial support for Oriental studies. Arguing first that the resources for promotion of Indian education have a "specific origin" and a "determinate application," Wilson charges that the 1835 measures violate such carefully deliberated and intentional acts as the King of Oude's provision of financial support for the promotion of Mohammedan education at Delhi College and the British government's founding of Benares College precisely to preserve the study of Sanskrit literature and Hindu law. Wilson's critique of the 1835 act resembles the arguments of other conservative writers (Dickens, William Arnold, and Tennyson, for instance), who attacked a colonial governance founded upon the fusion of mercantile expansion and moral duty advanced by Liberals such as Macaulay and his brother-in-law Charles Trevelyan. Wilson asserts that having exterminated "the patrons" of Orientalist studies, "usurped their power and engrossed their wealth," the British government has an unshirkable responsibility to the "learned classes of India" to allow them to continue study of their own literature. The distinction Wilson makes between study of literature for its own sake and as a means of "earning a livelihood" is an important one (9).

Together with other critics of mercantile colonialism, Wilson scorns the cool professionalism demanded by Macaulay's 1833 House of Commons speech that begins to shape British policy in the 1830s and 1840s. He declares that the "learned and influential classes" in India have not been inspired to study by the need to earn a living and that the less wealthy intellectual classes only need as much English as "will enable them to earn a subsistence" (12). In Wilson's argument, the study of Indian languages both by European Orientalists and by learned Indians is associated with disinterested intellectual practice, and the study of English is linked to material necessity. With some truth, Wilson claims that the Orientalists wish Indians to study so that they may elevate their own culture, religion, and morality and that the Anglicists wish Indians to study with the aim of training them to be servants of the newly fashioned British Raj. Summing up what he regards as the bureaucratic folly of the 1835 decision, Wilson acidly observes that the government had no reason "to resort to measures of spoilation to provide funds for rearing clerks and copyists" (12).

In an equally impassioned contribution to the debate, Charles Trevelyan argues for a civilizing effect of the study of English literature that ranges far beyond the local creation of a class of petty bureaucrats. Advancing a fantasy of colonial selflessness, he argues that India will gain much more in the implementation of the 1835 act than the British. In the West Indies, he asserts, Britain gave its language "to a population collected from various parts of Africa, and by this circumstance alone they have been brought many centuries nearer to civilization than their countrymen in Africa, who may for ages grope about in the dark, destitute of any means of acquiring true religion and science" (88). Trevelyan's paternalistic racism differs little from Carlyle's tirade about pumpkin-loving Quashee and praise of the white enchanter who brings the rank West Indian jungle to life, although, of course, Carlyle's low assessment of Exeter Hall benevolence is much closer to Wilson's nostalgic conservatism than it is to Trevelyan's Liberal politics.

Trevelyan initiates his argument grounded in an imperialist fable of British altruism and African groping-in-the-dark by reviewing the purposes of educating male Indians at the Mohammedan College of Calcutta (established in 1781) and the Sanskrit College at Benares (established in 1792). He claims that the study was "purely oriental and the object of it was to provide a regular supply of qualified Hindu and Mohammedan law officers for the judicial administration" (1–2). Trevelyan implies that if one believes the legal system in India to be functioning well, then providing it with Indian officers well educated in their own languages would seem to be a good thing. But the problem for Trevelyan and for most of his fellow Anglicists and Liberals was, of course, that the British believed the Indian "judicial administration" to be a complete mess. If one remembers Macaulay's stern call, in his 1833 speech, for a reformation of a legal system in which Hindu Law, Mohammedan law, Parsee law, and English law are all "perpetually mingling with each other and disturbing each other, varying with the person, varying with the place" (713–14), it is not surprising to discover that Trevelyan links the need for English education with legal reform. In the early Victorian discourse of correct colonial governance in India, the study of English literature and the reformation of an anarchic legal system are directly linked in the initiation of a comprehensive network of subjugation and control. Just as the patriarchal British Raj in the 1820s undertakes to save Indian women from the savage ritual of suttee (and, as Gayatri Spivak argues, deny them subjectivity), in the 1830s, it undertakes to save Indian men from their own learned but useless culture by training them to administer educational and legal systems organized along British lines and conducted in the English language.

The effect of these two patriarchal/imperial policies is to confine Indian women to the status of helpless victims of their own barbaric religion and to subordinate Indian men to the status of ancillary bureaucrats. To be sure, the burning of live women and the education of men in the English language are hardly comparable, but the British attitudes toward the elimination of one and development of the other share, at best, a benevolent paternalism and, at worst, a contemptuous dismissal of Eastern cultures.

Resting his argument upon vague and patronizing reference to the "past history of the world," Trevelyan claims that the "character" of colonized peoples is always improved "by the extensive study and imitation of the literature of foreign countries" (36). In his emphasis upon character and imitation, Trevelyan implies that through mimicry of the sort Homi Bhabha claims eventually and inevitably deforms and disrupts a "master" text,[9] Indians will be cured of their fondness for mingling rather than managing ideas and will become as a consequence efficient servants of the empire. Guided by their Liberal colonial masters, English-educated Indians will improve their weak moral characters and learn to be mimic Englishmen of the sort to be found all over Britain's twentieth-century empire — "clerks and copyists" such as Joyce Cary's sadly comic character, Mister Johnson, or the young, educated Trinidadians, described by George Lamming as waiting eagerly by their radios to hear their own poems and short stories (written in English, of course) to be transmitted from London back to them in the West Indies through "the magic of the B.B.C." (*The Pleasures of Exile* 66).[10] This is not to argue, though, that the Orientalists necessarily articulated a more positive view of the Indian mind and morals. Horace Wilson, for example, while urging British support for the Indians to study their own literatures and develop their own institutions of learning, also advised that the British must "chasten" Indian tastes, "correct" superstitious views of science, and provide "purer sources of religious belief" (8). Orientalist and Anglicist views of the native mind are, at core, Eurocentric and patriarchal, but the important difference is the latter group's interest in developing a class of civil servants for the empire. Macaulay's "Minute," although brief, is the document that most fully justifies Brit-

---

[9] See Homi K. Bhabha, "Signs Taken for Wonders."

[10] See Cary's *Mister Johnson* for the story of a "copyist" for a district officer in Nigeria. As Lamming notes, "it was not only the politics of sugar which was organised from London. It was language, too" (*The Pleasures of Exile* 67).

ain's need for such a social class. In addition, its alignment of a poetic, feminized imagination with a colonized people and a factual, masculine mind with colonizing Britain shows how Victorian writing about empire appropriates influential ideas about gender and intellectual practice.

In framing his case for the development of a group he deems essential for the maintenance and reproduction of British power, Macaulay concedes one point of agreement with the Orientalists, "that it is impossible for us, with our limited means, to attempt to educate the body of the people." He believes, however, that the British government is able to focus and isolate its politically directed educational aims: "We must at present do our best to form a class who may be interpreters between us and the millions whom we govern; a class of persons, Indian in blood and colour, but English in taste, in opinions, in morals, and in intellect. To that class we may leave it to refine the vernacular dialects of the country, to enrich those dialects with terms of science borrowed from the Western nomenclature, and to render them by degrees fit vehicles for conveying knowledge to the great mass of the population" (729). Initially, it might seem as if Macaulay calls for a class of interpreters, hybrid creatures produced by the Victorian empire, who will mediate between vernacular speaking Indians and their British rulers. But Macaulay proposes that the function of the Indian interpreter must be to refine and to enrich his own language with Western nomenclature and thus make it fit for the transmission of Western knowledge. Essentially, what Macaulay demands is the incremental eradication of Indian knowledge through the labor of intellectual advance men, a group that will form the ranks of a pacific cultural army whose target is the invasion and transformation of Indian languages and cultures.

The invasion and colonization by British military and civil forces however, are inescapably (and almost simultaneously) accompanied by a counterinvasion by the colonized. The history of a looted Indian diamond disrupts English country house life; a deranged woman from Jamaica destroys a world thought safe from what she represents; palm trees and tropical fruit find their way to the metropolis; and Macaulay's interpreters, having softened up their own language and culture for the reception of what he calls superior scientific thought, in the history of India's move to independence, become the agents of political change. What Macaulay envisioned as a one-way interpretation became more transformative than anything he could have imagined in 1833. As I shall soon argue, the fictional Ezra Jennings in Wilkie Collins's

The Moonstone and the actual Kalicharan Banerjee are figures born of Macaulay's discursive creation of hybrid cultural identity, one providing selfless and feminized assistance to the empire and the other posing a potential danger to its patriarchal and racist social order. Ezra Jennings's interpretive skills, acquired through an Anglicist education, enable the restoration of a fabulously imagined pre-Orientalist and pre-Anglicist time in British imperial culture. But Banerjee, lounging on Mary Pigot's verandah, undermines the patriarchal British Raj's subordination of male Indians and of its own women, who, even if they consented to be grilled alive in Calcutta, were not willing to relinquish their hard-won professional independence.

According to Macaulay, the insurmountable problem with the Indian dialects is that they lack "information," although he does allow that "the department of literature in which the Eastern writers stand highest is poetry" (721–22). When it comes to hard knowledge, however, poetry just won't do: "When we pass from works of imagination to works in which facts are recorded, and general principles investigated, the superiority of the Europeans becomes absolutely immeasurable" (722). The Indian mind is thus aligned with poetic imagination and the British mind with facts and intellectual speculation, its literature abounding in texts unsurpassed as the means of moral and political instruction (722).[11] Given the prevalent gender division in Victorian culture between female feeling and male intellect, it seems reasonable to inflect Macaulay's argument with an implied association of the Indian mind with female, sensitive, and intuitive modes of thought and the British mind with robust, vigorous, and factual male thinking. Educating the Indians in the English language will connect them with their fellow colonized subjects around the world, Macaulay argues, millions of indigenous peoples who inhabit Marlow's treasured red spaces on the Victorian map of empire. English, Macaulay asserts, is the language of commerce, the language of "two great European communities which are rising, the one in the south of Africa, the other in Australasia; communities which are every year becoming more important, and more closely connected with our Indian empire" (723). As Britain's im-

---

[11] British notions of the "Oriental" mind as poetically imaginative became common in the Victorian period. In a biography of a late-Victorian missionary, Charlotte Maria Tucker, she is recorded as having said to a friend before going out to India: "I want to Orientalise my mind," but, her biographer notes, "she seemed to have been born with an Oriental mind. Parable, allegory, and metaphor were the very language in which she thought" (Giberne, *A Lady of England* 213).

perial history shows, Macaulay's vision of an empire connected by the English language came to pass: Native education in the colonizing language, whether in India, Africa, Australasia, or the West Indies, created a global economic and cultural network that served to enlarge and consolidate Britain's mercantile imperialism, transport millions of indigenous peoples from one part of the empire to another, and create a counterinvasion from the colonized space into the invading center of empire. The arrival of West Indians in an imperial metropolis eager for their labor after World War II originates, in part, in their education in the English language. These West Indians were the descendants of slaves who, according to the breathtakingly racist thinking revealed in Charles Trevelyan's arguments for the Anglicist position, by virtue of their education in the English language were "brought many centuries nearer to civilization than their countrymen in Africa." A brief discussion of the curriculum initiated in Indian missionary and government schools as a consequence of the 1835 English Education Act will suggest the cultural retooling of the native mind that led in India to the presence of Banerjee in Barrackpore Park and elsewhere in the Victorian empire to transformations in local trading patterns and to the migration of indigenous peoples from one British possession to another. A firsthand account of the important curricula changes of 1835 is provided by the wife of the commander of a Sikh regiment who traveled to India in 1846.

A fervent Presbyterian, Mrs. Colin Mackenzie visited many mission schools and zenanas. For the purpose of missionary fundraising, she gathered copious details of how the schools were run, and while in the zenanas, she dispensed homeopathic remedies and offered religious counsel to women. When she returned to England, she published *Life in the Mission, the Camp, and the Zenana; or Six Years in India.* Her observations of Anglo-Indian and native life emphasize the "picturesque," and in this regard, *Life in the Mission* is similar to Emma Roberts's *Scenes and Sketches* (1835) and Fanny Parks's *The Wanderings of a Pilgrim* (1850). The dark servants at table are always "dressed wholly in white, with white and crimson turbans—very picturesque" (1:28); the people, in general, are "so beautiful in their forms, so free and graceful in action, and so remarkably still when in repose, that it was like seeing a succession of pictures, or a gallery of antique bronze statues" (1:30). It is the impetus for her writing—raising money for the mission schools— that distinguishes her from Roberts and Parks, however, and it is also with that purpose in mind that she gives in its entirety the curriculum in 1851 of the College division of the Free Church Institution in Bombay (a Presbyterian institution).

Male pupils at the Free Church Institution studied general history and church history, with an emphasis upon the overthrow of the Roman Empire and the momentous transformations wrought by the Reformation; constitutional history and political economy included Jane Marcet's *Elements of Political Economy*, readings in James Mill, and the article in the *Encyclopaedia Britannica* on these subjects; mathematics attended to Euclid; natural history relied heavily upon the *Encyclopaedia Britannica;* and English classics and composition mainly covered the favorite poet of the Evangelicals, Cowper, whose "Tyrocinium" and almost all the books of *The Task* are listed in the curriculum (2:331–32). That students read *The Task*, a poem that delights in English rural scenes, the joys of gardening, and the domestic pleasures of the English countryside, provides ironic evidence of how young Indian men were indoctrinated in a culture that, if one considers the difference between mid-Victorian Bombay and the late-eighteenth-century bucolic scene evoked by Cowper, must have seemed strangely different from their own. The peculiarly English gratifications of visits from the village postman, chats with the wagoner in the snow, the sounds of the woodman and his dog, and so on, provide useful didactic aids in the constitution of an educated, docile social class, happy with the quiet and simple pleasures of the countryside in contrast to a more politicized life in the city.

Overall, *The Task* evokes the humble joys of English village life to indict worldliness and corruption. The tremendous popularity of this text in the training of Indian "clerks and copyists" as "fit vehicles for conveying knowledge to the great mass of the population" (as Macaulay puts it) shows how the moral renovation of British colonial practices that began in the early part of the Victorian period was in the process of being extended to the colonized. To create Macaulay's desired group of interpreters ("Indian in blood and colour, but English in taste, in opinions, in morals, and in intellect"), the poetry of Cowper would seem to have been an excellent choice, certainly safer, say, than the work of Byron or Shelley, whose satire and impassioned lyrics were not the stuff of training in acquiescence. Second to Cowper in popularity, in the curriculum quoted by Mrs. Mackenzie, was Milton, whose *Paradise Lost* provided inspiration for the "needy boys" flocking to the British seminaries to learn, according to Trevelyan, "without fee or reward, all that English literature can teach them."[12] But whether found in the missionary or the government curriculum, whether by Milton, eighteenth-century neoclassicist, or Romantic, whether taught by teachers who were sympathetic to the Orientalist or Anglicist positions, English poetry primarily served an unstated political purpose: to teach male Indians about British moral and cultural values, to wean them from idolatry, and to place them in positions of bureaucratic responsibility in the Victorian empire. That they would be fit for this responsibility (that is to say, liberated from what was seen as mumbo-jumbo) was never doubted by Macaulay. Writing to his father in 1836, he declared that the effect of English education on Indians is "prodigious. No Hindoo, who has ever received an English education, ever remains sincerely attached to his religion. . . . It is my firm belief that, if our plans of education are followed up, there will not be a single idolator among the respectable classes in Bengal thirty years hence" (*Life and Letters* 329–30).

Less sanguine about the salutary effects of English education upon natives, and ridiculing the Utilitarian social thought of Macaulay and Trevelyan, the Orientalist *Asiatic Journal* in 1835 published an anonymous article that attacked the metropolitan doctrine of "degrading literature and exalting science and depreciating the pretensions of poetry and eloquence," a doctrine that calls for the Indian mind to be made a "*tabula rasa*, a blank sheet, upon which new characters can be traced."[13] Although the Anglicists conceded that poetry served its own particular function in teaching Indians about the joys of English life, they wished to trace upon the *tabula rasa* of the Indian male mind the "facts" about "the superiority of Europeans," which Macaulay believed should form the pedagogical centerpiece of education in English ("Minute" 722).

[12] For useful details of the curricula of missionary and government schools after the 1835 English Education Act, see Viswanathan, 54. Viswanathan does not, however, discuss Mackenzie's *Life in the Mission, the Camp, and the Zenana,* from which I gained much useful information about the Presbyterian missionary school curriculum. It is interesting to see, incidentally, that the study of Milton was not restricted to boys. The education of a ruling-class girl, Toru Dutt, is described by a Mrs. Chapman in her *Sketches of Some Distinguished Indian Women* (1891): Toru Dutt and her sister shared the English lessons given to their brother by "Babu Shib Chunder Banerji, for whom she always entertained a grateful affection, and who seems to have been the first person to instil into her mind a love for the study of English literature. . . . The stern, grand poetry of Milton is hardly what one would expect to find as the chosen study of young Indian girls, yet these two sisters knew large portions of 'Paradise Lost' by heart, and apparently understood and appreciated it far more thoroughly than most English girls of the same age" (92).

[13] *Asiatic Journal*, vol. 18, p. 239.

If not as alarming as the curriculum inflexibly expounded by Thomas Gradgrind and sweetly resisted by Sissy Jupe in Dickens's *Hard Times*— "Facts alone are wanted in life. Plant nothing else, and root out everything else. You can only form the minds of reasoning animals upon Facts" (1)—English education in India was initially predicated on the assumption that Indian dialects, however appropriate for poetic expression, were deficient for the cultivation of rational, scientific thought. The attempt to collect, organize, and distribute "facts" is a distinguishing mark of detective fiction and will be important in my discussion of Wilkie Collins's *The Moonstone*. First, however, I want to look at the offensive conducted in the 1830s by the British against the thuggee gangs in India. In this campaign, the British attributed their victory to the efficient acquisition of facts about the thugs' nefarious activities. Unable to retain its hegemonic grip on colonized subjects through the Anglicists' development of consensus in place of coercion (precisely because that process was in fact developing), Britannic rule engaged in all-out military warfare. Plotting the kind of robust male exploits that defines the Victorian adventure story, the British capture the thuggee bandits, extract their nefarious secrets, and purge India of one of the most violent expressions of resistance to its governance, at least until the uprising of 1857.[14]

ELIMINATION OF THE THUG

The word "thug" has entered the English language, part of the Raj's linguistic loot from its Indian empire, and the original meaning of these two words in Indian dialect and Anglo-Indian idiom is long forgotten. "Loot," according to the *Oxford English Dictionary*, is derived either from a Hindi word meaning to break or from a Sanskrit word meaning to rob; "thug" is derived from *thuggee*, an Anglo-Indian transformation of a Hindi word *thagi*, deployed by the British in India to refer to the practice of ritualized robbery and murder. Believed by the British, not without foundation, to be inspired by a fiendish worship of the goddess Kali, thugs organized themselves into professional gangs, roamed the countryside, and practiced "thuggee." Revealing a process whereby rebel violence is transformed by British military power into discourse—

---

[14] See chapter 2 of Patrick Brantlinger's *Rule of Darkness* for an informative discussion of the Victorian male adventure story's complicity with imperial conquest.

thuggee becomes thug—the thuggee literature celebrates a restoration of social stability: first, to the local communities beset by gang violence, and then, as a consequence, to Anglo-Indian political order. British initiation into the secrets of organized violence becomes the means of its victory over thuggee.[15]

In the literal war waged by the British on thuggee and in the symbolic battle for complete and controlling knowledge of the colonized that may be said in part to characterize Victorian imperialism, one finds that the more the British decode the secrets and rituals of thuggee, the more is revealed to them by captured bandits. As Thomas Richards has argued, "the production of certain kinds of knowledge was in fact constitutive of the extension of certain forms of power" ("Archive and Utopia," 105). In early Victorian British India, this pattern of incremental acquisition of knowledge, occurring alongside the incremental acquisition of political power, reveals a determined ambition to conquer (and thus control entirely) the colonized subject through acquiring complete knowledge of that subject. Practicing the scientific, rational thought that is identified with male minds in Victorian gender politics and that is also the desired goal in educating the male Indian to transmit what was considered to be superior European knowledge to his people, brave male figures who seem to step out of early Victorian adventure tales become the heroes of their own narratives of superior military strategy, rational detection, and just victory. Two representative texts from the writings about thuggee provide graphic evidence of how the British won this particular war. The first is John William Kaye's *The Suppression of Thuggee and Dacoity* published in 1853 (Kaye is the author of *Peregrine Pultuney*, which I discussed in conjunction with *Dombey and Son*'s interrogation of mercantile colonialism); his narrative describes the elimination of the linked practices of strangulation and robbery by roving gangs and shows how Britain cleared the countryside in a fashion similar to Tennyson's Arthur, who "broke the bandit holds and cleansed the land ("Geraint and Enid"). The second, *Report on the Depredations Committed by the Thug Gangs of Upper and Central India,* was written by Sir William Henry Sleeman who was British Resident in Oudh from 1849 to 1856 and known affectionately as Thuggee Sleeman. Writing not long before Henry Mayhew asserted in the opening

---

[15] As early as 1839 we find reference, in Carlyle's essay on Chartism, to "Glasgow Thuggery," a symptom of the diseased society under moral examination in this essay (*Selected Writings* 152).

of his *London Labour and the London Poor* that Victorian ethnologists confirm "almost every tribe of people who have submitted themselves to social laws, recognizing the rights of property and reciprocal social duties . . . are surrounded by hordes of vagabonds and outcasts from their own community" (1:1), Kaye justifies his text with descriptions of outlaw violence. At the same historical moment, an official network of residencies, legal circuits, and schools is being rigorously organized by the British, thuggee vagabonds and outcasts are organizing themselves into clandestine operations. As the thug gangs create dangerous political affiliations (Foucault's "horizontal conjunctions" designed to resist a dominant political power), the British Raj launches its campaign of civil subordination in the form of mandating English studies and reforming an anarchic legal system. Contributing to this campaign, Kaye's discursive weaponry glorifies the British as investigators of the secrets of a violent cult waging "systematic war against life and property" (1). It is significant that Kaye constructs an enemy both lucidly coherent and ridiculously superstitious, an enemy worthy of being defeated by British male heroism and ingenuity and yet also captive of the absurd worship of a vengeful goddess. Revealing the frequent inconsistency of Victorian writing about empire in his contradictory images of the thugs, Kaye has them deploying amazingly systematic tactics and efficiently grouped into bands of "professional and hereditary murderers . . . committing the most monstrous crimes with as much forethought and ingenuity as though murder were one of the fine arts, and robbery a becoming effort of human skill" (1). Nevertheless, Kaye scornfully announces he knows of a no more "absurd chapter in all that monstrous farrago of absurdities, the Hindo mythology" than that which sanctions thuggee and its diabolical practice of strangling victims after robbing them with an armband magically provided by the goddess Kali. The thugs, therefore, are gifted with a kind of demonic forethought and ingenuity that enables them to turn highway robbery into one of the fine arts, but at the same time they are brutal captives of a barbaric mythology. British colonial subjectivity is thus constituted by vanquishing a worthy enemy and by eradicating its pagan practices. This paradoxical pattern also suggests some of the complex Victorian attitudes toward social groups that resist the dominant social order (whether they be working-class Chartists in Manchester in the 1840s or rebellious laborers in Jamaica in 1865). Perceived as driven by irrational political demands, such groups are also credited with the talent to plan structured political resistance.

"Various were their artifices—great their cleverness," admits Kaye; the thugs are "consummate actors" (4). But the British are craftier, learning to appropriate the arts of deception, which are revealed, for instance, in *The Moonstone* as Betteredge's Indian "rogues" disguise themselves as conjurors wearing white linen frocks and trousers and carrying small hand drums (94).[16] These are the arts of disguise in which Kim is schooled at the end of the century. In a signal example of the success of the British disciplinary project initiated in the 1830s through the institution of English studies and the military eradication of thuggee, in Kipling's novel, Kaye's "consummate actors" have long ago had their skills commandeered by the British and found themselves transforming a young sahib into a holy beggar who conceals a revolver in his sand-colored robes and a compass in an old purse belt (232).In *Kim,* having wiped out thuggee, the empire uses its tricks, deceptions, and disguises to fight another enemy, the Russians eager to play the Great Game on the Northwest Frontier. The historical violence of imperialism, visibly present and celebrated in the thuggee literature, is present in *Kim* only as an instance of the cultural and social changes that followed Britain's conquest of India: the fragments of a Buddhist monastery on display in the Lahore Museum, the teeming lower Simla bazaar filled with the people "who minister to the wants of the glad city" (194), the memorable Babu Hurree Chunder Mookerjee, M.A., of Calcutta University. In Kaye's narrative, Victorian violence meets native thuggee, and hegemonic power eradicates resistance. Surrendering his bloody vow to Kali in the face of British force, one captured insurgent is quoted as saying, "before the sound of your drums, sorcerers, witches, and demons take flight" (11). These are the drums (and guns) of the East India Company, whose "servants," Kaye announces at the beginning of his narrative, have "extirpated" all these sorcerers, witches, and demons.

How is it that the thuggee gangs thrived until the late 1830s, despite British civil and military power? How is it, given the fact that the British had been working their own special magic in India for more

---

[16] *London Labour and the London Poor* provides fascinating details of the Indians to be seen in the metropolis: "Within the last few years East Indians playing on the tom-tom have occasionally made their appearance in the London streets. The Indian or Lascar crossing-sweepers, who earned their living by alternately plying the broom and sitting as models to artists—the Indian converted to Christianity, who, in his calico clothes, with his brown bosom showing, was seen, particularly on cold days, crouching on the pavement selling tracts, have lately disappeared from our highways, and in their stead the tom-tom players have made their appearance" (Mayhew, 3:185).

than a century, deploying their own political demons to gut the Indian provinces of their wealth and turn the subcontinent into a dependent colony, that these leagues of thugs still flourished? Dealing with this issue in some detail, Kaye asserts that it was due to British ignorance of certain mysterious rituals: "We knew little or nothing about them. They were mighty secrets—hidden mysteries—dimly guessed at, not all understood" (13). Colonel Sleeman and his fellow detectives now arrive upon the scene, armed not only with drums, but also with an intelligence network heavily invested with patriarchal and racial meaning.

The winning attitude, so to speak, that Sleeman brought to his campaign to wipe out the gangs is suggested by his remarks about the king of Oude, who has been corrupted by the "society of fiddlers, eunuchs, and women" (*A Journey through the Kingdom of Oude* 1:29). The gangs may be tough, but the British are tougher; the thugs may display guerilla male cunning, but they are scorned in Sleeman's account for their allegiance to a goddess and their ready divulgence of secrets; the thugs may be men, but the British are manlier. Sleeman and his associates "initiate themselves into all the secrets of the craft," and the more knowledge of native ritual, violence, and superstition the British obtain, the more they receive: "It was astonishing what a mass of serviceable information was locked up within our prison-walls" (36), says Thuggee Sleeman. This is information that is serviceable in the accrual of power through the acquisition of knowledge, which in turn leads to more knowledge and thus more power. Finally, captured thugs reveal absolutely all they know when they are convinced that the British know it all anyway, having learned it through their own superior sorcery and witchcraft and, Sleeman implies, through their firm scorn for feminized idolatry. "Astonished and alarmed by this display of knowledge—all his secret history laid bare," a thug, Sleeman observes, confesses every secret of thuggee allegiances, strategy, and tactics. In this reciprocally enforcing triad of power, knowledge, and control, the British eradicate resistance and make the community safe for the education in English of their Indian subjects.[17] In the discourse of thuggee, the ground is cleared, as it were, for the planting of consensus in place of coercion, for the cul-

---

[17] Patrick Brantlinger provides an excellent and informative discussion of the first best-selling Anglo-Indian novel, Philip Meadows Taylor's *Confessions of a Thug* (1839). Brantlinger points out that Taylor's novel, based on his experiences as superintendent of police in part of Hyderabad, has a "definite reformist purpose" and argues that it should be regarded as "one of the great Victorian crime novels" (87).

tivation of the babu in place of extermination of the thug, for a kind of properly feminized work of translation between colonizer and colonized in place of a brutal, yet unmanly, resistance to British power.

Throughout his report, Thuggee Sleeman attributes the British success to an organization of facts, which leads to the decoding of secrets and dismantling of mysteries. In the introduction, Sleeman authorizes the existence of his text by declaring, "I was anxious to place on record, in an authentic shape, the proceedings of the Thug Associations in all parts of India from the year 1827 down to their gradual suppression under our operations." The placing on record of his proceedings in an "authentic shape" suggests the process described by Foucault in which disciplinary writing becomes "the accumulation of documents, their seriation, the organization of comparative fields making it possible to classify, to form categories, to determine averages, to fix norms" (190). Sleeman's report is constituted by multiple narratives of the expeditions in search of thug gangs, accompanied by an extraordinary map covering that "Portion of the Kingdom of Oude most infested by Gangs of Thugs or Professional Assassins who range the High Roads and under the guise of Friendship win the confidence of unsuspecting Travellers and after accompanying them for a Stage or two on reaching the first selected and retired spot or Bail, Murder them by Strangulation! and plunder their property." The map traces 1,406 miles of road and 274 bails, and Sleeman concludes with an alphabetical list of thugs at large, or unaccounted for, in all parts of India, up to 1 January 1840, with name, age, caste, birth, village and district. The astonishing thoroughness of this cartographic record of the defeat of thuggee literally displays what Foucault defines as the aim of discipline: in an accounting that even covers the birth dates of "thugs at large," the map conclusively, to use Foucault's phrase, "clears up confusion" (219).

The trope of explicit colonial eradication of local resistance and implicit establishment of a colonial economy to be found in Sleeman's report is made literally visible, some hundred years later, in the British Empire Exhibition of 1924, to which I referred in my earlier discussion of the way Victorian writers about empire create a fable of salvation of the native. Claiming that the Exhibition has collected not only examples of "all the natural products to be found in the regions of the world over which the British flag waves, but specimens of the articles made from these materials, examples of every known industry in the world, models of the greatest wonders, natural and artificial in the Empire, besides a complete display of all the methods of transport and communication used in every part of that Empire" (39), the catalog reveals the Exhibition as a political perfection of the transformations detailed by Kaye and Sleeman. Making manifest the material base of empire, the displays from Nigeria and Sierra Leone presented a forestry show of mahogany panels, canoes, rice, and ground nuts, and the Australian pavilion, in a show that would have gratified Charles Rowcroft's settler in Van Diemen's Land, exhibited oats, hay, wheat, tobacco, flour maize, sisal, dried fruits, cotton, electrical machinery posters, and wines. The geopolitical process whereby in India the elimination of thug gangs secures the subcontinent for material exploitation by the Victorian empire and whatever economic self-sufficiency it might have enjoyed is irrevocably altered by Britain's global patterns of world trade is brilliantly revealed in the 1924 Exhibition.

Finally, just as the elimination of thug gangs enabled imperial wealth, the thugs themselves become an imperial curiosity, a transformation theatrically realized during the Prince of Wales's visit to India at the end of the nineteenth century. One of his Indian subjects provided a dramatic demonstration of how thuggee strangulation had been executed back in the 1830s. Moreover, where it had once been necessary to travel to far-flung outposts of empire to observe subjugated lands and peoples, at the British Empire Exhibition in 1924, visitors who may well have admired the technological wonders of the Palm House at Kew could see another of Macaulay's important facts revealing European supremacy: "There can be no doubt" declares the catalog, that the Exhibition "has for those interested in our far-off possessions, annihilated distance. The intelligent visitor, whether trader, settler, or merely tourist, can in the many Overseas Pavilions learn on the spot anything he desires to know, and reach a sound conclusion on any subject without incurring the outlay of time and money involved in a long journey" (43). The Exhibition is a pedagogical wonder, a material emblem of the surveillance, subjugation, and preparation of economic exploitation enacted by Thuggee Sleeman and his lieutenants, an anticipation of the colonialist police state so chillingly evoked in Nadine Gordimer's *Burger's Daughter* where nothing, the narrator bitterly observes, is off the map of South African surveillance. In 1924, the colonizer does not need to go to the colony, does not need to suffer the grilling heat, the dirt, the smell, the absolute foreignness of it all: the natives who have "survived and prospered" thanks to British imperialism, according to the catalog, have been brought to the heart of the empire and are exhibited in its disciplinary space.[18] Meeting the challenge to patriarchal imperialism of securing its grip on colonized peoples, the conquest of Indian male thuggee by British male power is implicitly displayed in the Empire Exhibition of 1924. Knowledge becomes so sophisticated for the triumphant colonizer that he or she no longer needs to see what has been colonized, appropriated, and refashioned to write the British imperial nation. Its metonymic representation is displayed for immediate inspection.[19]

INTERPRETING EZRA JENNINGS

In emphasizing the ways in which the resistance of thug gangs to British extirpation was to be found in their devotion to the goddess Kali and to each other, Kaye compares them to London criminals; he refers to a recent report from the Chaplain of Newgate, which records that "the metropolis contains gangs of men who not only live together for the purposes of stealing, but who educate young persons of profligate habits in the most ready and dexterous methods of stealing" (46). If the savage thuggee gangs in India are bound to each other through allegiance to what Kaye viewed as a "farago" of superstition, then in the literature of the criminal city, the artful Dodger characters of London were bound together by fidelity to Fagin-like leaders. In yet another instance of the trope of invasion and counterinvasion central in Victorian writing about empire, the savage vows of the thugs are likened to the barbaric loyalties of English working-class street gangs.[20] Conversely, the colonizer's fear that the enormous numbers of colonized

[18] As Richard Altick has shown, in Victorian Britain, the exhibition of imperial curiosities (sometimes human) accompanied imperial expansion, a phenomenon that crested at the grandest Victorian imperial show of all: the Great Exhibition at the Crystal Palace in 1851 (*The Shows of London* 269–87).

[19] The perfection of imperially gathered information that is displayed at the British Empire Exhibition may be seen as similar to the process of information gathering into the archive described by Thomas Richards: "Victorian England was one of the first information societies in history, and it charged a variety of state facilities with the special task of presenting and representing the conditions and possibility of comprehensive knowledge. The operational field of projected total knowledge was the archive. The archive was not a building nor even a collection of texts but the collectively imagined junction of all that was known or knowable, a fantastic representation of an epistemological master pattern, a virtual focal point for the heterogeneous local knowledges of metropole and empire" ("Archive and Utopia" 104).

[20] As V. G. Kiernan observes, the British ruling-class man in the Victorian period tended to view "discontented native in the colonies, labour agitator in the mills" as the "same serpent in alternate disguises" (*The Lords of Human Kind* 316).

people under its governance might get out of hand is sometimes expressed through talk of a revolutionary English working class, as we see from Kaye's reference to Newgate. In the race, class, and gender relationships of colonizer and colonized, ruling class and lower class, and, to a lesser extent, Victorian man and woman, one sees a complex political problem manifesting itself in different forms: the problem is how to secure the acquiescence of subaltern groups in their subordination. The figure of Ezra Jennings in Wilkie Collins's *The Moonstone* may be said to fuse—and to resolve—the different forms of this political problematic. He is a colonized figure from the empire, sympathetic to the lower classes, and feminized in terms of Victorian gender politics by virtue of his sympathetic sensitivity.

By the time that *The Moonstone* was being serialized in *All the Year Round* (from January to August 1868), Wilkie Collins had become a highly successful novelist, his books displayed on the library tables of middle-class drawing rooms and on the shelves of back kitchens.[21] Its plot originating in a moment of colonial violence in 1799 and its work of successful detection performed by a figure imaginatively created by the English Education Act of 1835, *The Moonstone* is a novel densely involved in empire. The narrative ambition of *The Moonstone* is a scrupulous "record of the facts" (39) so that English ruling-class life may resume a complacent serenity untroubled by memories of who looted India fifty years ago and unmolested by relentless Indians whose religious beliefs, if not as fanatical as those of the thug gangs, are regarded by the English characters in the novel as misplaced in Yorkshire and London. If the English Education Act of 1835 aimed to transmit British knowledge to Macaulay's "great mass" of Indians through native translators, and if Kaye, Sleeman, and their thuggee campaigners pin the eradication of thuggee to the acquisition of Indian knowledge, then Ezra Jennings in *The Moonstone* may be said to be empowered through his knowledge of the English language and possession of a poetic imagination.

The Moonstone is divided into Prologue, Story, and Epilogue; the story is told by some eight narrators who have been instructed by the central male character, Franklin Blake, to reveal only what they knew of events at the time they occurred. Known to be the thief of the diamond taken from Rachel Verinder's room in the middle of the night

[21] See Page, *Wilkie Collins* 19.

(he is actually seen by her doing so), Blake, having no memory of the incident, authorizes the collection of different accounts of events surrounding the theft with the aim of discovering the facts. As things turn out, he took the diamond out of fear it would be stolen by the Indian rogues loitering in the neighborhood, but he did so under the influence of opium given to him by the Verinder family doctor, Mr. Candy, as a practical demonstration of the efficacy of sleeping draughts (heatedly denied by Blake). When he leaves Rachel's bedroom, he gives the diamond to Godfrey Ablewhite, a professional philanthropist famed as a speaker at charitable meetings and administrative manager of various Benevolent Societies of the Exeter Hall sort lambasted by Carlyle in his "Nigger Question" essay. In desperate need of money to support a secret life that runs to a suburban villa and a mistress, and also to repay money he has embezzled from funds for which he is a trustee, Ablewhite pawns the diamond in London. Meanwhile, Candy falls into a fever and his medical assistant Ezra Jennings transcribes, translates, and interprets Candy's delirious account of how he drugged Franklin Blake. Jennings's work eventually leads to the discovery and despatch of the English villain of *The Moonstone*, revealing him as a colonized figure so trusted by his masters, so purged of the native savagery that flourished at the time of the thuggee gangs, that he can be assigned the labor of cleansing the center of empire itself of its own corruption.[22]

A figure from what Mary Louise Pratt labels the "contact zone," a literal and imaginative space between the imperial metropolis and its periphery,[23] Jennings's physical description is extraordinary and its blunt evocation of a dissonant racial mixture demands lengthy quotation: "His complexion was of a gipsy darkness. . . . His nose presented the fine shape and modelling so often found among the ancient people of the East. . . . Add to this a quantity of thick closely-curling hair,

---

[22] Ronald R. Thomas argues that the "assembly and construction of the complicated machinery and personnel" to complete Jennings's experiment "forms the main action of the novel, completely replacing the primal political crime of colonial conquest with which it had begun and enabling its transformation into a story of bodily passion denied" ("Minding the Body Politic" 237). Thomas believes that Collins's romantic plot "effectively cancels out the political intrigue at the root of all these problems in the first place" (237).

[23] Pratt argues that while "the imperial metropolis tends to understand itself as determining the periphery, . . . it habitually blinds itself to the ways in which the periphery determines the metropolis." For Pratt, the "contact zone" is the "space in which peoples geographically and historically separated come into contact with each other and establish ongoing relations, usually involving conditions of coercion, racial inequality, and intractable conflict" (*Imperial Eyes* 6).

which, by some freak of Nature, had lost its colour in the most star-
tlingly partial and capricious manner. Over the top of his head it was
still of the deep black which was its natural colour. Round the sides of
his head—without the slightest gradation of grey to break the force of
the extraordinary contrast—it had turned completely white. The line
between the two colours preserved no sort of regularity. At one place,
the white hair ran up into the black; at another, the black hair ran down
into the white" (371). The child of an Englishman and a non-European
woman (in his words, from "one of our colonies"), he would seem to
be Indian born, his exposure to British customs and education having
symbolically penetrated his native identity but having left starkly separated the two cultures that have formed him.

Jennings is invested with two significant qualities that construct him
as a figure through whom the political problem of how to maintain the
subordination of figures essential to the maintenance of class, colonial,
and gender hegemony is resolved. He is a sympathetic calming presence
among the rural lower classes surrounding the Verinder estate (with one
notable exception, who serves to show the fully achieved state of consensus in ruling- and lower- class relationships), and he possesses an
ability to subordinate his own desires to a dominant code of values and
behavior that, in the Victorian period, is more commonly associated
with women than with men. A figure against whom "a horrible accu-
sation" has been lodged (we never learn its nature), he seems to have
come to England to practice medicine. Due to the unspecified slander
of which he would seem to be a victim, he can only work as a medical assistant in increasingly remote parts of the country. Suffering from
what he terms an "incurable internal complaint," he doses himself with
opium, works tirelessly among the rural poor, and hopes to leave money
to a woman from whom he parted long ago.

Jennings is significantly different from Limping Lucy, a lower-class
character in the novel who, in her own way, is as wounded a figure
as Jennings. Where he melancholically accepts his unhappy life, she
does not. A fisherman's daughter, "battling" as Betteredge puts it, "her
lame foot and her leanness," Lucy vents her class and gendered anger
upon Franklin Blake, emblem of white male ruling-class authority,
with whom the drowned Rosanna Spearman, a lady's maid and Lucy's
friend, has been hopelessly in love: "Ha, Mr. Betteredge, the day is
not far off when the poor will rise against the rich. I pray Heaven they
may begin with *him*. I pray Heaven they may begin with *him*" (227). In

contrast, Jennings is reconciled to his illness, his isolation, his marginal place in English life. Where Lucy screams out her class and female rage, Jennings directs his "dreamy brown eyes" to English wildflowers and wistfully observes, "How beautiful they are! . . . And how few people in England seem to admire them as they deserve!" (420). These "dreamy brown eyes," and his gentle demeanor, and self-characterization as "female" show him to be the feminized figure that Lucy cannot be by virtue of her unflinching confrontation with Franklin Blake.

Explaining how he has managed to cure Mr. Candy of a life-threatening fever, he recalls that when he saw that Candy was recovered, he broke down: "An hysterical relief, Mr. Blake—nothing more! Physiology says, and says truly, that some men are born with female constitutions—and I am one of them!" His resigned acceptance of his sad life, his female constitution, and, as I shall now show, his babu-like talents, fuse into a symbolic image of class, race, and gender subordination achieved without violent coercion.[24]

Jennings discloses the details of his most symbolically significant act in the novel by revealing to Blake that he is completing a book "on the intricate and delicate subject of the brain and the nervous system" (423). Believing that the loss of coherent speech does not necessarily imply the loss of an ability to think coherently, Jennings records, transcribes, and interprets Candy's fevered ramblings about having drugged Blake. A hybrid figure of empire, he performs a textual service that paradoxically leads to the eradication of any sign of empire in its metropolitan center—Jennings's labor precipitates the eradication of anything that might remind Britain of its violent colonial past and also the geopolitical expansion occurring at the historical moment of publication of *The Moonstone*.

Taking down what he terms Candy's "wanderings" in shorthand, he then reproduces those notes "in the ordinary form of writing—leaving large spaces between the broken phrases, and even the single words, as they had fallen disconnectedly from Mr. Candy's lips" (423). Imaginatively blending the native poetic imagination ascribed to Indians by

---

[24] In his perceptive analysis of relationships between sensationalist fiction and gender politics, D. A. Miller observes that in Collins's *The Woman in White*, women are enclosed and secluded in the patriarchal institutions of marriage and madhouses: male "bodies" of incarceration. The "sequestration of the woman takes for its object not just women, who need to be put away in safe places or asylums, but men as well, who must monitor and master what is fantasized as the 'woman inside' them" (Miller, *Representations* 112). Jennings, it seems to me, because of his internalized subaltern status, has less need to "master" the "woman inside" him.

Macaulay with the talent for intellectual speculation taught him by the British, Jennings fills in each blank space on the paper with what on either side of the space seems plausible. Revising "over and over again" the manuscript he has created out of the union of Candy's incoherent words and his own interpretive skills, he hones it until his additions seem to fall naturally into place, all the while working as a sensitive editor to remove anything Candy might not want disclosed. The result is a manuscript of two large folio leaves of paper, one containing writing with blank spaces (Candy's words) the other containing writing in red and black ink (Candy's words and his additions).[25] What he discovers, of course, is confirmation of the theory he seeks to prove in his book: that incoherent speech does not necessarily register incoherent thought. Finally, he shows the manuscript to Blake, knowing that it will reveal to him his innocent part in taking the diamond from Rachel's bedroom, and correctly predicting that Blake's repetition of this action will disclose the truth, Jennings arranges its dramatic reconstruction. This leads to the revelation that Blake gave the diamond to Ablewhite.

Clearly, then, Jennings is one of the Raj's new social class of interpreters, a figure produced by the resolution of the Orientalist and Anglicist debate of the 1830s ("Indian in blood and colour, but English in taste, opinions, in morals, and in intellect"), his admiration of English hedgerows and wildflowers a telling instance of his English "taste." Moreover, Jennings is not the only character in *The Moonstone* who may be linked to the Orientalist and Anglicist arguments of the 1830s. Godfrey Ablewhite's interest in the diamond as a material commodity rather than religious relic identifies him with the venal John Herncastle who in 1799 steals the stone; Ablewhite's greed also links him with the corrupt East India Company and thus with an Orientalist culture different from that devoted to the supposedly disinterested study of Eastern literatures and languages. The steely, rational, scientific intelligence of Sergeant Cuff (a Scotland Yard detective called in privately by Lady Verinder) may be said to be grounded in the Anglicist claim for the superiority of facts over imagination as articulated by Macaulay

---

[25] Gauri Viswanathan observes that Adam Smith's "concept of the impartial spectator was embedded in the rationale of literary instruction in India, which presupposed a divided self-consciousness" (129). It seems to me that with his gift for filling in the blanks, for being able to think as Candy might have thought and at the same time be distant from that process, Jennings may be said to resemble Adam Smith's impartial spectator in the context of Viswanathan's argument and my emphases in this chapter.

and Trevelyan. Significantly, both Ablewhite and Cuff are failures—the former a corrupt disgrace and the latter incapable of solving the mystery. In *The Moonstone*'s high-Victorian "writing the nation," the figure associated with tainted colonialism is the villain of the piece, and the figure associated with Anglicist values of rational thought is strangely impotent. It is left to Jennings to effect a magical restoration of a time before empire intruded upon ruling-class domestic order. It is as if the novel itself performs an ideological labor that parallels Jennings's subaltern work. In its recording of facts, rational accrual of information, and fictive eradication of greed and hypocrisy, *The Moonstone* also enacts a fabulous restoration of a pre-Anglicist and pre-Orientalist time, or, perhaps, an Orientalist time imagined as existing before the corrupt practices of the East India Company began to dominate British colonial governance. It is a time that Murthwaite, the Orientalist of *The Moonstone,* symbolically occupies at the end of the novel as he records the moment of unity and coherence that imaginatively transports the reader away from the dirty business of empire to a spot where the hills seem to melt into the grassy plain and three rivers meet. Here, thousands of pilgrims gather to see the moon god, bearing on his forehead, in Murthwaite's words, "the yellow Diamond, whose splendour had last shone on me in England, from the bosom of a woman's dress" (525–6).

In sum, *The Moonstone* relies upon a figure produced by Victorian empire to enable continuation of ruling-class enjoyment of wealth derived from empire. Ezra Jennings embodies the most significant quality required for cultivation of peaceful acquiescence in Victoria's colonial subjects: selfless acceptance of dominant class, race, and gender codes for thinking and behavior.[26] Desires realized in the world of the novel, however, are rarely so easily gratified in historical actuality, a critical truism demonstrated by the events and their aftermath that were said to occur in Barrackpore Park in 1882.

[26] Ezra Jennings's acceptance of imperialist ideology and of isolation in Victorian society is similar to the experiences of the twentieth-century colonized recently described by Stuart Hall. Discussing the problematical cultural identity of black people in the British empire, Hall writes, "The ways in which black people, black experiences, were positioned and subject-ed in the dominant regimes of representation were the effects of a critical exercise of cultural power and normalisation. Not only, in Said's 'Orientalist' sense, were we constructed as different and other within the categories of knowledge of the West by those regimes. They had the power to make us see and experience *ourselves* as 'Other'" ("Cultural Identity and Diaspora" 394).

SHAKING THE EMPIRE

In 1829, in *The Bengalee: Or, Sketches of Society and Manners in the East,* the essays, poems, and short stories of H. B. Henderson, a re- tired officer in the Bengal Civil Service, a character observes that "every time an Englishman shakes hands with a Baboo, he shakes the basis on which our ascendancy in this country stands" (189). The reports of the Mary Pigot case reveal that some fifty years later, it was the act of a British woman shaking hands with a babu, which, if it did not rock the empire, certainly shook up the Anglo-Indian missionary community in Calcutta.

In 1870, Mary Pigot arrived in Calcutta to take charge of the Church of Scotland's orphanage and zenana mission. Nine years later, the Rev. William Hastie arrived to direct the College for Indian men run by the General Assembly of the Church of Scotland. An irascible figure, Hastie quickly entered into theological disputes with Kalicharan Baner- jee, who was a teacher at the orphanage and a close friend of Mary Pigot's; these disputes took the form of heated exchanges of letters in the Calcutta newspapers. After the picnic in Barrackpore Park in 1882, Hastie brought charges of improper conduct against Pigot, and in Calcutta in March 1883, she filed counter charges for defamation of character. After a long trial presided over by a Justice Norris, who, it seems, engaged in relentless harassment of Pigot, she was awarded the insulting amount of one anna. In 1884, she appealed the judgment to the Appellate Bench of the High Court and in April of that year, was awarded three thousand rupees in damages with costs. Consequently, Hastie was relieved of his post as head of the college and recalled to Scotland. Returning to India to participate in the Foreign Mission Committee's enquiry into the matter, Hastie was arrested on arrival for nonpayment of the damages, spent one month in the Presidency jail, and was released on the grounds of his insolvency. He returned to Scotland. Ten years later, he was professor of theology at Glasgow Uni- versity, and Pigot, as far as one can tell, remained in India, the recipient of a pension awarded to her by the Foreign Mission Committee.

The events sketched briefly here, provide, it seems to me, suggestive evidence of how an educated Indian man and an unmarried indepen- dent British woman challenged the authority of late Victorian patriar- chal imperialism. Hastie's response to Banerjee's friendship with Pigot shows a white male's fear of native molestation of British women, and the responses of the legal, social, and church authorities to Pigot's startling refusal to remain quietly chastised by her male superior in the Church of Scotland hierarchy show white male fear of losing control of hitherto docile women to a dangerous ideal of fraternization. Among many charges and rumors, Pigot was said to have organized social gatherings of Indian and British groups, in addition to having invited Banerjee's advances. In this messy case, the body of a British woman (the encircled waist) becomes the site of contestation between threatened colonizer and insubordinate colonized.[27]

In the various accounts of what happened, Banerjee, by virtue of his English education, acquires a more theatrically intense identity than that possessed by the undifferentiated, uneducated, ordinary middle-class native. It is this developed late-Victorian identity, I think, that constitutes the babu figure as less politically manageable than before and as more sexually dangerous to the governing British Raj. What Macaulay ridiculed in 1853 in connection with a provision of the India bill to permit Indians to be nominated to the Civil Service—the Tory belief that an educated "Hindoo" will be armed with "such an accession of intellectual strength, that an established Government, with an army of 250,000 men, backed by the whole military and naval force of England, are to go down before its irresistible power" (*Life and Letters* 592)—seems, thirty years later, to have become a felt political actuality, if the Pigot case is any guide. Moreover, as Kenneth Ballhatchet points out, the British "often suspected that Indians were by nature more lascivious than they were themselves. Child marriage and polygamy seemed to prove it" (5).[28] Dressed almost always in European clothing and his imagined lasciviousness highlighted by European manners, the

[27] In discussing the imagery of rape in colonialist discourse, Sara Suleri observes that "When the colonial dynamic is metaphorically represented as a violated female body that can be mourned over with sentimentality's greatest excess, its rape is less an event than a deflection from a contemplation of male embattlement, the figure of which more authentically dictates the boundaries of colonial power" (61). In the Mary Pigot case, however, I do not see the obsessive interest in her possible violation by Banerjee as a deflection from anything. The male embattlement Suleri refers to is literally about possession of women as an expression of male control. In another connection, David Arnold points out that the actual bodies of Indians became immensely significant in medical work in India in the last years of the Victorian period. In "Touching the Body: Perspectives on the Indian Plague, 1896–1900," he argues that "The plague dramatized the importance of the body—the body, that is to say, of the colonized—as a site of conflict between colonial power and indigenous politics" (392).

[28] Benita Parry makes the useful observation that "the huge interest which Anglo-Indians took in the sexual conduct of Indians suggests that they attributed to them the erotic fancies and fantasies forbidden by their own society." Parry finds evidence of this interest in an English obsession with "obscene" temple sculpture, dancing-girls, male courtesans, bestiality, and so on. (*Delusions and Discoveries* 60).

educated Indian gains a kind of dark glamour, becomes a figure sexually threatening to British male control of its own women. He is very different from the Anglicists' refining and enriching go-between, the agent of British superior rational thought.

It would seem that in the Victorian India of the 1830s and 1840s—before the uprising of 1857—the native male Indian was regarded as barely threatening in sexual terms. Sexual assault appeared unlikely, an attractive Indian unthinkable, and the violence of 1857 unimaginable.[29] In the early years of Britain's vaunted moral renovation of colonial governance, the English-educated male Indian had not yet become sufficiently visible to threaten British male dominance, and the male Indian tended to be regarded by British women either as a flashy dynastic ruler dependent on the East India Company for military protection, or as a superstitious peasant—ignorant, poor, and totally in subordination to British forces.[30]

Harriet Tytler, for example, describes how in the late 1830s at the age of eighteen, she traveled some nine hundred miles entirely alone (by this she means without a female companion): "It was an awful risk, but in those days the peasants of India would no more have thought of harming an Englishwoman than of flying, for they knew they could not have escaped punishment" (57-8). Emma Roberts crossed India in the late 1830s, when Britain's acquisition of territory was being secured by the queen's regiments, and describes a journey undertaken with twelve camels, a persian cat, two female servants, and a large guard of sepoys: they were "peasants," she confides, "not inclined to purchase an ill

---

[29] My argument here, and elsewhere, is similar to that made by Jenny Sharpe. Sharpe argues that during the 1857 rebellion, "the idea of rebellion was so closely imbricated with the violation of English womanhood that the Mutiny was remembered as a barbaric attack on innocent white women. Yet Magistrates commissioned to investigate the so-called eyewitness reports could find no evidence to substantiate the rumors of rebels raping, torturing, and mutilating English women" (2). Sharpe's excellent study argues that the Western fear of interracial rape emerges when colonial governance feels itself to be losing its grip.

[30] V. G. Kiernan observes that the presence of Englishwomen in India led to the Englishman turning his back on Indian women, and also on India altogether: "His wife, whose susceptibility to the ravages of the climate was notorious, was less uneasy about him because he ostentatiously avoided all Indian society. It may be surmised that a broad moat between the races helped the white paterfamilias also to feel easy in his mind. There were other too well-known effects of a hot climate; young Indian men were often handsome, in a raffish Italian style; they were believed by prudish Victorians to be inordinately, unnaturally lascivious. Altogether, the peace and quiet of the family were safer if Indian company was excluded from the spacious bungalow" (*The Lords of Human Kind* 57-58).

name by acts of tyranny or oppression" (2:163). And a woman missionary writing in 1876 recalls that in the 1840s, she slept "with *not a soul
in the house but myself,* and the house seems so strangely open; but I
was not afraid" (Giberne, 234–35). One can argue, of course, that an
emphasis on how unafraid these women were, and how unthreatening
the peasants appeared, indicates something quite the contrary: that the
women dealt with their perceived sexual vulnerability by erasing even its
possibility. This may very well be the case, but it seems more critically
interesting to consider how certain people could have believed, or at
least recorded, certain things at certain historical moments. After 1857,
no Englishwoman would have registered such feelings, for it is doubtful
she would have felt them. Allowing for the luridly embellished accounts
of rape that incited punitive counteratrocities on the part of the British,
historical accounts of the uprising in 1857 show that the trope of the
Englishwoman as a sacrificial agent of empire assumes a brutal literal-
ness.[31] But in terms of far-reaching disturbances to the political power
of the British at the end of the Victorian period, the babu figure in
many ways becomes more dangerous than the defiant troops in Meerut,
Cawnpore, Delhi, and Lucknow. From the British perspective, the babu
could not be dispatched with the military measures applied to rebellious
sepoys and unruly peasants—and, his services were important in the administration of Victoria's enormously profitable empire. But these male
Indian figures, Horace Wilson's "clerks and copyists," and English-
educated teachers, from their ancillary yet powerful position, gained
social contact with British women—perhaps became close enough to
put their arms around Anglo-Indian female waists, to touch bodies controlled by the gender codes of Victorian patriarchy. The Anglo-Indian
community was well aware of these possibilities. In a letter published
in the Calcutta newspaper, *The Statesman,* on 3 October 1883, when the
charges of libel brought by Mary Pigot against the Rev. Hastie were
being heard, a district judge warns that "in these days of social antipathy
between the races," it is asking for trouble to allow unmarried British
women to visit the houses of middle-class Hindus for the purpose of
teaching the women in the household.[32] Mary Pigot's transgressive visits

---

[31] A tense moment in *A Passage to India* suggests the resonance of the uprising in the British
colonial imagination: "The club was fuller than usual, and several parents had brought their children into the rooms reserved for adults, which gave the air of the Residency at Lucknow" (180).
See Sharpe's well-researched chapter on the events of 1857 in *Allegories of Empire* 57–82.

[32] Quoted in *Opinions of the Indian Press* 23.

to Hindu households and defiant links to the educated Indian community were met with a battery of sensationalist charges. She was said to be an "illegitimate half-caste," to keep her female orphans in a filthy condition, to have been "the ruin of several innocent girls" by admitting men to their dormitory, to be an agent of the Jesuits, to favor "certain Baboos," and, finally, to have wasted orphanage money on "native brass bands."[33] For me, she emerges from newspaper accounts of the events precipitated by the picnic at Barrackpore as a woman unwilling to navigate the slippery spaces between being a pedagogical object and a performative subject. Jane Eyre, a politically symbolic character in a novel published almost forty years before the feminist climate that, in essence, produced Mary Pigot, is enabled by Brontë to recognize the demanding terms of her agency. Mary Pigot either refuses this recognition or denies the existence of such terms. I suspect the latter.

Contemporary Indian newspaper accounts of the events (to be found in *Opinions of the Indian Press on the Defamation Case, Pigot vs. Hastie* published in 1883) begin with Hastie's "Note Explanatory" on the *Report of the Consulting Committee to the Ladies' Association*, which found both Pigot and Banerjee to be innocent of any wrongdoing. For Hastie, its poor English "would disgrace our Bengali schoolboys"—hardly testimony to the success of the English Education Act of 1835—and he charges that entirely without evidence it excuses Pigot from misdeeds, "which no amount of falsehood or imbecility could conceal" (i). Hastie claims that the Female Mission over which Pigot presided is "a reproach and a by-word wherever its real ongoings have been known" (i). These ongoings, by which he obviously means sexual activity concealing itself behind the respectable facade of a female mission school, have been abetted by Indian female feminists, the most prominent of whom (unnamed) he calls "that greatest living founder of Female Reformers" (ii–iii). Hastie inflects his fevered fantasies about female sexuality with conservative male fear of late-Victorian feminist movements and then flavors the misogynistic tirade with race by charging that Pigot's school is "largely attended by illegitimate half-castes," a group with whom she has "naturally the strongest affinities" (iii). In a concluding torrent of antifeminist anger, Hastie finds the logic of the entire report of the

[33] *Statesman*, 1 October 1883. Quoted in *Opinions of the Indian Press* 20.

Consulting Committee to be grounded "on some new female system that may have been worked out in Edinburgh of late" (v).[34]

Articles printed in the *Indian Daily News* found it hardly credible that Mary Pigot could have been guilty of the charges brought against her. Who could possibly believe, asks the paper on 18 September 1883 (during the trial) that if Hastie knew Pigot "had committed adultery with one man, he would have been willing to receive her as a fellow-worker on any terms whatsoever?" (*Opinions* 5). "We are asked to believe," this account continues, that Mary Pigot "united in herself the loose principles of a gay abbess of the seventeenth century, a shameless-ness beyond that of the hardened courtesan, and the lust of a Messalina" (*Opinions* 7). The *Statesman* also found the charges impossible to believe simply on the grounds that Pigot's life as director of the orphanage was an open book; the fact that her accusers "are driven to declare her immoralities to have been enacted in the open Park in the midst of a picnic" (*Opinions* 12) persuaded the *Statesman* that she must have been innocent. The *Liberal* added that all the charges were rendered ridiculous by the evidence, especially since Banerjee "told the Judge in so many words that he regarded Miss Pigot as mother. . . . Mother is a sacred name in India; one who could pronounce the word with reference to any woman could not by that very fact look to her in any other improper light" (44). In general, Pigot was strongly defended by the native Indian newspapers, primarily because of her efforts to improve racial relations and also because of Banerjee's unblemished reputation as a principled Christian. As the newspaper of the "Educated non-Christian Natives," *The Bengalee*, asked on 22 September 1883, "What Hindoo, unless he were sunk in a depth of infamy which is inconceivable, would apply to a woman with whom he was holding immoral relations, language such as Baboo Kal Churn Banerjee employed toward Miss Pigot?" (53).

Newspaper accounts of evidence presented at the 1883 trial show that Pigot was not guilty of any of the charges brought against her: of being illegitimate, of being a Jesuit, of committing adultery with Banerjee, of running a brothel instead of an orphanage, of wanting Hastie's job

[34] In *Empire and Sexuality,* Ronald Hyam examines the Purity Campaign launched in the mid-1880s and dedicated to codes of sexual restraint, eradicating promiscuity and prostitution, and preserving the "imperial race"; this movement and Hastie's misogyny may both be seen as expressive of the patriarchal fears of assertive women that I am concerned with here.

for one of her "admirers," and of splurging orphanage money on band music. What she is guilty of is forming a friendship with a male Indian and, through this action, eluding the control of her white male superiors. Essentially, the trial exemplified the fears of patriarchal imperialism that the babus educated to transmit the facts of Western knowledge to their native brothers were no longer the docile, translating, interpreting, bodies that we see imaginatively exemplified in Ezra Jennings. The trial was also about the fears of patriarchal imperialism that British women had moved out of the cantonment bungalow, that they had become resistant to social and moral control either because of the pleasures afforded them by Anglo-Indian life (what Maud Diver called the endless "shawlings, fannings," and so on) or because of dangerous feminist thought invading from the metropolis out to the reaches of empire (Hastie's "new female system" from Edinburgh). Writing in 1926, Hastie's biographer perfectly summarizes these fears. Charging Pigot with being an independent-minded, inefficient, and morally lax manager of an orphanage that had become "a byword in the city" because of the conduct of its female teachers and senior girls (95), Donald Macmillan ridicules the male members of the investigating committee for trembling "in fear of serious consequences of a domestic nature" and siding with their wives in protesting Pigot's innocence. Furthermore, he records that after the judgment in the libel action in the High Court found in favor of Pigot, her female friends "let themselves loose upon him [Hastie] like a band of furies, and tried to make the Church believe that he was a sort of anti-Christ" (109). In his association of Pigot and her female defenders with the vengeful furies, Macmillan elaborates the late-nineteenth-century patriarchal fear that female missionary labor had eluded the direction of a male establishment. The female missionary evoked by St. John Rivers in his unsuccessful pitch to Jane Eyre has become a figure "grilled alive in Calcutta" not by the burning sun, but by the vituperative charges of an enraged authority. In his "Song of the Cities," Kipling eroticizes, without censure, the British conquest of Madras in the lines "Clive kissed me on the mouth and eyes and brow, / Wonderful kisses, so that I became / Crowned above Queens." Yet in illuminating contrast, an Indian man is hounded for a rumored touch upon the waist of a British woman, and she, in turn, is grilled at the trial by being asked some 333 questions in two hours.[35]

---

[35] Ballhatchet, 114.

THE INVASION OF ADELA QUESTED

As a way of concluding my discussion of the challenges to white male power in India at the end of the Victorian period, I would like to look forward, in a sense beyond the ending of this book, to E. M. Forster's *Passage to India*, which almost uncannily revises the meanings of what may or may not have happened in Barrackpore Park in 1882. Mary Pigot's experiences are exactly unlike those of Adela Quested in Forster's novel. The British woman, rather than accusing the educated Indian of molesting her (as Adela Quested does Aziz), sues the man who charged her with improper sexual conduct, is awarded damages, insists that Hastie be jailed until he pays up, and retires from the orphanage some years later with a comfortable pension. In a sense, this late-Victorian actuality promises a twentieth-century diminution of the power of patriarchal imperialism to govern the lives of British women and Indian men (needless to say, in utterly different degrees of imposed restriction). Forster's novel cautiously skirts the prospect of such a change, but then the brilliance of *A Passage to India* lies not in fidelity to historical fact but in imaginative exploration of political ideas through literary language, a radical vision, and an expression of utopian desire of what must take place for Aziz and Fielding to be friends—a prospect denied by the horses, the earth, the temples, the palace, and the birds, who say, "in their hundred voices, 'No, not yet' " and the sky, " 'No, not there' " (322). Forster's vision of what must happen before the voices can say "Yes" and the sky "Here," is, it seems to me, articulated in the description of Adela Quested after she leaves the court, her charge against Aziz of sexual misconduct in the Marabar Caves retracted, her reputation as a "pukka memsahib" (further linguistic trophies from the Victorian empire that belong with "loot" and "thug") destroyed.[36]

Here is Forster's description: "The faint, indescribable smell of the bazaars invaded her, sweeter than a London slum, yet more disquieting: a tuft of scented cotton wool, wedged in an old man's ear, fragments of pan between his black teeth, odorous powders, oils—the Scented East of tradition, but blended with human sweat as if a great king had been entangled in ignominy and could not free himself, or as if the heat of the sun had boiled and fried all the glories of the earth into a single mess.

[36] I am grateful to Gauri Viswanathan for pointing out to me that late in the Victorian period, the British Raj developed a judicial system as one further means of confining the potentially disruptive educated Indian in his subaltern place.

They paid no attention to her. They shook hands over her shoulder, shouted through her body—for when the Indian does ignore his rulers, he becomes genuinely unaware of their existence" (231). The invasion of Adela Quested by the smell of India is a sweet, pungent movement of the colonized into the body of the British woman, who, in so much Victorian writing about empire, is idealized as a symbol of superior civilization, culture, and morality, or, by virtue of her own historical moment, is vilified as a traitor to established codes of race and gender. Here, in this moment outside the courthouse, the symbol ceases to signalize suffering, sacrifice, and service to male imperialist power, and neither does it represent resistance. Adela becomes finely receptive to the experience of another culture: disquieted but not wasted by India, moved not "grilled" by a sun that seems to boil, fry, and mix "all the glories of the earth," ignored by natives, and in need of no white male protection. The British woman's body becomes transparent, as others "shouted through" her and Indians shake hands over her shoulder. In a moment strangely similar to the ending of *The Moonstone* where the diamond and the reader are restored to a time before colonial greed, *A Passage to India* imagines a time free of babu and memsahib, either back before these two figures of the Victorian empire were created or forward to a time when they no longer exist. In either case, in a moment of imaginative desire, the transmission of superior British knowledge through native education, acquisition of colonial power through knowledge of thuggee, performance of subaltern restorative service by a fictional babu figure, and knowledge possessed by patriarchal imperialism at the end of the Victorian period that its racial and sexual objects were gaining a dangerous kind of subjectivity do not seem to matter.

CHAPTER FIVE

LABORING FOR THE EMPIRE:
OLD PATRIARCHY AND NEW IMPERIALISM
IN TENNYSON AND H. RIDER HAGGARD

"The bow of Ulysses is unstrung. The worms have not eaten into the horn or the moths injured the string, but the owner of the house is away and suitors of Penelope Britannia consume her substance, rivals one of another, each caring only for himself, but with a common heart in evil. They cannot string the bow."
— James Anthony Froude,
The English in the West Indies, or the Bow of Ulysses

"Colonialism is the very base and structure of the West Indian's cultural awareness. His reluctance in asking for complete, political freedom . . . is due to the fear that he has never had to stand. A foreign or absent Mother culture has always cradled his judgment."
— George Lamming, *The Pleasures of Exile*

In my discussion of *The Old Curiosity Shop* and *Dombey and Son,* I suggested that in the process of negotiating the moral difficulties entailed in a Wordsworthian "getting and spending" made possible by Britain's burgeoning colonial wealth, Dickens appropriates certain prevailing middle-class ideas about woman's social role. In part, Little Nell is driven to sentimental death in an expression of Dickens's desire that Britain abandon self-deluded "civilization" of the "savage," and Florence Dombey is beaten so that the mercantile colonialism once practiced by her father may continue unmolested by further moral interrogation. In this chapter, I am interested in the ways mid- and late-Victorian culture is engaged by a similar project of moral negotiation. But where writers such as Dickens addressed the complex demands of an expanding, volatile, almost unknowable empire, later Victorian writers were confronted by an empire whose vast geopolitical scope was indelibly marked in red on Marlow's map, whose outposts were managed by a corps of professional colonial servants, and whose monumental existence served almost entirely to define British national identity. The issue, then, for Victorian writing about empire produced after mid-century is less one of refashioning the nation to fit the rapid acquisition of colonized territories than it is of securing Britain's continued imperial power. In the later period, the empire is not so much under construction as it is under a discursive inspection designed to shore up rocky foundations, ward off agitation, and ensure that the cost of imperial power not unbalance the political, social, and cultural order of the metropolitan center.

In a pattern of adjacent developments, in the time between publication of *The Old Curiosity Shop* and *Dombey and Son* and the poems and fiction discussed in this chapter, well-documented changes in sexual politics and class relationships accompanied the transformations in scope and meaning of empire.[1] Whether New Women or Odd Women — or just ordinary middle-class daughters, wives, mothers, and sisters — British women, in the last quarter of the nineteenth century, created and witnessed profound changes in their domestic lives, eligibility for higher education, and acknowledged fitness for professional careers. In novels and social actuality, they were subject to loosened gender codes, and as an obvious consequence, their participation in constructing the Victorian imperial nation also changed. From the perspective of patriarchal imperialism, this was not always a change for the better, as one sees in the case of Mary Pigot, a late-Victorian woman who refused to be cowed by male authority and who was willing to place her private life on humiliating display in the cause of self-vindication. Moreover, her friendship with Babu Kalicharan Banerjee revealed that the British reliance upon English-educated Indian civil servants, law clerks, and teachers also led to altered social and political opportunities for

---

[1] As Elaine Showalter has argued, the last decades of the nineteenth century in Britain were characterized by social contradiction and malaise. The making of vast industrial fortunes was accompanied by the political ascendancy of the Labour Party, the imperialist adventures abroad brought attention to metropolitan blight and misery, and women's political agitation had led to the passing of the Married Women's Property Act of 1882 and the Guardianship of Infants Act of 1886 (*Sexual Anarchy* 7). For a comprehensive history of the development of political feminism in late-Victorian Britain, see Olive Banks's *Faces of Feminism*. Banks identifies three intellectual traditions that shaped late-nineteenth-century women's political action: Evangelical Christianity, Enlightenment philosophy, and socialist feminism.

these servants of empire. In the more conservative quarters of patriar-chal imperialism, Mary Pigot and Banerjee were viewed as trespassers across the social and geographical boundaries that dictated and pre-served racial separation. These are boundaries traced, for instance, in Flora Annie Steel's Anglo-Indian novel *Miss Stuart's Legacy* (1897): the British live in a space marked by "parallelograms of white roads cen-tered by brown stretches of stubbly grass, and bordered by red and blue houses"; the "lines of the native regiment" are visited by the hero of Steel's novel who goes "in and out among his men, knowing them by name, and sympathising with their lives"; and the local population is "a race apart . . . the tillers of soil, the hewers of wood and drawers of water, who pay the bills for the great Empire" (71–72). Pigot and Baner-jee traversed the guarded lines of racial demarcation evoked in Steel's mapping of the cantonment, the sepoy tents, and the native bazaar.[2]

After more than a century of acquisition of Indian land, resources, and labor, the British Raj at the end of the Victorian period faces a resistance occasioned by the restlessness of the educated Indian male subject and the appearance of the independent New Woman.[3] In the case of the colonized Indian, identified as the laborer who produces the global economic wealth of the empire and the bureaucratic servant who administers its local business, the political movement culminates in the gaining of Indian independence in 1947. In the case of the British woman, whose political identity as subaltern assistant trusted with the moral management of empire—wife, teacher, missionary, and imperish-able symbol of civilization—becomes similarly subject to change, there is a transformation signaled by an expanded purpose for female emi-gration to the colonies. Spurred by a domestic population of a million more women than men, the Women's Emigration Society was founded in 1880 in Britain to provide loans, a free registry for employment in such places as Queensland, Canada, and South Africa, and encourage-ment for women to "look upon colonial life in the same way in which their brothers do—not only as an inevitable necessity to be encountered

[2] Sandra Gilbert and Susan Gubar note that the fact that women and natives "simultaneously began to manifest frightening drives toward independence just as England's great century of em-pire drew to its uneasy close would, of course, have sealed the *fin de siècle* connections between these two previously silent and disenfranchised groups" (36).

[3] In *New Women, New Novels,* Ann Ardis provides an interesting discussion of the formal significance of the New Woman novels in terms of narrative innovation, together with a useful selected bibliography of New Woman fiction published between 1880 and 1920, and other writ-ings about the New Woman.

bravely and cheerfully—but as an opening for ability and perseverance" (Ross, 316). The old female political identity as subaltern may be said, finally, to expire with the end of the British empire. Or perhaps not, if one considers the visible presence in British culture and society after World War II of its once colonized subjects. The working-class white ladies' room attendant in Claridge's Hotel, after all, who believed that Brixton market had been changed for the worse by the availability of tropical fruit, inherited the undaunted belief in British superiority to the "wogs" that was exhibited by the women who actually traveled to the outposts of empire in the Victorian period, or, if they stayed at home, elaborated this sense of superiority in their daily lives.[4]

During the forty years or so between publication of Dickens's early novels and late-Victorian literary engagement with empire, political and economic power in Britain became securely housed in the social group bitterly indicted and gingerly redeemed in Dickens's Paul Dombey: the mercantile middle class. Such significant shifts in the balance of class power during the second half of the nineteenth century are equal in importance with the transformations in service to the empire performed by British women and native bureaucrats. It is the negotiation of these multiple and related transformations—in the scope of empire, the parts played by women and natives in maintaining the empire, and in the changing class relationships occasioned by shifts in economic and political authority—that will be examined in this chapter. As texts representative of the sort of discursive management I have in mind, I have focused upon Tennyson's poems of the nation and two novels by H. Rider Haggard.

Recalling Dickens's complex ideological maneuvers and voicing a late-Victorian desire for disengagement from the fret and cost of empire, Tennyson's tortured celebrations of Britannic rule reveal a patriotic pride in Britain's rapidly increasing colonial power and a distaste for an aggressive middle class. Produced, for the most part, at a time when the empire he valued so ambiguously was, in the view of many conservative writers, being undermined by feminist and colonial agitation, Tennyson's poems express a longing for the stern maternalism of Queen Victoria, a nostalgia for the cradling of the colonies evoked by George

---

[4] See Paul Gilroy, *"There Ain't No Black in the Union Jack,"* for an examination of the complexity of racial politics in Britain in the 1960s to 1980s and for documentation of fear of tropical fruit in Brixton.

Lamming. Indebted to the figure of a subservient yet dominant middle-class Victoria that Margaret Homans argues is integral to the monarchy in nineteenth-century parliamentary democracy, Tennyson's poems of nation and empire deploy gendered images of imperial stability in a particularly resonant and historically specific way.[5] Nostalgia for a lost, or eroding, imperial order is also a recurrent theme in the strongly masculinist fiction of H. Rider Haggard. In his adventure tales, women are either pliantly submissive or fiercely assertive, and natives tend to be noble fellows or bloodthirsty savages. In what follows, I explore two of his novels, *King Solomon's Mines* and *She,* primarily from the perspective of their revelations of male panic about wayward women's bodies.[6]

In *King Solomon's Mines* and *She,* and in some of Tennyson's empire poems, the laboring body becomes a site of deep anxiety and political desire. By the "laboring body," I mean the actual, historical body of the colonized native, whose work sustained Britain's imperial power throughout the nineteenth century, from the Jamaican sugar plantations omitted from Rochester's tale of tropical passion to the African diamond mines ambiguously glimpsed in Haggard's adventure narratives, and the laboring body of the British woman, desired as both the literal means of imperial reproduction and the vehicle of significant, gendered metaphors of imperial control.[7] That the bodies of British women, for instance, might be developing a political life of their own is registered in the alarmed writings of Maud Diver, who together with Flora Annie Steel, dominated the field of Anglo-Indian fiction at the beginning of the twentieth century. Diver, a conservative in sexual and race politics, positioned herself against feminist agitation in the im-

[5] See Homans, " 'To the Queen's Private Apartments': Royal Family Portraiture and the Construction of Victoria's Sovereign Obedience."

[6] Joseph Bristow has usefully analyzed the fantastic aspects of late-nineteenth-century male adventure fiction. He argues that a number of "interrelated European anxieties about religion, sexuality" get played out in myths about savage Africa and that the journeys of male adventurers "across the desert, along the river, and into the jungle were just as significantly travels into two troublesome zones: first, the urban squalor of major cities, and second, what were increasingly recognized as the unknown underworld passages occupying the labyrinthine depths of the supremacist psyche" (131).

[7] Paul Kennedy has pointed to a climate of fear at the end of Victorian period: "Late nineteenth-century imperialism, so far as the British were concerned, was increasingly an imperialism of fear, of *weltpolitsche Angst* and a growing 'siege' mentality . . . which makes it altogether different in form from the decades prior to 1870, when the empire's trade and territories were expanding in a power-political vacuum" ("Continuity and Discontinuity in British Imperialism, 1815-1914" 34). Kennedy argues that after 1870, Britain's imperial power was considerably diminished owing to rival manufactures and foreign tariffs.

perial metropolis and on the side of male mastery of insubordinate British women and politically restless native men in the outposts of empire. I begin my exploration of the meaning of the laboring body in Victorian imperial culture with Diver's elegy for a lost social order and then will consider Tennyson's disdain of a middle class made rich by the technology of empire. Although they bear no trace of Diver's blunt deployment of literature for didactic harangue, Tennyson's poems of empire betray a politics that is at times not too different from her conservative alarmism. Elucidation of the meaning of the new imperialism in late-Victorian Britain follows, and the discussion concludes with an exploration of the richly gendered terrain of *King Solomon's Mines* and *She*, a place of swelling breasts and withered female bodies.

"SHE OF ASIA"

In her guide to Anglo-Indian life, published in 1909, Maud Diver traces a nervous and moral decline in the late Victorian memsahib. Asserting that the climate "tends to promote an astonishingly rapid waste of nerve tissue" (*The Englishwoman in India* 6), Diver implies that the body of the British woman, essential in the most literal way to reproduction of empire, is enervated by a grilling sun, not just in Calcutta but throughout the feverish spaces of the British Raj. Indulged by a parade of servants unavailable in the Home Counties and cossetted by a male phalanx of officers and civil servants, the memsahib, Diver warns, begins "to develop the emotional, pleasure-loving side of her nature, to blur her girlish visions of higher aims and sterner self-discipline" (16–17). She turns away from the moral authority symbolized in Jane Eyre's governess sensibility and degenerates from neurasthenia into giddy hedonism. Through guarded references to "domestic tragedies" caused by "amateur theatricals and the military man on leave" (24), Diver infers that British women are unbuttoning their moral corsets and directing their sexuality away from biological reproduction to erotic pleasure.[8] Diver reiterates the durable Victorian myth of woman as salvational angel in an age of secular materialism and reminds us of the redemp-

---

[8] Martha Vicinus aptly observes that "imperialism, while extolling the self-sacrificing single man who gave his life to tame some remote part of the empire, called for women to return to their traditional roles in the home. The eugenics movement attempted to reform working-class mothers and to pressure upper-class women to marry, lest the race lose its best stock" (*Independent Women* 285).

tive domestic heroism incarnated in Little Nell and Florence Dombey. She urges that it is not enough for women "to be just women": they must do more, they must "keep alive the grace, the poetry, the soul— so to speak—of a material age" (52). In her novel *Awakening* (1911), Diver sharpens these warnings about the slide into female pleasure encouraged by Anglo-Indian luxury, and she directly links the decline of Britain's imperial power to feminist agitation. The novel also sounds some reactionary alarms about degeneration of the white race; Diver attributes this degeneration to white woman's truancy from motherhood and her gender-specific role as moral policewoman of the colonizer and moral instructress of the colonized.

Less about India than about the corruption of a sentimental ideal of British rule, *Awakening* traces the romance of an English upper-class painter of the Alma Tadema sort, Nevil Sinclair, and Lilamani, a high-caste seventeen-year-old Hindu—always referred to in Diver's arch style as "she of seventeen summers" or "she of Asia"—who has been brought to Europe to study medicine by a feminist physician, Audrey Hammond. In *Awakening,* the British female renovation of the colonizer that we see symbolized in Jane Eyre's handling of Rochester has become the actual work of a British woman devoted to her Indian female patients and to the training of Indian women in the practice of medicine. Audrey regards Lilamani as "the one tangible, practical result of my three years' crusade" (19). *Awakening,* however, proves Audrey's crusade to be a waste of feminist energy by having Lilamani abandon her studies in favor of marriage to Nevil. Rather than becoming a physician in service to her own people, Lilamani becomes an artist's model in service to Nevil's Orientalist fantasies. It seems as if *Awakening* were written in almost direct response to the egalitarian arguments of Olive Schreiner's *Woman and Labor* (also published in 1911).

Schreiner's passionate demand that in the "strange new world" of the early twentieth century women must have their proper "share of honored and socially useful human toil" (65) is, in effect, ridiculed by *Awakening*'s portrayal of Audrey Hammond. From the narrator's perspective, the female sexuality that should be directed to making strong babies for the empire has, in Audrey's sad case, been damaged by her ambition, intellectualism, and career—indeed, one might argue, by her adherence to Schreiner's claim that it is possible for sexual relations between men and women to exist "apart entirely from physical reproduction" (*Woman and Labor* 20). When dancing with Nevil, Audrey experiences "no stir of pulses," which causes the narrator to remark, "It is a question whether girls of her type—products of extreme reaction from mid-Victorian ideals—are not cultivating brain and ego at the expense of the natural emotions; a doubtful gain for themselves and for the race, in an age already over-loaded with intellectuality and all its works" (52). This criticism of Audrey Hammond's career and ideals, rooted in early-twentieth-century gynophobic attitudes toward women and careers, and in antagonism to Schreiner's demand that women perform "socially useful human toil," is shared by Nevil, who quizzes her about her "progressive schemes," her treatment of "zenana ladies," and her "advanced views on the Woman Question" (16). Not surprisingly, Diver's fictional New Woman remains celibate, implicitly barren by virtue of the brain work that has sapped her reproductive energy and condemned her to life as a zenana doctor and an educator of young Indian women who want to become physicians. The fear-mongering suggestion that brain work performed by intellectual women impaired their powers of biological reproduction was hardly unique to Diver's novel. At a time when Britain's imperial hegemony was being threatened by France, Belgium, and the Netherlands,[9] reactionary physicians regularly warned that too much female thinking would result in maternal anemia, that female careers would produce weak infants unable to become brave defenders of the empire.[10]

Maud Diver's fear of a transforming sexual politics that would steer women away from making babies to making careers is also expressed in the sentimental stereotyping of dusky Lilamani, who gazes at Nevil with "her dark unfathomable eyes" in a "passion of adoration, such as the modern man rarely looks for in marriage, and still more rarely receives" (130). In late-Victorian and early-twentieth-century writing about empire, it is rare to find the suffering and civilizing woman of empire figured, say, in Emma Roberts's narrative of Anglo-Indian misery. Either this figure is consciously resisted, as we see in Schreiner's political writings, or another figure, the native woman, assumes the unhappy

[9] See Barbara Kanner's comprehensive bibliography of late-Victorian and early-twentieth-century texts dealing with "Race Improvement" in Vicinus, *A Widening Sphere* 258–60. Anna Davin offers a comprehensive historical analysis of the efforts of turn-of-the-century patriarchal imperialism to indoctrinate lower-class mothers in patriotic allegiance to empire and in bearing strong babies for the national good. See her essay "Imperialism and Motherhood."

[10] Elaine Showalter provides a helpful discussion of patriarchal fears of higher education for women; she quotes Sir James Paget (*Clinical Lectures and Essays* 1867) as arguing that brain work for women tended to induce "development of the nervous constitution" (*The Female Malady* 125–26).

burden of sentimental self-sacrifice, as we see in *Awakening*. Lilamani is the obedient and generic "she of Asia" whose subservience reproves Western women and natives eager for their different but related forms of independence, and as is so often the case in Victorian writing about empire, the East functions ideologically in relation to the West, either as unhappily deficient or as fortunately instructive. When British writing about empire vaunts its intrinsic superiority to Oriental cultures (one thinks of Macaulay's nonchalant announcement that "one half of a good European library" is worth "the whole native literature of India and Arabia"), the East is clearly the loser. But when writing about empire laments an attrition of Western idealism, then the East becomes the site of an ideal sexual politics (as we see in *Awakening*) or the place where Western individuals, usually male, discover and integrate into their personalities suppressed destructive tendencies (as we see in *Heart of Darkness*).[11] In Diver's novel, the mindless fidelity of an educated Indian woman to a fatuous ruling-class Englishman registers a recurrent charge in early-twentieth-century conservative circles: British women had sunk far below the gendered standards of obedience to patriarchy and sacrifice for empire that were inscribed for them throughout the Victorian period. Although not promoting as sanguine a view of protected Indian women as one finds in the observations of a British woman writing earlier in the century—"They are happy in their confinement; and never having felt the sweets of liberty, would not know how to use the boon if it were to be granted them"—in the cause of conservative sexual politics in the West, Diver perpetuates a thoroughly racist view of women in the East.[12] Finally, Maud Diver is but one of several early-twentieth-century women writing about empire who turns to the Indian female as chastening and instructive model for errant feminist women—"free, strong, fearless and tender" (Schreiner, *Women and Labor*, 271). In Flora Annie Steel's *On the Face of the Waters* (1896), set in Lucknow and Delhi at the time of the 1857 uprising, Indian characters similar to those in *Awakening*—"learned, well-born, well-doing folk"—give "firm adherence to civilization" and

---

[11] Chinua Achebe's voice is perhaps the strongest in making this argument: "I have no doubt that the reason for the high rating of this novel in Europe and America is simply that there it fortifies fears and prejudices and is clever enough to protect itself, should the need arise, with the excuse that it is not really about Africa at all. And yet it is set in Africa and teems with Africans whose humanity is admitted in theory but undermined by the mindlessness of its context and the pretty explicit animal imagery surrounding it" ("Viewpoint" 113).

[12] See Mrs. Meer Hassan Ali, *Observations on the Mussulmans of India* 1:313.

know something of their empress, "the mysterious woman across the sea" (101). The British heroine, Kate Erlton, stranded in Delhi (as was the actual Harriet Tytler, whose memoirs contribute to the powerful Britannic narrative of female sacrifice for the empire), escapes massacre through assuming Indian female disguise. Wearing an Indian bracelet she feels an "odd thrill" at the "touch of that gold fetter" (285). In other words, she feels something of the masochistic excitement imagined by Maud Diver and Flora Annie Steel as the experience of erotically enslaved Indian women. Kate spends the four-month siege of Delhi as a "screened woman," losing track of time, eating rice and fruit rather than the bungalow fare of mutton stew, and finally achieving a previously unknown sense of contented acquiescence in whatever life may unfold.[13]

Awakening also trots out a number of stereotypes in fashioning its political critique. Audrey belongs to a type whose brain work has erased her female sexuality (no "pulse" beats for Nevil); Hebraic Germans are the money-making type;[14] Nevil is the Orientalist painter type; cut from the Anglophillic model is Lilamani's father, Sir Laksham Singh, about whom the narrator remarks, "If modern India produced more of his type we should hear little or nothing of political unrest" (53). A form of worlding, stereotyping is an integral aspect of the elaboration of British racialism that accompanied expansion of empire in the Victorian period. The deployment of types worlds the space of identity of a colonized individual and fixes that individual in place, much as Emma Roberts's *Scenes and Characteristics*, published some seventy five years before *Awakening*, frames and fixes a colonized culture in a stereotype of sloth and neglect, or as Nevil Sinclair, in painting Lilamani, fixes her as the adoring Indian woman. Moreover, the son of Nevil and Lilamani is endowed, in stereotypical fashion, "with the best that two great races can give—the spirituality of the East, and the power and virility of the West" (431). This fable of East and West resonates with the gendered affiliation of native bureaucratic service to empire with a poetic

---

[13] See Nancy L. Paxton's "Complicity and Resistance in the Writings of Flora Annie Steel and Annie Besant" for analysis of Steel's ambiguous identity as privileged, racist, and authoritarian memsahib, and campaigner to improve the social rights of Indian women. See also Jenny Sharpe's discussion of *On the Face of the Waters*, which emphasizes the ideological significance of the memsahib figure in Anglo-Indian writing (*Allegories of Empire* 85–110).

[14] Anti-Semitism appears in another Anglo-Indian novel, Flora Annie Steel's *Miss Stuart's Legacy:* a character who is an accountant in the Indian Civil Service, John Raby, covets power "not so much for its own sake as for the use he could make of it. For just as some men inherit a passion for drink, he had inherited a greed of gain from a long line of Jewish ancestry" (86).

imagination, and the virile direction of empire with a masculine intellect, which I explored in my earlier discussion of the Orientalist and Anglicist debate of the 1830s and the subsequent generation of an often feminized babu figure, as we see in Ezra Jennings.[15]

TENNYSON'S COLONIAL MOTHER

In his exploration of Tennyson's imperial politics, V. G. Kiernan argues that for Tennyson, empire provided a myth of valiant ideals and actions that he could value in the distasteful world of capitalist greed. In addition, Kiernan claims, the class insecurities rooted in Tennyson's genteel childhood in a run-down vicarage, were assuaged by an identification with heroic, if flawed, figures such as Ulysses and Arthur. About Tennyson's fascination with Arthur in the context of Victorian empire, Kiernan observes: "England's combats might be righteous and unsought, but they were gaining for it the widest-ranging empire in history, for Tennyson a bastion against his haunting sense of mutability and impermanence. It was something tangible and vast, which could be admired from every point of view from commercial to moral." ("Tennyson" 134). Kiernan believes that from empire Tennyson derived "a simple certitude of rightness, a simplification of moral and political issues, unattainable in his own ever-complicated country" ("Tennyson" 136). To complicate Kiernan's important readings of Tennyson, Tennyson's poems about nation and empire serve more complex functions than offering the certitude of moral positions or an uncomplicated sense of political security. Disliking a metropolitan society driven by mercantile capitalism and looking to the myths of empire as a noble alternative to Wordsworth's "getting and spending," Tennyson must negotiate his way out of an ideological bind: what he values as an alternative to what

---

[15] This fable of East and West appears in a piece of steamy gothic fiction published a century before *Awakening*. *The Missionary*, by a Miss Owenson (1811), tells a lurid tale of erotic temptations in early-seventeenth-century Goa, and describes the romance of a "Christian Saint" and a "Heathen Priestess," a couple "finely opposed, the noblest specimens of the human species, as it appears in the opposite regions of the earth; she, like the East, lovely and luxuriant; he, like the West, lofty and commanding" (1:150). The contrast continues in this way: "the one radiant in all the lustre, attractive in all the softness which distinguishes her native regions; the other, towering in all the energy, imposing in all the vigor, which marks his ruder latitudes; she, looking like a creature formed to feel and to submit; he, like a being created to resist and to command: while both appeared as the ministers and representatives of the two most powerful religions of the earth; the one no less enthusiastic in her brilliant errors than the other confident in his immutable truth" (1:150).

he despises is, in fact, being produced by the social class and the Gladstonian Liberal politics that he finds so abhorrent. As a consequence, Tennyson creates myths that enable him to embrace empire: His empire is located in the exalted past and is rooted in the mythic vows of the Round Table, not in the grubby dealings of cotton-mill owners. For Tennyson, coarse Manchester bullies, who in his "The Third of February, 1852" poem are described as having "niggard throats," are greedy for profit and stingy in patriotism. Kiernan carefully identifies Tennyson's idealization of empire but does not perceive the corner into which Tennyson writes himself. It is a middle-class Queen Victoria who bails Tennyson out of his tight political spot.

In March 1851, the year of his first publication as poet laureate, Tennyson dedicated his *Poems* to the queen, hoping that "the care / That yokes with empire" (9-10)[16] might yield Victoria time to consider his verse, averring that she has "A thousand claims to reverence closed / In her as Mother, Wife, and Queen" (27-28). In these lines, he elaborates a powerful image that pervades nineteenth-century society: Victoria as the great colonial mother and revered monarch of all her colonized children and domestic subjects, the spotless emblem of marital loyalty, maternal firmness, and moral rectitude. In "Opening of the Indian and Colonial Exhibition by the Queen" (the poem was published in 1886 and the exhibition opened in May of that year), the speaker salutes the filial gifts of empire presented to Victoria and the mother-nation:

> Sons and brothers that have sent,
> From isle and cape and continent,
> Produce of your field and flood,
> Mount and mine, and primal wood;
> Works of subtle brain and hand,
> And splendours of the morning land,
> Gifts from every British zone.
>
> (3-9)

Horticultural produce, mined resources, intellectual labor—these are the material fruits of an economic expansion born from Victoria's actual and symbolic fertility; these "gifts," the poem continues, will reveal "The mother featured in the son" (12). Moreover, this colo-

---

[16] All further citations to Tennyson's verse are taken from the 1969 edition of his poems edited by Christopher Ricks.

The Voyage of the Sable Venus, from Angola to the West Indies. From W. Grainger, *The History, Civil and Commercial, of the British Colonies in the West Indies* (1801). By permission of the Library Company of Philadelphia.

nial mother possessed what Tennyson saw as absent from eighteenth-century British government: a maternal hand that might have stayed departure from the colonial home. This is the ideal hand that guides the amazing Sable Venus on her voyage from Africa to the West Indies. In the American colonies, British bungling, "Drove from out the mother's nest / That young eagle of the West / To forage for herself alone" (27–29), a charge that reminds one of the "Magna Britannia" figure, her severed limbs representing the rebellious American colonies. The prevalent Victorian image of Britain as colonial mother and the colonies as obedient daughters is to be found in almost all of Tennyson's poems of empire: America, greeted in "Hands All Around!" (1852) as "Gigantic daughter of the West" (36), has been forced to forage "for herself alone." And in Kipling's numerous poems about the colonies, Britain is always a stern yet benevolent mother watching over her female colonies who are linked in a sororal chain of obedience. In the last stanza, for example, of his 1897 poem celebrating a trade agreement between Britain and Canada, Kipling figures Canada in this way:

> "Daughter am I in my mother's house,
> But mistress in my own.
> The gates are mine to open,
> As the gates are mine to close,
> And I abide by my Mother's House,"
> Said our Lady of the Snows.

If one recalls the eroticized imagery of a woman's body as America in Donne's "To His Mistris Going to Bed"—"O My America! my new-found land, / My kingdome, safeliest when with one man man'd, / My Myne of precious stones, My Emperie, / Howe blest am I in this discovering thee!"—then the domestication of sexuality in these Victorian poems of empire becomes particularly vivid.

Tennyson's fusion of maternal care and colonial command appears prominently in "To the Queen," published in 1873 as a closing to *Idylls of the King*. The poem recalls a moment when Victoria and Albert attended a thanksgiving service after his illness and were gratified to hear the cries of joyful, thankful subjects—London is "one tide of joy"—echoing throughout the empire and heard in "The prayer of many a race and creed, and clime" (11). The speaker declares that those loyal to the crown:

> Are loyal to their own far sons, who love—
> Our ocean-empire with her boundless homes
> For ever-broadening England, and her throne
> In our vast Orient.
>
> (28–31)

These lines domesticate empire, make it an extension of British loyalty to the Queen, in the image of "boundless homes" spreading throughout Britain's "broadening" territories, the emphasis on a rounded unity intensified by the strong assonance.[17] The poem also expresses the imperialist desire to make what is not-Britain into what is Britain. In the furthest reaches of the ocean-empire, one will find an English home, a place that is a colonial metonym of the unblemished domesticity presided over by Victoria and her female subjects, of whom Florence Dombey is an ideal representative. If one considers for a moment the soured domesticity of the *Idylls* in the context of these celebrations of domestic harmony in the colonies, then, as is often noted by Tennyson's critics,[18] it seems clear that Arthur's empire falls apart because he lacks a Queen Victoria to reign alongside his own Albert-like self: "Thou hast spoilt the purpose of my life," Arthur chillingly announces to Guinevere. The "spoiling" of Arthur's world implies that for Tennyson the perfect empire (that is to say, one not fueled by monetary greed) requires the perfect woman—selfless; faithful throughout all trials to father, husband, and children; and prepared to suffer. With the exception of Victoria, who in her immensely long reign was transformed in the public imagination from young wife presiding over a rapidly expanding family composed of her many children, her millions of domestic subjects, and her colonies, to an aged widow/queen/empress who reigned supreme over an enormous empire, none of Tennyson's female figures seems to suit.[19] Tennyson's reconciliation to mercantile imperialism is achieved, in the main, under the maternal auspices of an idealized colonial mother. Distaste for the middle-class materialism that has created empire is erased by the fusion of imperial might and middle-

[17] As Tricia Lootens has noted, Felicia Homans's perhaps best-known poem "The Homes of England" (1827) links grand and lowly dwellings and constructs a stable national hierarchy with the hearth as woman's empire; by extension, Lootens argues, "in an imperialist country . . . the hearth must be an imperialist site" (248). Tennyson's domestication of empire builds upon what one might call the imperialization of the home.

[18] See, for example, Elliot L. Gilbert, who argues that because of Victoria's immense power, a queen who is "the repository of enormous inherited authority," Tennyson has Arthur play a number of parts "assigned by culture to the woman"; that is to say, in the absence of a figure like Victoria in the *Idylls*, Arthur takes on some of her maternal authority.

[19] Adrienne Auslander Munich argues that a patriarchal ambivalence about Victoria's immensely long reign, very different from Tennyson's laudations, finds comic expression in the stereotyped overbearing female characters in Gilbert and Sullivan: for example, the Duchess of Plaza-Toro, Lady Blanche, Lady Jane, and of course, Katisha. See " 'Capture the Heart of a Queen': Gilbert and Sullivan's Rites of Conquest."

class propriety to be found in his images of the queen. In addition to his salutes to Victoria, he also constructs this positive ideal through the negative images of lustful and enraged women who are to be found in poems less explicitly about Britain's nineteenth-century empire. The obvious place to begin looking at these figures is the *Idylls.*

The *Idylls of the King,* written, Kiernan observes, during a long succession of imperial victories, creates a fable of benevolent colonial government. Without question, Arthur's rule involves many fierce and bloody battles, but it is a rule dedicated to "our fair father Christ" not to the prospect of economic gain that Tennyson believed (correctly) to be the foundation of Victorian colonial government.[20] As all critics have observed, in "The Coming of Arthur," Tennyson imagines a leader devoted to the establishment of moral and social order in a time of violence and destruction, and his writing of the nation in the *Idylls* constructs a barbaric Roman Britain not unlike Macaulay's highly imaginative notion of what India looked like before the British arrived; to Macaulay, India was a place "to which history scarcely furnishes a parallel" (*Prose and Poetry* 702).[21] Arthur's coming initiates moral, political, and social renovation:

> For many a petty king ere Arthur came
> Ruled in this isle, and ever waging war,
> Each upon other, wasted all the land;
> And still from time to time the heathen host
> Swarm'd overseas, and harried what was left.
> And so there grew great tracts of wilderness,
> Wherein the beast was ever more and more,
> But man was less and less, till Arthur came.
>
> (5-12)

[20] Kiernan notes that the writing of the *Idylls* coincides with the following imperial victories: the conquest of the Punjab in the late 1840s and of Lower Burma in 1854; the Second China War of 1856–60; the attack on Persia in 1857; and the defeated Indian uprising of 1857. Also, there was a fifty-five-year lapse between the writing of the "Morte d'Arthur" in 1833 and publication of the complete *Idylls* in 1888. Kiernan also suggests that Tennyson's support of Governor Eyre in 1865 was influenced by the events in India in 1857.

[21] See John D. Rosenberg's *The Fall of Camelot* for a sensitive exploration of Arthur's tragic failure. Linda Shires has usefully identified what she sees as the Victorians' need to "invent a patriarch to run the country on behalf of the young Victoria" (403). For Shires, Tennyson's Arthur is one such symbolic, if doomed, patriarchal figure.

In imagining an ancient, mythical Britain doubly devastated by the wasting disputes of its own petty kings and the invasions of heathen hordes, Tennyson creates a political wilderness where the colonized are unable to govern themselves and where their heathen invaders lack the ability to institute effective colonial control. But when Arthur arrives, he is Tennyson's ideal colonizer and someone whom Macaulay would surely welcome. The readiness with which Macaulay's political thought comes to mind when thinking about Tennyson's ideal empire suggests, I think, a complex similarity and difference between them.

The clear difference between the gloomy, romantic conservative and the optimistic, practical whig may lead one to argue that, because Tennyson disdained the bureaucratic social class to whom Macaulay appealed, any argument about similarity becomes suspect. There is more affiliation between these two Victorian writers about empire in terms of political myth making, however, than there is difference. Both construct fables of benevolently wise colonialism—of subjugation through moral right not martial strength. Macaulay projects a serene British India inhabited by enlightened, high-minded British rulers and educated, subservient Indian people. Tennyson creates a fantastic ancient Britain inhabited by noble knights who can vanquish heathens and bandits, throw out the degenerate Romans, and rule Britain as a symbolically "stronger race" of colonizers. The political challenge for Tennyson (not one ever faced by Macaulay) is to reconcile his sheer pleasure in the vital empire building symbolized by the Arthurian project in the *Idylls* and admired by him in Victorian Britain with the values of the social class most responsible for its existence.

The imaginative alignment of Arthur with an idealized form of colonialism depends upon his symbiosis with the new Christian order that defeats Roman colonists, weakened as they are by corruption and brutality. The banquet in honor of the arrival of Guinevere heralds the beginning of political renovation: the "great Lords from Rome" demand their tribute "as of yore," but the times of yore are in fact just that:

> The old order changeth, yielding place to new;
> And we that fight for our fair father Christ,
> Seeing that ye be grown too weak and old
> To drive the heathen from your Roman wall,
> No tribute will we pay.

> (*Idylls* 508–12)

In Tennyson's myth of empire, Arthur's martial verve and moral intensity vanquish the Roman colonizers who have neither subdued the British barbarians nor the heathen invaders. Arthur, then, although king of Britain, is never colonized by Rome because, as mythic figure, he exists outside the historical actuality of the fierce battle between Roman colonizer and British barbarian. Tennyson's mythic empire thus ventures the desire for a history in which Britain defeated its Roman colonists more by virtue of its Victorian idealism and less by virtue of the violence and savage taste for battle we find powerfully embodied in Tennyson's Queen Boadecia (a figure in historical actuality defeated by the Romans in the middle of the first century). Boadecia's female rage and her fiery resistance to the Romans provide a vivid contrast to the fable of Arthur's somber, measured, and responsible usurpation of Roman governance.

Tennyson's "Boadecia" (1864) is a rollicking exercise in galliambic verse. Boadecia exhorts the tribes of Britain to vengeful action in a blood-curdling fashion:

> Burst the gates, and burn the palaces, break the works of the statuary,
> Take the hoary Roman head and shatter it, hold it abominable,
> Cut the Roman boy to pieces in his lust and voluptuousness,
> Lash the maiden into swooning, me they lash'd and humiliated,
> Chop the breasts from off the mother, dash the brains of the little one
>   out,
> Up my Britons, on my chariot, on my chargers, trample them under us.
>   (64–69)

If one juxtaposes the measured, rueful, tones of Arthur with the alliterative brutality of Boadecia's cries, then the male voice of moral reproach roundly admonishes—in effect silences—the female voice of fury, the voice of the Eumenides come to Britain. In addition, Boadecia's anger may be affiliated with Guinevere's utterly different but still gendered female destructive powers as they are manifested in the *Idylls* and, I would suggest, also with the furious contempt in which Edith Dombey holds her husband, however obvious the moral and formal difference between Paul Dombey and King Arthur. The fury of bellicose Boadecia and the licentious sexuality of regal Guinevere emerge in instructive contrast to the venerated moral serenity and middle-class propriety of Victoria. In the *Idylls* and "Boadecia," texts that disclose Tennyson's effort to imagine some kind of decent imperialism he can live with, he substitutes Victorian moral earnestness for Roman corruption, heathen greed, and indigenous British violence. It is interesting to see, incidentally, that Tennyson not only distorts for political effect Boadecia's reign, but he creates a very different poetic figure from that to be found in William Cowper's 1780 poem, "Boadecia." Cowper's queen flies into battle "with all a monarch's pride," and in her marvelous death hurls at her Roman foe the cry "Empire is on us bestow'd, / Shame and ruin wait for you" (43–44).[22]

As Kiernan, then, and other critics have argued, Tennyson's figures of the Round Table are antecedents of the figures he wished were running the Victorian empire. In this process of substitution, however, Tennyson must accommodate the historical fact that the architects of Britain's colonial wealth were beyond his conservative pale, a group also disdained, one recalls, in William Arnold's attack upon the East India Company in *Oakfield*. In a poem written in response to Louis Napoleon's coup d'état of December 1851,[23] "The Third of February, 1852" (published on 7 February), the speaker, who would appear to be addressing the House of Lords, exhorts Britons to rally against the dangerous doings across the channel. Evoking the noble honor of Arthurian moments fast fading in a society driven by the desire for profit, Tennyson's poem urges remembrance of how Britain "wrung" its claims for parliamentary freedom from Charles I and "flung the burthen of the second James" when "Prick'd by the Papal spur." The last stanza puts the social group primarily responsible for Britain's industrial wealth in its vulgar place:

[22] In the *Idylls*, of course, some of the qualities of Tennyson's Boadecia are to be found in Vivien. The disruptive energy of Vivien, Boadecia, and Guinevere represent a Victorian fear analyzed by Anita Levy, a dread "that the bourgeois female and with her the middle class itself were always in imminent danger of slipping back into the chaotic, sensual depths from which they had emerged" (68–69). In her exploration of cultural links between women and the primitive, Marianna Torgovnick asserts that "gender issues always inhabit Western versions of the primitive. Sooner or later those familiar tropes for primitives become the tropes conventionally used for women" (17). The figure of Tennyson's Boadecia would seem to exemplify very well this double-trope of women and the primitive.

[23] It is interesting to contrast Tennyson's political critique of the coup with Elizabeth Barrett Browning's impassioned defense of Louis Napoleon. For her, he was exactly the heroic figure for whom Tennyson seemed to be in search. See my essay, "The Old Right and the New Jerusalem: Elizabeth Barrett Browning's Intellectual Practice."

Though niggard throats of Manchester may bawl,
What England was, shall her true sons forget?
We are not cotton-spinners all,
But some love England and her honour yet.
And these in our Thermopylae shall stand,
And hold against the world this honour of the land.

(43–48)

The emphasis upon true sons of England and allusion to Thermopylae implies, of course, the crass cowardice and ignorance of classical learning to be found in Victorian businessmen, a sentiment that appears also in "Maud": the poem scorns the pacifist, "Whose ear is crammed with his cotton, and rings / Even in dreams to the chink of his pence" (1:371–72), "Britons, Guard Your Own," published in January 1852, was also written with the threat of Louis Napoleon's coup hovering over England. The eighth stanza of the poem cries:

We were the best of marksmen long ago,
We won old battles with our strength, the bow:
Now practice yeoman,
Like the bowmen,
Till your balls fly as their true shafts have flown.
Yeomen, guard your own.

(43–48)

In rousing lines that exhort Englishmen to retrieve their heroic pasts, forgetting the fact that Victorian battles for empire were being won with firepower, not with bow and arrow, and fought by professional armies, not by knights and yeoman gathered under colorful banners, Tennyson casts his Francophobic sentiments in a retrospective mood. But his writing of the Victorian imperial nation does not always look back.[24]

Perhaps the most jingoistic of the empire poems set in the present historical moment is "Hands All Round" (1882).[25] The poem is a call to pledge the queen and drink to England:

[24] In some ways, my argument about Tennyson's ideological dilemma is similar to that of Alan Sinfield's in his assessment of Tennyson's class attitudes: in discussing "Hail Briton!" (1831–33), Sinfield claims that Tennyson "cannot prevent bourgeois freedom from intruding on the margins where he locates imaginative freedom" (45). Sinfield's model is derived from an image of center and margin; mine, rather, is one of overlapping attitudes and beliefs.

[25] A version of the poem was first published in 1852 and then the first stanza recast to be published alone in 1882. I cite the 1882 version.

To all the loyal hearts who long
To keep our English Empire whole!
To all our noble sons, the strong
New England of the Southern Pole!
To England under Indian skies,
To those dark millions of her realm!
To Canada whom we love and prize,
Whatever statesman hold the helm.
Hands all round!
God the traitors' hope confound!
To this great name of England drink, my friends,
And all her glorious empire, round and round.

(13–24)

In a manner similar to that deployed in "To the Queen," the speaker of the poem creates an organic image of empire through the emphasis upon wholeness, roundness, and unity that is initiated in the assonance of the first line. It is easy to scoff at this jingoistic verse and ascribe its blatant flag-waving to Tennyson's desire for royal and popular acclaim, but his patriotic poetry is part of the labor by Victorian literary culture to secure Britain's imperial power. To recall, for a moment, the comforting red spaces on Marlow's map of empire, Tennyson fills those spaces in with sentiments toasting the "dark millions" under England's realm. To be sure, lines such as those found in "Ode Sung at the Opening of the International Exhibition" (composed for a choir of four thousand voices — no easy task), which celebrate world trade as "Polar marvels, and a feast / Of wonder, out of West and East, / And shapes and hues of Art divine! All of beauty, all of use, / That one fair planet can produce" (20–24), encourage one to think the poet laureate is earning his bread and butter (and not too well). But to explain the chauvinistic verse in this way, preferring as we do to praise the painful beauty of "In Memoriam" or the pithy elegance of the "The Eagle," is to believe that the only sincere verse is that about the self.[26] Why not see Tennyson's patriotic verse making as an expression of a genuine admiration for the technology that has produced the marvels on exhibition? The nagging

[26] It is interesting that a recent special volume of *Victorian Poetry* devoted to Tennyson focused almost exclusively upon issues of patriarchy and gender. All the contributors seem to skirt Tennyson's flag-waving. See, for example, Ian McGuire's essay "Epistemology and Empire in *Idylls of the King*," which in its effort to connect "Freudian sublimation and colonial discourse" hardly refers to the historical actuality of the empire Tennyson figures so prominently in his poems of the nation.

problem for Tennyson is, of course, how to reconcile this admiration with a contempt for such princes of the city as Paul Dombey and Manchester cotton spinners bawling in their niggardly way about profit.

"Locksley Hall" (1842) and "Maud" (composed between 1834 and 1856) contain strong critique of a new social class in charge of mercantile empire building. Spurned by Amy and orphaned by a father killed in "Mahratta-battle," the speaker of "Locksley Hall" yearns "for some retreat / Deep in yonder shining Orient, where my life began to beat" (53–54); he is, in fact, a child of empire, the son of an army officer killed by Bombay soldiers in 1818. To modern readers, the most alarming section of the poem occurs in the speaker's prolonged fantasy that he will take "some savage woman" and that she will "rear his dusky race," a moment of exotic erotica that for Victorian readers is contained by the speaker's recognition that he counts the "gray Barbarian lower than the Christian child" and that he cannot "herd with narrow foreheads."[27] Consoled by this racist thinking, he calls for Britain to move "forward": "Let the great world spin for ever down the ringing grooves of change. / Through the shadow of the globe we sweep into the younger day: / Better fifty years of Europe than a cycle of Cathay" (182–84).

The stunning Eurocentricism of these lines can be representative of an attitude elaborated by Tennyson and many others in Victorian literary culture, and they can also serve to characterize the speaker of this dramatic monologue, a fiercely disappointed young man whose beloved has married a lout rather than remaining faithful to him. Yet what is it in the Victorian experience of empire that enables Tennyson to provide with confidence for the speaker of the poem this fantasy of cultural and racial supremacy? In this regard, Philip Curtin has usefully described the development of European racist attitudes throughout the nineteenth century. Pointing to the effects of the industrial revolution upon European technology, Curtin argues that European armies "could now win battles virtually anywhere" and that in psychological terms, "Europeans could now see and measure their superiority—in factory production, agricultural yields, or the cost of transportation by railway or steamship. Where superior feelings had once rested on little more than religious arrogance and ordinary xenophobia, they could now be

---

[27] In a recent unpublished paper, Gerhard Joseph usefully notes that "in this rejection of the gray barbarian, Tennyson is representative of most of his contemporaries" but that his racism is complicated by the romantic desire for a retreat from the press of urban life.

buttressed by demonstrable superiority in power and knowledge" (*Imperialism* xiv).

Moreover, Curtin continues, this sense of superiority in power and knowledge was "fortified" by "a new, racially oriented view of human beings and their civilizations" that was based upon a scientific arrangement of the different races, with European man at the pinnacle. Such hierarchical structures facilitated a sense of cultural superiority on the part of the British based on racial difference: "If men were seen to be markedly different from one another in physical racial traits, and if some cultures were seen to be vastly superior to others, it seemed to follow that the racial difference must have been the case of the cultural superiority" (xv). It is exactly this belief that informs so much of Tennyson's poetry of nation. Consider, for instance, "The Palace of Art," first published in 1832, much revised in 1842, and taken by most critics to be Tennyson's most deeply self-conscious statement about his own poetic craft. The fantastic palace contains "every legend fair / Which the supreme Caucasian mind / Carved out of Nature for itself" (125–27). Before attempting to explain away the offensive beliefs of Victorian writers such as Tennyson as aberrations in otherwise politically untainted art, I think we need to remember that Tennyson, like many, many others, believed that "narrow foreheads" were indeed a defect, that "fifty years" of European culture far surpassed anything produced by China, and that "Caucasian minds" were superior to black ones.[28] Class snobbery, perhaps, is easier for us to live with than racism; but this does not mean, either, that we should overlook the scorn Tennyson expresses for certain social groups.

In "Maud," the speaker seems wounded by romantic and social blows similar to those felt by the speaker of "Locksley Hall": his ancestral home inherited by Maud's "local millionaire" father and his beloved Maud virtually betrothed to an ill-mannered "new-made lord." Her "worldly" brother (in Orientalist fashion termed "The Sultan") his sworn enemy, the speaker searches for a fabled and lost idealism, a way to defend Britain's tottering decency and valor under the onslaught of Lancashire materialism. Finding that the money-making metropolis encourages middle-class boorishness rather than the fabled good man-

---

[28] The term "Caucasian" was established Victorian usage. The comparative anatomist Johann Friedrich Blumenthal (1752–1840) in the 1780s classified the "races" as American, Caucasian, Ethiopian, Malayan, and Mongolian. See Christine Bolt, *Victorian Attitudes to Race,* for comprehensive analysis of the issues discussed here.

ners of the upper classes, the speaker seeks (and finds) his salvational cause in the Crimean War. Ironically, this is a conflict not exactly fought for the Arthurian British heroism he seeks but rather a war in defense of British interests in India, and elsewhere, against the advances of the Russian bear.[29]

"Maud" seems both to want to glorify British military power and to evade the fact that this power is affiliated with the grandfather of the rude new-made lord who is pursuing Maud. This grandfather's lust for profit has sent him to a "blacker pit" than the coal mines where "Grimy nakedness dragging his trucks / And laying his trams in a poison'd gloom / Wrought, till he crept from a gutted mine / Master of half a servile shire, / And left his coal all turn'd into gold / To a grandson" (1:336–41). In "Maud," Tennyson weaves his poetic way through the thematic tension between desire and disdain for imperial power by removing the speaker to the Crimean battlefield where,

> Let it go or stay, so I wake to the higher aims
> Of a land that has lost for a little her lust of gold,
> And love of a peace that was full of wrongs and shames,
> Horrible, hateful, monstrous not to be told;
> And hail once more to the banner of battle unrolled!
>
> (3:38–42)

What seems unmanageable in "Maud"—a simultaneous acceptance and interrogation of British military power in pursuit of imperial wealth—is achieved by "Locksley Hall Sixty Years After" (1886). In this poem, the cynical young speaker of the earlier Locksley Hall is chastened by experience (he is eighty years old), and rather than imagining empire as a space wherein he might unleash his fury at being rejected by a flighty girl and a materialistic society that has no place for the impoverished son of an old gentry family, he questions Britain's material and military progress: "Russia bursts our Indian barrier, shall we fight her?" (115). "Those three hundred millions under one Imperial sceptre now / Shall we hold them? shall we loose them? take the suffrage of the plow" (117–18). Evoking the imagery of an imperial scepter that may continue to

---

[29] In his interesting discussion of ideological ambivalence in "Maud," Antony Harrison argues that the poem would be more coherent had Tennyson concluded with the speaker's madness rather than apparent recovery and commitment to the Crimean War. In my view, Part 3 exists, in a sense, so that Tennyson may attempt an acceptance and interrogation of imperial wealth. See Harrison, chapter 3.

hold Victoria's subjects or that may, as Macaulay ventures at the end of his July 1833 Charter speech, "pass away" from Britain, Tennyson recognizes the true burden of empire: how to hold on to it. And in almost all his poems of empire, he turns to the strict maternalism embodied in Victoria as the rein for rebellious colonies and angry women. In his imaginative containment of the resistance found in restless millions and assertive women, who, if not as terrifying as his shrieking Boadecia, were waiting at the gates of patriarchal imperialism, he evokes Victoria, a figure who so securely cradles her colonies that any rocking from restless natives and feminist women gets slapped down by a firm maternal hand. It is in Victoria that he creates a curb for the rage of his Queen Boadecia, a cure for the moral frailty of his Guinevere, a rebuke to the worldliness of his Amy in "Locksley Hall." Tennyson's celebration of Victoria's motherliness and middle-class propriety both erases the historical reality that her empire was founded upon competitive individualism and not Arthurian valor and expresses a desire that her female subjects emulate her moral and biological fecundity, dedicating their laboring bodies to preservation of the imperial nation.

LABORING NATIVES

The maintenance of Britannic rule is of deep concern to the upper-class Indian character in Maud Diver's *Awakening,* Sir Laksham Singh. A perfect English gentleman, Sir Laksham Singh speaks frankly and in excellent upper-class English idiom on the subject that "lies nearest the heart of all thoughtful Indians in this our day of agitation and transition" (113): namely, a failure of leadership at the center of empire. Lamented by the conservative British characters in the novel as belonging to a minority, Sir Laksham is urged to come to the aid of an empire in jeopardy by speaking out against the sexual politics of feminist New Women, the disruptions of Bengal agitators, the weakness of soft-hearted colonial officials, and the irresponsibility of inflammatory journalists. In the most laudatory of his speeches about British rule, Sir Laksham worries that Britain seems to be losing its grip on "those noble ideals of straightforward strength and courage that we learnt in early days to couple with the name of the British Raj" (115). Ever hopeful that Britain's essential decency and moral superiority will prevail, however, he affirms "his fervent belief in ultimate accord between 'mother and eldest daughter'" (113). This common metaphor for the state gains particular resonance in the Victorian discourse of empire, considering the moral and biological importance of the British woman in writing the Victorian nation.

In Sir Laksham's image, the great imperial mother country gives birth to obedient daughters, and pliant and faithful colonies: Kipling's Canada, Tennyson's America before she is forced to forage for herself, and the amazing "Sable Venus," her filial fidelity to European rule suggested in her mimicry of Botticelli's Venus and in her serene acceptance of having her nubile black body shipped from one part of the Britannic empire to another. As in *Oroonoko*, all traces of an actual Middle Passage are erased. In Victorian culture, no image of mother country can fail to be derived in some way from the fecund Victoria herself as the symbolic mother of her domestic and imperial subjects. Despite and because of the historical fact that the management of Britain's Victorian empire was in male hands, the sustaining image of control that the culture of empire constitutes for itself is always female—authoritative, regal, and satisfyingly fertile—which is not surprising if one considers that a metaphor for imperial rule evoking an authoritative father country begetting virile colony sons implies the filial usurpation of patriarchal power.

The female service to empire whose tracing in Victorian culture has been an important part of this study is clearly related to, generated adjacently to, the pervasive and nonthreatening images of the mother country and the mother queen. And all this imagery must be seen as derived from the actual labor of childbirth. The mother country, Queen Victoria, British women: in this important political symbolization, each and all must labor to produce colonies, to deliver the native labor to work those colonies, and to bring forth the virile male leaders to run those colonies. In *King Solomon's Mines* and *She,* the laboring bodies of the native and the laboring bodies of the British woman continue the late-Victorian desire to constitute and reproduce imperial power by creating material wealth for their masters and robust sons and dutiful daughters for their patriarchal culture.

If Dombey's blow to his daughter's breast imaginatively suggests male panic in the face of unspeakable reliance upon women's bodies for generation of patriarchal privilege, then the symbolic exploration of woman's body in *King Solomon's Mines* and *She* reveals a magnification of this panic. These exemplary works of male fantasy take the male characters (and the reader) on a Magical Mystery Tour of what in Lear's tirade against his daughters is figured as demonic: "But to the girdle do the gods inherit, / Beneath is all the fiends." *King Solomon's*

Mines and *She* perform a significant labor of political evasion, which Haggard's critics have tended to ignore when analyzing his importance in the history of the novel of empire.[30] What is conspicuously absent from the novels of adventure exemplified by *King Solomon's Mines* and *She* is reference to the material base of empire: The actual physical labor of subjugated peoples, which in creating capitalist wealth, creates the readership and fictional landscape for Haggard's novels, never appears. In *King Solomon's Mines* and *She*, it seems to me that a Gladstonian new imperialism forms an ideological alliance with a conservative race and gender politics in the construction of two fictions of empire: that white influence in Africa exists without economic exploitation and that adventurous men may discover, explore, and control the secret places of woman's reproductive powers. In these fictions, money is the root of imperialistic evil, and brainy women are the root of imperialistic decline. Africa, the major site of late-Victorian capitalist expansion, is the setting for political critiques of old imperialism and for symbolic penetration of feminized landscapes.

In *Heart of Darkness*, Marlow is accused by the young man supposedly in charge of brick making of being like Kurtz, "an emissary of pity, and science, and progress, and devil knows what else. . . . You are of the new gang—the gang of virtue" (26–27). Allowing for Conrad's irony in having the reader divine the twisted nature of Kurtz's virtue, the young man deploys the language of a new way of handling imperial business. Self-defined as humane, scientific, and progressive, and notably similar to the ideal colonial governance outlined in the 1840s by Macaulay,

[30] Two notable exceptions are the essays by Anne McClintock on *King Solomon's Mines* and Laura Chrisman on Haggard's imperial ideology. My argument about the evasion of black labor for the empire to be found in Haggard's fiction is similar to McClintock's contention that "the Victorian obsession with treasure troves, treasure maps, and the finding of treasure may be seen as a symbolic repression of the origin of capital in the labour of people" (125). McClintock's primary interest, however, is in the way *King Solomon's Mines* may be seen in the context of an attempt in southern Africa to reorder "black female labour within the homestead" (97), an effort on the part of white colonizers to break the control held by black men over the labor of black women. My argument is more focused upon the issue of erased black labor than it is upon whether the labor is male or female. Laura Chrisman observes that *King Solomon's Mines* "explicitly confronts issues surrounding one material practice of imperialism—namely the mining of mineral wealth (gold and diamonds) that began in late-nineteenth-century South Africa" ("The Imperial Unconscious?" 507). In addition, Chrisman argues that *She* discloses "how far imperialism is already profoundly split in its identity and value-scheme, utilising an other in order to dramatise its ambiguities, ambivalences, and indeterminacies" (504). I can agree that Ayesha is the figure through whom Haggard's worries about the threat to imperial hegemony are expressed, but it seems an exaggeration to say that imperialism at the end of the nineteenth century is "split" in its identity. Rather, I would argue, imperialism finds its identity besieged by aggressive women and restless natives.

Trevelyan, and other Liberals, the new imperialism distanced itself from the rampant capitalism brought to lucrative perfection by its most notorious exponent Cecil Rhodes at the end of the Victorian period.[31]

Arriving in South Africa in 1870, Rhodes staked a claim at the Kimberley minefields, became immensely wealthy, founded the De Beers Mining Company, commanded troops in the Boer War of 1899–1902, and had a sizable piece of Africa named after him. Until its occupation in 1893 by white South Africans supported by the De Beers Company, the 150,000 square mile territory that became Rhodesia (now Zimbabwe) had been inhabited primarily by the Matabele peoples (a model for Haggard's Kukuanas in *King Solomon's Mines*).[32] Rhodes was a prime villain for critics of imperialism. He was driven by a seemingly inexhaustible appetite for territory, money, and power, which is revealed in Kurtz's "weirdly voracious" open mouth eager "to swallow all the air, all the earth, all the men before him" and in the gesture of Lord William Bentinck (governor general of India in the 1830s), who when asked about the future of the Gwalior state, "opened wide his mouth, and placed his thumb and finger together like a boy about to swallow a sugar-plum."[33] Late-nineteenth-century figures such as E. D. Morel, a defender of African rights who termed Rhodes's cravings "an intolerable national disgrace" (quoted in *The Lords of Human Kind* 224) and J. A. Hobson who in 1902 distinguished between colonialism as pacific transportation of European culture to foreign places and imperialism as bellicose grabbing of territory, made Rhodes their capitalist bogeyman. As a way of elucidating the political critique of what many believed were gangster practices masquerading as imperialism, of what James Sturgis has characterized as a period in African history marked by "one punitive action after another against recalcitrant tribes" (94), I will focus on an important essay by G. P. Gooch in *The Heart of the Empire*, published in 1901 and edited by C. F. G. Masterman.[34]

[31] Rhodes, like the Morgans and the Rockefellers who "were rearing empires of another sort in America," notes V. G. Kiernan (*The Lords of Human Kind,* 223), presided over the white appropriation of southern Africa's vast mineral wealth.

[32] See "The Real King Solomon's Mines" (20).

[33] Quoted in Ramesh Chandra Majumdar (251).

[34] See Sturgis for a useful discussion of the development of new imperialism. Sturgis notes that once the Boer War started, a mounting protest against British imperial expansion began: "Civil disquiet, Hobson's book, setbacks on the Veld and 'methods of barbarism' all touched off the soul-searching and intimations of decline which marked the period after 1902" ("Britain and the New Imperialism" 96).

The Heart of the Empire addresses the problems of what it terms in its subtitle "Modern City Life in England." Gooch's lengthy chapter on imperialism is argued from a position strongly opposed to the Boer War, to Rhodes's flagrant land grabbing, and to capitalist expansion. Regularly evoking Gladstonian Liberalism and defending the Liberal Party against Conservatives' charges that it was indifferent to expansion of empire in the 1880s, Gooch implies the possibility of a humane appropriation by Europeans of lands occupied by indigenous African peoples. Gooch directly cites Gladstone's hope that Britain would "never seek to extend the Empire by either violently wrestling, or fraudulently obtaining, the territories of other people" (333) and argues for what he terms a "true" imperialism without violence or fraud. Gooch's brand of imperialism does not impose itself on non-Western peoples in order to make a profit; it does so in order to educate those people to become politically responsible and economically self-sufficient. The true imperialism indicts the "destruction of natives" celebrated, Gooch charges, by Kipling, the wholesale massacre of Armenians by the Turks that began at the turn of the century, and the hypocritical "national conceit" that decides "England 'expands,' but Russia 'encroaches'" (312-13). Summing up by deploying the mother/daughter relationship for colonialism evoked by Sir Laksham Singh in *Awakening,* Gooch affirms his strong belief that "England and her daughter nations may be trusted to work together in common accord" (343). However serene this gendered image, the new imperialism is deeply problematical.

In aiming to unpack the ideological delusions of Gooch's argument, I do not mean to dismiss outright the opposition to Rhodes and his fellow South African capitalists or to scoff at those who refused to trade in that section of the London Stock Exchange derisively known as the "Kaffir Circus" (except to note the dualistic identification of Western lust for profit with what was perceived as African barbarism).[35] Rather, I am interested in how writing about the late-Victorian empire negotiates the difficulty confronted by Dickens, William Arnold, and others, some

---

[35] V. G. Kiernan observes that by "the end of the century moralists as well as socialists were complaining of a moral degeneracy among Europe's upper classes, now far on in their metamorphosis from aristocracy into plutocracy: rampant materialism, worship of wealth and luxury, contempt for moral scruples" (*The Lords of Human Kind* 224). Much as I admire Kiernan's analysis of imperial cultures, he seems to ally himself with those "moralists" and "socialists" who imply that the British ruling classes were once uninterested in money, luxury, and exemption from the moral behavior expected of other (lower) social classes.

fifty years earlier, of how to enjoy the wealth and national security of empire purchased with the labor of millions of subjugated peoples and engineered by a social class who, if not always displaying the bully tactics of Cecil Rhodes, evinced what seems now to have been a plausible, if unappealing, interest in material gain. Gooch's "Imperialism" attacks Rhodes for having invited the Dutch at the height of the Boer War " 'to drop all this business about the war and develop the country' " (316). From the perspective of those unhappy with a Britannic rule rather too nakedly directed to profit, Rhodes callously discards a nationalism that often leads to conflicts such as the Boer War, in favor of a kind of capitalist worldview that pits rich white men against poor black natives.

The unassailable political contradiction of the "true" or "new" imperialism as elaborated by Gooch is that it implicitly justifies the continuance of Britannic rule through a sanguine fable of domination founded upon altruism rather than exploitation. Once Britain realizes that the "Native Question" will be solved by recognizing that not all " 'natives' are on the same rung of the ladder of civilisation," the nation will be liberated to exercise its benevolent "white control" with the eventual aim of getting everyone in the empire on the same "civilized" rung. For the moment, colonial and imperial government must understand that "The Parsi is far higher than the Hottentot, and the Matabele is lower than the Maori. No two races require precisely the same treatment" (341). Arguing that the challenge to the early-twentieth-century empire will be to defeat "the power of organised money, . . . secularising our ideals, and poisoning the wells of our knowledge" (394), "Imperialism" echoes the disdain for the profit-minded social class identified in *Dombey and Son* and in much of Tennyson's political poetry. In its reference to England and her "daughter nations," and in Gooch's elegy for an increasingly secular society, the new imperialism also evokes the enduring Victorian instruction to women that they form a moral barrier against materialism and secularism, link their lily-white arms, so to speak, in the face of the Paul Dombeys of the nineteenth-century world. Furthermore, where the critique of mercantile colonialism of the mid-Victorian period makes Tennyson's "niggard throats" of Manchester the bawling culprit, turn-of-the-century mystifications of the economic foundation of empire indict Cecil Rhodes as the major villain. In convicting a single individual—in demonizing Rhodes for his grabbing of vast tracts of south central Africa—rather than giving a leg up to the natives mounting the ladder of civilization, the new imperialism evades the material base of empire upon which its own high-minded racism rests. Consciously or not, it ignores the field of exploited labor that anchors the racist ladder of civilization constructed by the benevolent paternalism of the Liberal Party.

In addition, by directing so much of its attack to one undeniably rapacious individual in a manner similar to the late-twentieth-century obsession with figures such as Robert Maxwell and Rupert Murdoch, the new imperialism, as it is expansively defined in *The Heart of the Empire*, implicitly fails to indict the innumerable British businessmen and companies for whom Southern Africa was a personal treasure trove of extraordinary wealth. As Peter Fryer demonstrates, the vast acquisitions of African territory by European powers during the last decade of the nineteenth century "were directly controlled by various capitalist groups and companies, such as the United Africa Company, a subsidiary of Unilever." Moreover, the ruling-class British, through their business affiliations with these enormous imperialistic conglomerates, secured for themselves their own sizable pieces of African land.[36] There is nothing new about the early-twentieth-century new imperialism. It replays Victorian mystifications of the empire as profit into mystifications of the empire as civilization.

In an ironic affirmation of Marx's assertion that the wages paid for labor eventually reproduce "the muscles, nerves, bones, and brains of existing labourers" (*Capital* 1:536–7),Rhodes viewed natives as necessarily reproductive bodies, whereas the new imperialism saw them as "impressionable children of nature" (Gooch, "Imperialism" 361). It is the latter view that most closely matches Rider Haggard's inhabitants of the heart of Kukuanaland in *King Solomon's Mines* and the Amahagger cave dwellers in *She*. Even if they engage in nasty savage practices that place them very low on the new imperialism's ladder of civilization (the hot potting practiced in *She* would prohibit even a toe on the first rung), they are not bodies laboring for empire, never figures from a diamond or a gold mine, never workers in the manganese, copper, and tin industries of Africa.[37] They labor not for the white man's profit

[36] Fryer, 35. Fryer notes, for instance, that in Kenya's Njoro district, "Lord Delamore acquired 100,000 acres of the best land in 1903 at the cost of one penny per acre" (*Black People in the British Empire* 35).

[37] For a fascinating description of what is left out of *King Solomon's Mines* and *She*, see Olive Schreiner's description of the South African diamond mines. She writes that in the crowd are "small naked Mohurahs from the interior, grotesque, hideous with spindle legs and swollen stom-

but for the entertainment of Haggard's readers, who relish graphic violence, misogynistic club talk, and some genteel eroticism—"She" going
topless, or as the narrator L. Horace Holly says, "baring the blinding
loveliness of her form" (*She* 320). Haggard's natives inhabit landscapes
and cultures untouched by labor for the white capitalist, and if they
work at all, it is to maintain their strange kingdoms. In effect, they may
be said to defy geography and history by living outside the world that
has, by virtue of their existence in best-selling adventure tales published
at the height of Britain's imperial wealth, brought them into being.[38]

As all of Haggard's critics observe, *King Solomon's Mines* is a rich
example of the male adventure, or male quest, genre. It constitutes
European male subjectivity through tropes of travel, hazardous adventure, and eventual mastery of the forces that both threaten and
define masculinity.[39] Allan Quartermain, the rugged narrator of *King
Solomon's Mines*, is a no-nonsense kind of fellow. As he notes in his brief
Introduction, accounts of differences between various African dialects,
family customs, or the "indigenous flora and fauna of Kukuanaland,"
were sacrificed to telling the "story in a plain, straightforward manner" (5). The story is also told in a manner that affirms patriarchal
inheritance. Traditions, maps, and documents signifying possession—
whether it be knowledge of hunting (as we see in Quartermain), knowledge of the terrain of valuable land (as we see in the treasure map), or
knowledge of extraordinary escapes from wicked forces (as we see in
the legacy of Quartermain's narrative to his son)—are passed from one
man to another. Sir Henry Curtis, almost immediately after meeting
Quartermain, tells him the legend of Solomon's Mines, gives him the

---

achs and beast-like faces. . . . The Zulus here too, and the Karrif: tall, finely developed creatures
they are with magnificent muscles, and not wholly devoid of brains. They are clad in ragged European clothing for the most part; as are their wizened, cute, most ape-like little Hottentot cousins"
(quoted in Monsman, 9).

[38] Mary Louise Pratt observes that travel writers deploy "strategies of representation whereby
European bourgeois subjects seek to secure their innocence in the same moment as they assert
European hegemony" (*Imperial Eyes* 7). In my view, the complete absence of any trace of European colonization, combined with the endangered condition in which Haggard's male adventurers
find themselves for almost the duration of their narratives, suggests the same kind of innocence
of European subjugation of African peoples.

[39] See Wendy Katz's comprehensive study of all of Haggard's writings. Katz regards Haggard as a "firm imperial defender." Patrick Brantlinger pays attention to the masculinist nature of
Haggard's novels and also regards *King Solomon's Mines* as the first in a series of what he terms
"imperial Gothic" texts, primarily romances that combine "the seemingly scientific, progressive,
often Darwinian ideology of imperialism with an antithetical interest in the occult" (227).

relics of a precious map, and shares the translation of the account of one Jose da Silvestra who died three hundred years earlier in search of the treasure. In *She,* the translations of writing on a priceless potsherd are relics "religiously passed on from generation to generation" (27), the most recent recipient of this male legacy being Leo Vincey, blond Apollo of the Oxford quad and direct descendant of a fourth century B.C. North African, Kallikrates, who was foolish enough to reject the love of "She-who-must-be-obeyed."

"Rather different from the ordinary run of Zulus," the character who goes variously by the names Ignosi and Umbopa in *King Solomon's Mines* is a magnificent physical and moral specimen. Initially guide to Sir Henry Curtis, Captain John Good, and Alan Quartermain, and later restored as rightful African king of Kukuanaland through their white male agency (men pass political and cultural power along the great chain of patriarchal being), he is described on his first appearance in the novel as "scarcely more than dark" (like Crusoe's Friday). He also bears a striking resemblance to the magnificent Zulu who appears in Haggard's short story "Black Heart and White Heart." A "splendid specimen," the Zulu is graced with "genial and honest eyes," a height of at least six foot two inches, a wide chest, and solid limbs: "In short, the man was what he seemed to be, a savage gentleman of birth, dignity and courage" (75). After sizing up Sir Henry Good (a magnificent specimen of the ancient Dane variety), Ignosi announces that "we are men, thou and I" (49). This discourse does not transcend racial prejudice through praising similarity (being "men") and acknowledging difference (coming from very different cultures). *King Solomon's Mines* presents a racist image of Umbopa as a dusky version of Sir Henry in which real men are magnificent broad-chested blonds, never less than six feet in height, and fearless fighters. They also have sidekicks who are generally short, dark, hairy, and sometimes stout—Good in *King Solomon's Mines* and L. Horace Holly in *She.*

The Kukuanas (Umbopa's tribe) have remained magically untouched by white encounters. They speak an old Zulu analogous to Chaucerian English, are comically awed by false teeth, white legs, and firearms, indeed anything associated with Victorian England, and their physical splendor seems implicitly to originate in their isolation from the white world. They bear no resemblance to colonized workers in a South African diamond or gold mine, nor to those dying "black shapes" who crouch upon the earth in "all the attitudes of pain, abandonment, and despair" in *Heart of Darkness*, Africans who have been "brought from all the recesses of the coast in all the legality of time contracts" to build the railway (55). What I am trying to get at here is not that *King Solomon's Mines* interrogates imperialism through showing the British reader the magnificence of natives untouched by imperialism's greedy hand, nor am I assembling an indictment against Haggard for fictional infidelity to historical fact. Rather, these superb Africans suggest a number of ways that a conservative novelist such as Haggard might evade the brutal aspects of imperialistic capitalism in a story set in Africa at the end of the Victorian period and yet at the same time, glorify the male heroism engraved as characteristic of Britannic rule. The first way is to write imperialistic capitalism entirely out of the narrative picture and the second is to imply that the dirty work of imperialism has already been done—by others, long ago. Let me explain.[40]

Sir Henry, Good, and Quartermain journey to Solomon's Mines in search of Sir Henry's brother, not as capitalist imperialists in pursuit of the diamonds: "I am going to trace him to Suliman's Mountains, and over them if necessary, till I find him, or until I know that he is dead," vows Sir Henry (32). After the restoration of Ignosi to his Kukuana kingdom, the trio of adventurers sets off for the mines only at his insistence that they take home some of the "shining stones." When they leave this bit of fantastic Africa visited by white men uninterested in wealth, they come home with stones of such stupendous quality that they have to "sell by degrees" for fear of flooding the market. These are diamonds, according to Quartermain, which were mined "thousands of years ago" by North Africans. Thus, they were not mined by Europeans, a significant detail that Haggard elaborates in his essay, "The Real King Solomon's Mines."

Haggard explains that his fictional Kukuanaland is an area north of the Transvaal (now Zimbabwe), where one may find the ruins of a Semitic people, probably Phoenicians, who colonized Southern Africa and "enslaved the local population by tens of thousands to labour in the mines and other public works" (21). These fierce traders, he continues, broke the spirit of a peaceful agrarian community (a spirit memorial-

---

[40] Norman Etherington notes in the critical introduction to the annotated edition of *She* that in the manuscript (later revised), Haggard "let his Conservative sympathies run away with him. Leo Vincey is described as a 'red hot conservative' who regards William Gladstone as a tyrant and a demagogue. The Liberal party is blamed for 'plundering one class of a community to enrich the others'" (xx).

ized, one might say, in Ignosi) and "forced them to dig in the dark mines for gold, to pound the quartz with stone hammers, and bake it in tiny crucibles" (23). Ruefully admitting that "there was no historian to record it and no novelist to make a story of the thing," Haggard speculates that these subjugated peoples "having learned their masters' wisdom, rose up and massacred them to the last man." The ideological displacement, then, that Haggard effects in *King Solomon's Mines* is to locate imperialistic exploitation so far in the past there can be no record of it and simultaneously to suggest that exploitation in all probability may be traced not to white Europeans, but to the spirit-breaking Phoenicians. Whichever way one looks at it, late-nineteenth-century white Britannic presence in black Africa is untainted by abuse of native labor, and the natives in *King Solomon's Mines* may embrace the British as their broad-chested white brothers, not fight them as conquerors of their land and exploiters of their labor.

Quartermain also tells the reader that enough elephant tusks "to make a man wealthy for life" (276) are contained in the cave with the diamonds. But the tusks are not shipped out of Africa in Kurtzian fashion by the white adventurers, who are interested solely in retrieving lost relatives and restoring noble Africans to stable leadership. The trio of male altruists (the tall, blond hero, his comical sidekick, and the knowledgeable hunter) visits a magical African kingdom inhabited by brave warriors who fight in regiments named the Greys and the Buffaloes and who are ruled by a leader uncannily schooled in the ideals of new imperialism, which he will implement without the presence of white Europeans. At the end of the novel, Ignosi makes a number of significant promises to his white male friends: no white man will be allowed to cross the mountains into Kukuanaland; no traders with "guns and rum" will change the ways of men who fight like their forefathers with "the spear, and drink water"; no missionaries will be allowed "to put fear of death into men's hearts, to stir them up against the king, and make a path for the white man who follow to run on." Ignosi vows, "None shall ever come for the shining stones" (306). Here, Haggard admits the possibility that Britannic rule might be interested in Africa and paradoxically invests Ignosi's vision of Kukuanaland's peaceful future with some of the values of new imperialism: no violence, no alcohol, no missionaries, no exploitation of black labor for the acquisition of "shining stones" or elephant tusks. Haggard's ideological erasure of white exploitation of black labor opens the space for the decent, humane, wise employment of black Africans that is wishfully imagined by Gooch's "Imperialism."

Because the Africans in *King Solomon's Mines* do not even look African, they are less an image of exploited labor, which they were in the historical actuality of Southern Africa, than engaging exotic figures of Orientalist fantasy. The women, for example, are deemed "exceedingly handsome" by Quartermain by virtue of their hair being "rather curly than woolly," their features "frequently aquiline," their lips "not unpleasantly thick as is the case in most African races," and their manners suitable for a "fashionable drawing-room" (129). With the demonic exception of Gagool, Haggard's description of the Kukuana women in *King Solomon's Mines* locates them more in the Turkish harem than on the plains of what is now northern Zimbabwe.

In *She*, the male natives are built along the heroic lines of Ignosi's warriors in *King Solomon's Mines:* they are "of a magnificent build, few of them being under six feet in height"; "yellowish in colour," they have "thick black locks" rather than frizzy hair, and they possess excellent teeth. Again, they have the "aquiline features" of Ignosi's people and have remained magically unvisited by white men. Dominated by Ayesha, however, and because descent in Amahagger culture is traced "only through the line of the mother" (57), they do not seem to be the jolly and cooperative fellows of *King Solomon's Mines*, who were happy to organize into British-style regiments as if about to participate in the charge of the Light Brigade. The Amahagger are evil looking, cold, and sullen; they never smile, which is not surprising since their ruler, whom they see once every two or three years is likely to "blast" them to death with a movement of her magnificent arm if they fail to prostrate themselves correctly in her presence. Moreover, they are governed not only by the supernatural powers of a woman intellectual who is two thousand years old. They are also controlled by a matriarchal culture in which women are supremely powerful. As the old man Billali says to Holly, "In this country the women do what they please. We worship them, and give them their way, because without them the world could not go on; they are the source of life" (78). *She* is a wildly misogynistic text whose fears and fantasies disclose the late-Victorian panic about uncontrollable women. Before discussing this aspect of *She* in some detail, however, I want first to take a look at the feminized landscape of *King Solomon's Mines*.

LABORING WOMEN

The journey to Solomon's Mines is made in the company of Foulata, a "dusky . . . soft-eyed, shapely Kukuana beauty" (246), and Gagool, an ancient woman described by Quartermain as a "withered old bundle" who leads them through various portals, passages, and caves to the treasure. These two female figures—one desirable, the other repulsive—reveal Haggard's ideas about desirable and disgusting female behavior, especially as it pertains to the body. In a suggestive diary entry for 7 July 1921, he describes two images of a woman's body: one is a photograph of young women "doing violent and ungainly things, leaping into the air with their legs all over the place" (226), and the other is his recollection of a woman dancing in a "garment that revealed the whole side of her naked body from beneath the arm to the point of the hip. . . . I suppose the object was to excite the admiration of men with the vision of the surging flesh and muscles" (226). Haggard's preference, he confides to his diary, is for "the sweet simplicity of the savage in a row of beads." In *King Solomon's Mines,* in contrast to the flying legs, surging flesh, and supple muscles of women's bodies unrestrained by Victorian patriarchy, Foulata possesses the sweet compliance of the *National Geographic* savage.[41] In repellent contrast, Gagool is a grotesque, fantastic crone, an emblem of Haggard's despised female physical energy having become withered, decayed, gone very bad.

Through the agency of Gagool, this preternaturally ancient woman, the men gain entry into a space that houses the royal dead of the Kukuana people preserved as stalactites and that also symbolizes human life, figured as it is in terms of imagery associated with a woman's body. The chamber of death and life is the final stage in a male traverse through feminized terrain. On the way to Solomon's Mines, the travelers are shown a sight that renders Quartermain "impotent even before its memory": Sheba's breasts. These stupendous and beautiful mountains swell up "gently from the plain," and on the top of each is "a vast round hillock covered with snow, exactly corresponding to the nipple on the female breast" (85). Usually Sheba's breasts are "wrapped" in a

---

[41] In November 1922, he recorded his horror at the sight of young women drinking cocktails and smoking cigarettes in a London restaurant: "A sign of the recent 'emancipation' of the sex, I suppose! What will it all end in?" (*The Private Diaries of Sir H. Rider Haggard 1914–1925*). For a fascinating study of the way exotic cultures have been framed for the Western readers of *National Geographic,* see Lutz and Collins.

"curious gauzy mist" (86), an anticipation, perhaps, of the gauzy wrappings that shield Ayesha's magnificent body from her subjects' eyes. After the mist clears, Quartermain recalls that the men "were able to take in all the country before us at a glance. I know not how to describe the glorious panorama which unfolded itself to our enraptured gaze" (104). The enraptured gaze of Leo and Holly when they witness the glorious panorama of Ayesha's body in *She* repeats the bedazzlement of Curtis, Good, and Quartermain in *King Solomon's Mines*. In *King Solomon's Mines*, one set of male adventurers is dazzled by a lustrous feminized landscape. In *She*, another set is dazzled by the brilliance of Ayesha's actual body. In both stories, however, the female landscape/body is eventually mastered through exploration by the male traveler.[42]

Gagool is described as an appallingly wizened monkeylike creature, a figure "of great age, so shrunken that in size it was no larger than that of a year-old child, . . . made up of a collection of deep yellow wrinkles. Set in the wrinkles was a sunken slit, that represented the mouth"; Gagool's skull is "perfectly bare, and yellow in hue, while its wrinkled scalp moved and contracted like the hood of a cobra" (147). This a monstrous female body that reappears dramatically in *She* after Ayesha is demolished by what Gilbert and Gubar term a "perpetually erect symbol of masculinity," the pillar of flame. Gagool also resembles an old black crone to be found in Haggard's short story "Black Heart and White Heart." Known as "The Bee," she possesses eyes "fierce and quick as those of a leopard and shifts shape into the likeness of a colossal and horrid spider sitting at the mouth of her trap" (80). Gagool's trap is the site, the space of Solomon's Mines itself. What is also interesting about her meaning in late-Victorian patriarchal imperialism is her management of a male-authorized carnivalesque display of female

[42] No reader of Haggard's fiction can fail to notice this unsubtle pattern of male conquest of female terrain. Elaine Showalter, for example, argues that *She* is about "the flight from women and male dread of women's sexual, creative, and reproductive power" and that with the death of the "phallic and aggressive mother, the space is cleared for unbroken male bonding and creativity" (*Sexual Anarchy* 83; 87). Gilbert and Gubar, more elaborately, claim that the journey in *She* is a symbolic return to the womb, that the pillar of fire that gives Ayesha her two-thousand-year lifespan is a "perpetually erect symbol of masculinity," not just a "Freudian penis, but a fiery signifier whose eternal thundering return speaks the inexorability of the patriarchal law" (21). Anne McClintock provides a clever, Freudian reading of the map leading the men to Solomon's Mines. She argues that after crossing over the breasts to the pubic mound (the Three Witches covered in dark heather) they approach the entrances to two forbidden passages, "the vaginal entrance into which the men are led by the black mother, Gagool—and behind it the anal pit, from which the men will eventually clamber with the diamonds" (114).

rage. In a blood-curdling ceremony, we see a mob of withered women set loose in the vengeful shape of the "witch-hunters."

In a violent ritual representing that part of the Kukuana culture destined to be rehabilitated by Ignosi, the women are allowed once a year to identify male witches for extermination. Quartermain describes some twenty thousand men lined up awaiting their fate. Gagool and ten "aged women"—their white hair streaming in the wind, their faces painted in stripes of white and yellow, their backs hung with snake-skins, and their waists circled with a girdle of human bones—identify with their small forked wands those who must be killed. At the end of the ceremony, one hundred and three warriors have been killed by having spears driven into their hearts and their brains dashed out with clubs. If Haggard's distaste for powerful female bodies is registered in his depiction of the compliant Foulata, then his general fear of female flesh is conveyed in the massacre of African warriors by postmenopausal crones.[43]

Further man-hating violence is performed by Gagool at the mines when she traps the adventurers in the cave: "All the manhood seemed to have gone out of us" recalls Quartermain when the men realize they face death by suffocation in a womblike space. "Buried in the bowels of a huge snow-clad peak," separated by a long tunnel and five feet of rock from fresh air, they escape through a stone trapdoor, which leads them down a staircase and into various tunnels until they emerge into the open air through a narrow space the size of a large fox's "earth." Sir Henry, Good, and Quartermain, then, enter a symbolically female space. They escape imminent emasculation, and they explore, survey, and record that space so that what comes out of the female earth is not just the three men but a narrative mapping of the interior to be passed along to other men. On the general level of sexual symbolism, the men have mastered the power of interior female spaces, and on the more specific level of political symbolism, they have mastered the power of woman's reproductive capacity. At a historical moment when actual women such as Mary Pigot and fictional characters such as Audrey Hammond were failing in their reproductive duty to empire and when

[43] Dorothy Dinnerstein's theories of woman as the "carnal scapegoat-idol" (124) of Western civilization are particularly relevant in considering Haggard's distaste for female flesh. In an important argument, Dinnerstein claims that ambivalence toward woman's body arises from "our inevitable mix of feelings for the flesh itself. The unreconciled mix is projected onto the first parent" (148).

Victoria herself, by virtue of her age and her immensely long reign, was creating worries for patriarchal society, the laboring female body is brought into line.

The misogynistic fantasies of *King Solomon's Mines* are more theatrically vivid in *She* because the woman who must be obeyed and as a consequence destroyed is an erotic goddess. *She* is a steamy brew of late-Victorian soft pornography, homoerotic ties broken by female wiles, and the eventual restoration of those ties through the destruction of female beauty and intellect.

She is narrated by L. Horace Holly, fellow of an Oxford college and guardian of the physically gorgeous and morally upright Leo Vincey. When he takes charge of the five-year-old Leo, Holly unambiguously announces his desire that "I would have no woman to lord it over me about the child, and steal his affections from me" (15). Once they get among the Amahagger people, however, women become a definite problem. Traveling in search of a white African queen whose story is inscribed on the potsherd passed from one male Vincey to another, Holly, Leo, Leo's servant Job, and an Arab guide, meet up with women as ferocious as Gagool. They are, in fact, cannibals who select dinner by fondling, "snake-like," the flesh of the unfortunate Arab guide.

Ayesha, "She who must be obeyed," emerges from Haggard's novel as a mesmerizing mix of striptease artist, gifted chemist, learned intellectual, and vegetarian clairvoyant. She is at least two thousand years old having bathed herself in the fire of life to await the reincarnation of the lover she murdered in a fit of passionate jealousy—Kallikrates—who is, of course, no other than the broad-chested Leo Vincey. Compared to Ayesha, who is extremely intelligent and because of her immense age rather well-read, and to Holly, who is a donnish classical scholar, Leo is a dimwit, the sex object for whom Holly and Ayesha compete, although the novel loudly insists that Holly is infatuated with Ayesha and a rival of Leo's.[44]

As Holly waits for Ayesha to reveal herself, he wonders what lies behind the heavy curtains that screen her perfumed haremlike recess: "some naked savage queen, a languishing Oriental beauty, or a nineteenth-century young lady, drinking afternoon tea?" (96). These

[44] Wayne Koestenbaum argues that "Haggard's romances make room for pederasty by excluding marriage" (153). Eve Sedgwick's arguments about the ancillary function of women in relation to the bonding of male characters in Western literature are certainly relevant to the homoerotic bonding between Holly and Leo (see *Between Men*).

three stereotypes suggest the range of Holly's misogynistic imagination: women are either lustful savages, pliable odalisques, or prissy
guardians of social manners. Ayesha is something else. A "great chemist" who has a cave fitted out as a laboratory, a mind reader who can
project upon a pool of water what is "actually in the mind of some one
present" (144), she is a world-class intellectual given to lengthy philo-
sophical and political disquisitions. Judging Holly to be in possession of
a "thinking brain," she recalls "certain of those old philosophers with
whom in days bygone I have disputed at Athens and at Becca in Arabia"
(126). And upon learning that the "real power" in Britain resides "in the
hands of the people," she observes that then "surely there is a tyrant,
for I have long since seen that democracies, having no clear will of their
own, in the end set up a tyrant, and worship him" (169). Much more
directly than *King Solomon's Mines, She* discloses late-Victorian fear of
assertive intellectual women bent upon visibility in the public sphere.
Ayesha's unveiling, in fact, may be seen as more than erotic fantasy. In
unveiling herself, Ayesha also suggests, albeit from the male perspective that translates all female desire into sexual scenarios, the desire of
the female chemist/psychologist/philosopher/political scientist to reveal her professional acumen to a rapt male audience.

Most of Haggard's feminist critics plausibly interpret the conservative cultural fear expressed by Holly that the New Woman, if she gains
entrance into the public sphere, will be terrifyingly unstoppable.[45] But I
think we need to see that *She* is about more than fear of the brave New
Woman, although in literally reducing Ayesha to ashes, the novel destroys female ambition and opens the space for obedient reproductive
service to patriarchal imperialism. *She* is also about justifying Britain's
imperial wealth and governance. Ayesha's kingdom may be seen as a
bad, unproductive empire ruled not by the fertile middle-class mother
Victoria but by the sterile, elitist Ayesha, or as Nina Auerbach describes
her, "a galvanized and transfigured Victoria" for whom "love does not
tranquilize womanhood into domestic confinement" (*Woman and the
Demon* 37). The Kingdom of Kor produces no commodities other than
those needed for the kingdom's own sullen sustenance in a strictly pas-

---

[45] Ann Ardis, for example, suggests that if we read "the name of Haggard's terrifying powerful African queen generically," we may "recognize Haggard's cultural displacement of anxieties
specific to the situation in England at the turn of the century. What will follow from the New
Woman's entrance into the public world? What will happen when she addresses herself to national
politics rather than to domestic affairs?" (141).

toral economy. It performs no labor for Ayesha, their white queen, other than prostration in her presence. Ayesha's great line that hers is an empire "of the imagination" is temptingly suggestive of the rule by a tiny group of Europeans of millions of Indians evoked by Emily Eden in her description of the Simla celebrations of the accession of Victoria to the throne in 1838. But there is no textual evidence to support a reading of *She* as either glorifying or lamenting the British presence in Africa. The Amahagger people live in an uncolonized time warp, in a landscape composed at its outer edges of almost endless swamp and marked by volcanic plain grazed by cattle and goats—a "great morass" whose worst feature is a dreadful smell of rotting vegetation. At the edge of Ayesha's mountain residence/cum mausoleum, we find the Amahagger people practicing matriarchally managed cannibalism (what else?) and maintaining their self-sufficient community by, for example, sowing grain to make their own beer. Ayesha's empire, it seems to me, is far less of the imagination that it is of the female body. Because this is a barren body laboring not to produce strong sons and daughters for the empire but to reproduce endlessly its narcissistic power to terrorize Ayesha'a subjects, it must be destroyed. And it is.

As Dombey's blow to his daughter's breast dramatizes patriarchy's resentment of reliance upon women for its reproduction, so *She* seems obsessed with the revelation and destruction of Ayesha's breasts. When Holly spies upon her in her secret chemistry lab, she is wearing one of the only two garments she seems to possess, a gauzy white peignoir (the other is a black cloak): "She was clothed, as I had seen her when she unveiled, in the kirtle of clinging white, cut low upon her bosom." Holly recalls that as she begins to curse her enemies, she raises her arms above her head, "and as she did so the white robe slipped from her down to her golden girdle, baring the blinding loveliness of her form" (110). Declaring her passionate two-thousand-year love for Leo, she slides to her knees and draws her "white corsage still further down her ivory bosom" (168). And as she prepares to step into the life-giving pillar of flame, she throws off her gauzy wrapping and stands before Leo and Holly "as Eve might have stood before Adam" (192). Like Eve, but rather more theatrically, Ayesha is punished for her forwardness. The pillar of flame that announces itself with a dreadful, thundering, crashing, and rolling noise, destroys her marvelous body, shrinks her to the size of a monkey; her gorgeous breasts and ivory skin become dirty brown, pucker "into a million wrinkles," the lily-white hands become claws, and the magnificent eyes become covered with a "horny film." (194). "She, who, but two minutes before had gazed upon us the loveliest, noblest, most splendid woman the world has ever seen, she lay still before us, near the masses of her own dark hair, no larger than a big monkey, and hideous—ah, too hideous for words" (194). This gynophobic reduction of Ayesha to a monkey puts the dreadful power of woman's physical attraction in its proper place and provides a chilling lesson to women who might be inclined to parade their breasts merely as a sign of their powerful sexuality (somewhat like the woman in Haggard's diary with her surging flesh and muscles) rather than as a sign of their reproductive labor for the empire.

Holly and Leo escape from "the very womb of the Earth, wherein she doth conceive the Life that ye see brought forth in men and beast." They have originally entered Ayesha's round mountain home/mausoleum/body by going into "the mouth of a dark tunnel" (88). Having, like the traveling trio in *King Solomon's Mines,* explored, surveyed, and escaped from a place that is almost literally the site of human conception (Ayesha waits in the womb of the earth for the flame to impregnate her with life), Holly and Leo return to the male coziness of their Oxford digs where Holly completes his manuscript "with Leo leaning over my shoulder in my old room in my college" (208). Saved from emasculating female power—Leo recalls that after Ayesha stretches out her hand to him "he felt as though he had suddenly received a violent blow in the chest, and, what is more, utterly cowed, as if all the manhood had been taken out of him" (151)—they have witnessed the alarming destruction of a woman "clothed in the majesty of her almost endless years," a woman who gets "blasted" by a phallic flame into a monkey. And with her elimination, although the novel does not discuss it because it does not need to, must go the destruction of her violent matriarchal kingdom. Deprived of their supernatural queen, the sullen Amahagger men and the Amahagger women who, in Gilbert and Sullivan stereotypical fashion are either lascivious middle-aged monsters or proudly loving and subservient to male wishes, sink into the dismal swamps of Kor.

IMPERIAL THEFT

In Charles Johnson's *Middle Passage* (1990), a harrowing and magical parody of the male quest narrative, the picaresque narrator travels in 1830 to Africa and back on the slave ship *Republic*. A raffishly articulate African American survivor of the New Orleans underworld, Rutherford Calhoun recounts his own history as an emancipated slave, the tale of the ship's mad captain Ebenezer Falcon, who is a cross between Dickens's Daniel Quilp and Conrad's Kurtz, and the wrenching story of the suffering and surrealistic slave cargo. Calhoun connects his multiple narratives with the imagery of theft. Himself a petty thief, "a Negro in the New World, *born* to be a thief," he is a man whose pleasure in theft is sensual, narcotic. Entering Falcon's cabin, he says "I felt the change come over me, a familiar, sensual tingle that came whenever I broke into someone's home, as if I were slipping inside another's soul. . . . Theft, if the truth be told, was the closest thing I knew to transcendence" (46–47). But theft also has political meaning for Calhoun; if he breaks "the power of the propertied class," the thrill is intensified. "The crates of plunder from every culture conceivable" that he finds in Falcon's quarters make him realize that the captain must have a standing order from "his financiers, powerful families in New Orleans who underwrote the *Republic*, to stock Yankee museums and their homes with whatever of value was not nailed down in the nations he visited" (48–49). Calhoun, fingering the vases, carpets, and temple scrolls that cram Falcon's cabin, understands the principle of taking and collecting—of theft. In *Kim*, the Lahore Museum houses stone fragments from Buddhist monasteries, Lurgan's shop is crowded with daggers, prayer wheels, amber necklaces, portable lacquer altars, and Russian samovars. In *The Moonstone*, an enormous diamond is transported from the forehead of an Indian god to the fichu of a woman's dress, and what is not stolen in *King Solomon's Mines*—to ensure for imperialism the laboring body of the black African—in *Heart of Darkness* is taken out of Africa in staggering amounts. It is the principle of theft that literally and imaginatively directs Victorian colonial and imperial practices: theft of objects from subjugated cultures; theft of land from subordinated peoples; and, most vividly and graphically in *Middle Passage*, the theft of Africans from Africa to work the plantations of the West Indies and the Americas. The old Bushman paintings of oxen, elephants, rhinoceroses, and a "one-horned beast, such as no man ever has seen or ever shall" engraved on a shelving rock on the "kopje" in Olive Shreiner's *Story of an African Farm*, and the heavy stonework of churches and bridges in Conrad's *Nostromo* proclaiming "the disregard of human labour, the tribute-labour of vanished nations" (89) are the artistic traces of European larceny. The paintings are the mark of a people dispossessed of their culture by invading colonizers initially in search of land and later in quest of labor power for the diamond and gold mines of Southern Africa, the heavy stonework is the sign of vanquished Indians whose descendants raise their sad, heavy eyes to look at Emilia Gould as she rides to the silver mine. Although not about Victorian imperialism or Victorian culture, *Middle Passage* brilliantly suggests how theft can be a dominant trope for analysis of imperial subjugation, appropriation, and governance. This understanding is also possessed by Emilia Gould in *Nostromo*.

"MATERIAL INTEREST":
EMILIA GOULD SUMS IT UP

The doctor was loyal to the mine. It presented itself to his fifty-years' old eyes in the shape of a little woman in a soft dress with a long train, with a head attractively overweighted by a great mass of fair hair and the delicate preciousness of her inner worth, partaking of a gem and a flower, revealed in every attitude of her person
—Joseph Conrad, *Nostromo*

For the broken, embittered, skeptical Dr. Monygham, Emilia Gould is something to live for, something he can believe in despite his harrowing history of physical torture and political disillusion. For him, indeed for almost all of Sulaco society, Emilia Gould's delicate beauty, noble morality, and discerning manners have made her an emblem of everything civilized worth fighting for. It is for her that Monygham will don a short linen jacket in order to go to tea at the exquisitely furnished Casa Gould, and it is for her, because she is so completely identified with the history of the San Tome Mine, that the Europeans load the silver into the lighter to save it from Pedro Montero, "as if the silver of the mine had been the emblem of a common cause, the symbol of the supreme importance of material interests" (*Nostromo* 260). And it is because of that identification, and despite his adoration of Antonia Avellanos, that Decoud takes the silver out into the placid Gulf and eventually sinks himself into its indifferent depths. As an ironic consequence of Decoud's death and because imaginatively Emilia Gould is the silver, Nostromo survives to grow rich slowly from the hidden treasure. Finally, it is to Emilia, as he lies dying, that Nostromo makes his confession, which is in response to her whispered words that she has always hated the idea of the silver and which expresses the powerfully ironic meaning of her presence in the novel:

"Marvellous!—that one of you should hate the wealth that you know so well to take from the hands of the poor" (560). In other words, it is a ruling-class Englishwoman—intelligent, sensitive, sympathetic— around whom the imperialist project in *Nostromo* revolves, and to whom all its action is dedicated and directed. In *Nostromo,* Conrad shows that Emilia Gould is as much a part of the systematic colonization of Latin America by Europe as is her husband, Charles, the American capitalist Holroyd, and Sir John, the British head of the railway company. In the eyes of her husband, her friends, and Sulaco society, Emilia Gould is a gendered symbol of perfected, European "civilization, an incarnation of ideal womanhood deployed in the service of Victorian empire.[1] "Imperium in imperio," usually read to mean the empire of the San Tome Mine within Sulaco, may also be read (and perhaps more richly) as the empire of Victorian womanhood within the empire of appropriation of land and labor.

A trope of invasion by the colonizer and counterinvasion by the colonized has been a significant and organizing motif throughout my discussion of the meaning of Britannic rule in the Victorian period. The tropical fruit on sale in Brixton market; the West Indians, Africans, and Pakistanis living in Britain after World War II; the lush vegetation in the Palm House at Kew; Bertha Mason Rochester in the bleak midlands countryside; Abel Magwitch lurking outside Pip's lodgings in London; the Indian diamond that invades the serenity of English country-house life—all these images, and innumerable others, are evidence of how the possession of empire in Victorian Britain was always and necessarily stamped upon the imperial metropolis. In conjunction with this exploration and analysis of the paradigm of invasion and counterinvasion, I have been interested throughout this book in how Victorian women contributed in certain exemplary ways to the constitution of empire. I have been engaged by women as writers, from Emily Eden's epistolary invasion of Macaulay's parliamentary rhetoric to the travel writings of figures such as Emily Roberts to Maud Diver's reactionary fears of feminism and native agitation. And I have been interested in women as Victorian symbols of civilization, from Little Nell's sacrificial death and Florence Dombey's redemptive salvation of

---

[1] Since the frame for my discussion of Emilia Gould's meaning in *Nostromo* is that of the participation of women in the constitution of Victorian empire, I shall not rehearse the numerous critical approaches to this novel. For a fine overview of these approaches, see Benita Parry's superb chapter on *Nostromo* in her *Conrad and Imperialism* 99–127.

Queen Victoria with her Indian servant at Frogmore (1893). By courtesy of the National Portrait Gallery, London.

her father's materialism to Jane Eyre's impeccable rehabilitation of corrupt colonization. I have also tried to show in Tennyson and Haggard the male writer's panic (expressed on behalf of late-Victorian imperialism) that British society was losing control of woman's laboring and reproductive body, as well as that of the laboring native.

The participation of women writers in the construction of Victorian empire and the deployment of women as symbols of superior civilization are, I think, clustered in the figure of Emilia Gould. As a character in Conrad's 1904 novel—which whatever the interpretation one makes of it, is, fundamentally, about empire—she may be said to be produced by the history of European invasion and subjugation of native peoples throughout the nineteenth century. As a figure who is continuously represented and interpreted by others, she may be said to be the supreme symbol of superior Britannic civilization as it is constructed in the fictions of empire I have discussed throughout this book. What makes her, though, an especially rich female figure of empire is the fact that she embodies in her character, and in her sensibility and understanding, the characteristics of counterinvasion. She is both the gendered power that participates in the construction of British imperial greatness and the sensibility that interrogates imperialistic practices. What Conrad shows so brilliantly in *Nostromo* is the political fact that imperialism is not just guns, not just Thuggee Sleeman slugging it out with guerrilla gangs in India in the 1840s, Rhodes's white troops brutally subduing the Matabele at the very end of the nineteenth century, Jamaican planters in the postemancipation period devising ever more cruel ways to chain their former slaves through punitive legislation and apprenticeship systems. What Conrad shows is that empire is created by the forces embodied in Emilia Gould, the forces of the humane, wise, and putatively nonracist new imperialism. She is a figure who legitimates the mystifying idealism of Gould's capitalist enterprise: the mine, the railway, the telegraph lines that gut, plow, and invade the Costaguana countryside. Her arrival and presence in Sulaco coincide precisely with the new imperialism brought by American capitalism's marriage to English materialism.

As a way of bringing together the parts played by Victorian women in the construction of Britannic rule—as writers, characters, and symbols—I want to demonstrate the way in which Emilia Gould encapsulates the cultural work of the Victorian woman writer and the portrayal of Victorian woman as symbol of European civilization. Endings are as arbitrary as beginnings, and I could, say, conclude *Rule Britannia* by contrasting the ambiguity of Conrad's anti-imperialism in *Nostromo* with Kipling's robust flag-waving. Or I could pair Emilia Gould's ambivalence about empire with, perhaps, the straightforward resistance to it found in the work of actual figures such as Annie Besant. Yet for me, the character of Emilia Gould gathers together almost everything I have tried to argue throughout this book. As Benita Parry aptly observes, she is the vehicle through whom Conrad articulates his "most uncompromising criticism of the West's moral decline" and also his "ardent vindication of European values" (109).[2]

Despite Conrad's insistence in his author's note that Antonia—

---

[2] Alan Sandison argues that for Conrad, the imperial idea "while it exposes human avarice at its most naked and squalid, is, fundamentally, a symbol of man's isolation and his utter failure to communicate with his fellows" (195–96). This view seems to me to be at once sensible and far too simple; if the problem of the imperialist is his isolation from his fellow men, then imperialist practices constitute and are constituted by this sense of solation. Race from race, class from class, these different forms of isolation enable capitalism, imperialism, and patriarchy.

"simply by the force of what she is"—is the gendered figure of idealism in contrast to Decoud's boulevard-style skepticism, it is Emilia Gould who is idealized by Conrad and the Sulaco community and who is the idealizing center of South American imperialism. Emilia Gould actually participates in the construction of the mine, symbolically giving birth to the silver that emerges from the ravaging of the hillside and performing the ideological reproduction of the values of new imperialism. Graced by Conrad with an intelligence purely feminine—"It must not be supposed that Mrs. Gould's mind was masculine. A woman with a masculine mind is not a being of superior efficiency; she is simply a phenomenon of imperfect differentiation—interestingly barren and without importance" (66–67)—she invades and conquers Sulaco society by virtue of her possession of qualities conventionally ascribed to ideal women in the Victorian period. She can converse charmingly but is not talkative, she is sympathetic but never intrusive, and she is not materialistic, nouveau riche, or showy (nothing like Tennyson's grubby Manchester manufacturers and their wives). Rather, she knows how to use money so that it seems as if she has no interest in money; albeit unconsciously, she helps propagate subjugation of indigenous peoples so that it seems as if without the European presence they would be savage, unemployed, and have no interest in mining silver from their countryside.[3]

When her husband tells her he would never have touched the mine "for money alone," she presses her head to his shoulder "approvingly" (74). Her artistry in effecting this ideological erasure of the source of her wealth imaginatively places her with the Victorian women who justify Britannic rule in their writings. Her life, her house, her marriage, are all aesthetic constructions designed as monuments to the superiority of European civilization. Believing that the bandits who are aligning themselves with a guerrilla leader would have been better off working in the mine, many an outlaw, she says, "would be living peaceably and happy by the honest work of his hands" (109). She speaks like a colonizer when at the lunch given to celebrate the arrival of the railway, she observes, "All this brings nearer the sort of future we desire for the country" (120). And Conrad's imagery of the literal invasion of the land by colonization symbolically links Emilia to these imperial practices.

[3] This is a point made by Benita Parry, who argues that the "ultimate effect of dignifying Emilia Gould's ardent idealism is to illuminate how her nobility is perverted by complicity in reprehensible decisions and participation in idolatry" (117). Parry's reading of politics in *Nostromo* finely identifies the antimonies of embrace of capitalism and retreat from history.

With the establishment of Ribiera, "great regenerating transactions were being initiated—the fresh loan, a new railway line, a vast colonization scheme" (144). Part of the scheme is the march of a "sparse row of telegraph poles . . . bearing a single, almost invisible wire far into the great camp—like a slender, vibrating feeler of that progress waiting outside for a moment of peace to enter and twine itself about the weary heart of the land" (166). In ways that are barely symbolic, however, Emilia Gould is the "slender, vibrating" feeler of European capitalism that winds its way across the land. The language suggests a conventionally feminine movement; the delicate, slender single telegraph wire will twine its clinging way across the countryside. As is so often the case in Conrad's brilliant use of language, the phrase "weary heart of the land" suggests a colonial gutting that has occurred from the time of the conquistadors.

That she is an artist of the conventional watercolor sort is indicated by the drawing she produces of the waterfall and tree ferns that hangs in Gould's study. This is painted before the re-opening of the mine. That she is an artist of another sort, imaginatively a figure who creates a work of art out of profit making (not a "touch of materialism" in her efforts), is seen in the way Conrad links her to the mine from the moment of its inception, or conception. Her childlessness as an emblem of the sterility of capitalism has been suggested by a number of critics; it is invested with a symbolic meaning distant from the kind of political heavy-handedness one finds in Maud Diver's indictment of Audrey Hammond's celibacy or H. Rider Haggard's misogynistic constructions of barren, withered female bodies. Emilia's childlessness serves to emphasize, to construct in a sense, the fruit of her marriage, which is of course the San Tome Mine itself. She is present at its conception— the moment on the Tuscan hillside when Gould lifts her off her feet in a sexual embrace after he has told her of his father's death and asked her to marry him and go to Sulaco to "grapple" with his inheritance of the abandoned silver mine. And she is present at every stage of its growth, literally and in the womb of her idealizing imagination, as she watches the erection of the frame-houses for the offices, listens for the sound of the machinery, and in a scene described by Conrad in such a way to suggest childbirth, waits "till she had seen the first spongy lump of silver yielded to the hazards of the world by the dark depths of the Gould Concession; she had lain her unmercenary hands, with an eagerness that made them tremble, upon the first silver ingot turned out still warm from the mould; and by her imaginative estimate of its power she endowed that lump of metal with a justicative conception, as though it were not a mere fact, but something far-reaching and impalpable, like the true expression of an emotion or the emergence of a principle" (107).

Her coupling with Gould conceives the silver. It is a Victorian marriage to which he brings the literal fact of his inheritance and to which she brings the idealism of her upbringing, so that what is born is something they both believe transcends the ordinary business of making money. On the political level, what she does is invest the commodity produced through the labor of thousands of Indians (to which I shall return in a moment) with a principled meaning, the mystifying justification that what she and Gould are doing in Sulaco is something more than, better than, superior to, the money making of Holroyd. Holroyd's view of Costaguana is that it is a "bottomless pit of 10 per cent loans and other fool investments" into which European capital has been flung for years. At some point, he says America is bound to step in since the wealth of the country determines a destiny of running "the world's business whether the world likes it or not" (77).

The description of the journey of the silver as it descends to the sea, the infant born from the hillside, packed in ox-hide boxes and loaded on two-wheeled carts, is graphic, visceral, aural: the procession is accompanied by the sound of spurs, the cracking of whips, and the deep rumbles as the carts go over the bridge down to the plain. Conrad's superb characterization of Emilia Gould emerges in the way he sustains this imagery of conception, birth, and growth. The silver/child becomes a "fetish," something that takes on "a monstrous and crushing weight," the "inspiration" of her early married life becomes a "wall of silver-bricks" within which her husband dwells, "leaving her outside with her school, her hospital, the sick mothers and the feeble old men, mere insignificant vestiges of the initial inspiration" (222). His decision to pin his faith to material interest—"Only let the material interests once get a firm footing, and they are bound to impose the conditions on which alone they can continue to exist"—becomes a sham to her. His obsession, framed by the comedy and brutality of internecine Central American politics, is "to keep unchecked the flow of treasure he had started single-handed from the re-opened scar in the flank of the mountain" (148). Spurs jingling, ginger mustachios twirling, riding crop in hand, he has forced open the land and generated the birth of the treasure.[4]

---

[4] In a wonderfully ironic moment, the silver that has been released from the mother earth through the coupling of Charles and Emilia, is returned by Nostromo to a symbolically female,

Eventually, Emilia becomes like a mother whose male child has grown and identified himself with the father, and it is an image that seems to rework the conventional one of great colonial mother and subservient dutiful colonized daughters. *Nostromo* revises the late-Victorian symbol of the mother country to show that the mother has been supplanted by the father-country; that is to say, Britain has been replaced by America in anticipation of a late-twentieth-century map of geopolitical control. At the end of the novel, Emilia Gould, the colonial mother, the good fairy, the gendered artist of empire whose art has served to mask the brutal economic reality at the heart of Gould's enterprise, becomes "weary with a long career of well-doing, touched by the withering suspicion of the uselessness of her labours, the powerlessness of her magic" (520). Her cherished child/mine/silver has become a deformed material creature. It is at this moment that in the "indistinct voice of an unlucky sleeper, lying passive in the grip of a merciless nightmare," she stammers two words: "Material interest" (522).

If Conrad invests Emilia Gould with the conventional attributes of idealized Victorian womanhood, which I have suggested are deployed by colonial and imperial discourse in the service of constituting and legitimating the takeover of lands and subjugation of peoples, then her husband is invested with qualities associated with the efficient colonial administrator. And if she is associated with the silver that comes spongy and warm from the hillside and then works its way, its life, down the hill to the sea, then he is associated less conventionally with the dangerously placid Gulf in his calm repellence of emotion. He has a mind that "preserved its steady poise as if sheltered in the passionless stability of private and public decencies at home in Europe" (49), and he accepts unmoved the political changes that to his wife seem a "puerile and bloodthirsty game of murder and rapine played with terrible earnestness by depraved children" (49). Completely a creature formed by Victorian gender politics, he believes that material interest and morals, feelings, and spirituality may be kept divided, and he relies upon his wife to preserve that divide.

It is in the Casa Gould that Emilia achieves her most perfect work of

---

sexual place on the Great Isabel: "In the shallow cove where the high, cliff-like end of the Great Isabel is divided in two equal parts by a deep and overgrown ravine . . . Where the ravine opens between the cliffs, and a slender, shallow rivulet meanders out of the bushes to lose itself in the sea, the lighter was run ashore" (295).

art: sumptuously comfortable, it contrasts significantly with the shabby palazzo where she has been living when she agrees to marry Gould. The principal room in that Jamesian space, "magnificent and naked, with here and there a long strip of damask, black with damp and age, hanging down on a bare panel of the wall," is furnished with a single, broken gilded armchair and cracked, heavy marble vase. Its decaying dampness is replaced by a domestic perfection centered around her patio and sala, each perfectly furnished with exquisite flowers and comfortable English chairs. Most of all, she loves the flower-filled patio, especially in the early morning as servants pass to and fro—laundry girls, the baker, her own maid "bearing high up, swung from her hand raised above her raven black head, a bunch of starched under-skirts dazzlingly white in the slant of sunshine" (68). "Like the lady of the mediaeval castle" (68), she may witness from her balcony all the departures and arrivals of the casa.

In the extraordinary imagery of sound in *Nostromo,* Emilia Gould's small murmur of "material interest" is the contrapuntal voice, similar to that of Emily Eden's, heard against the bells of the city that strike when Barrios sets sail to fight Montero. The rumble of wheels of the Gould carriage is "traversed by a strange piercing shriek" as the great bell of the cathedral clangs out explosively "dying away in deep and mellow vibrations. And then all the bells in the tower of every church, convent, or chapel in town, even those that had remained shut up for years, pealed out together with a crash" (381). It is not merely that these crashing bells bring all the Gould servants out on to the patio, and thus into the sight of a master who did not know he had employed so many, they also are the official sound, as it were, of the church and the state, against which the small voice of the idealized Victorian woman makes her protest and through which, in fact, she is licensed to speak her objection. Her small contrapuntal voice of protest is not unlike the screams of Hirsch— "Hirsch went on screaming all alone behind the half-closed jalousies while the sunshine, reflected from the water of the harbour, made an ever-running ripple of light high up on the wall" (447). He screams unheard, except by the reader. She murmurs unheard, except by the reader. His is a scream against the incomprehensible horror to which he has been subjected; hers is a murmur against what is chillingly revealed to her: the truth of her gendered contribution to empire. This is not to argue that *Nostromo* is a an uncomplicated attack upon empire, or that Emilia Gould is spokeswoman for that attack. *Nostromo* is more subtle, more demanding than such a reading would suggest. What it does, and

I see this happening primarily through Emilia Gould, is show the construction of empire, the forces that make it: the money, the railway, the
telegraph wires, the schools, the hospitals, the Casa Gould—in sum the
military and civil powers that combine to transform a South American
country from sleepy exploitation of Indians by the rancheros to energetic twentieth-century empire building.

"History," in Fredric Jameson's reading of *Nostromo*, I take to mean
something that Jameson believes Conrad does not like, something that
restricts individual freedom—or at least, the myth of the individual
subject possessing freedom of individual perception. Confronted by the
late-nineteenth-century erosion of even a belief in such myths of au-
tonomy, Conrad, according to Jameson, "recodes" the world in terms of
perception as a semi-autonomous activity so that eventually his stylistic
practice becomes a symbolic act. Jameson's political analysis of what he
terms "strategies of containment" in *Nostromo* is wonderfully suggestive. One sees the European containment of South America through
capitalist expansion, but one also sees Conrad's containment of political
chaos within the narrative frame of his novel as well as a containment
within the novel itself through the "sensorium," through Conrad's extraordinary "sentence production," of the fear of loss of individual au-
tonomy in the face of history. My problem with this reading, however,
is Jameson's failure to understand the rich political meaning of Emilia
Gould in the novel, someone he dismisses as "Conrad's only interesting
woman character" (240) and whose interest for him lies merely in her
presence in the richly sensuous proposal scene. For me, Conrad inherits
and revises into his narrative of containment the symbols of Victorian
womanhood deployed in the service of empire, so that we see in Emilia
Gould the most profound and most ambiguous aspects of colonial and
imperial practices. In sum, she is both a pedagogical and a performative
figure, similar in this way to Jane Eyre.

Pedagogically constructed as an object by ideologies of late-Victorian
empire, as we see in her absolute identification with the project in
Sulaco, she is also a performative subject everywhere enacting the
agency that is granted her by imperialism. In my discussion of *Jane
Eyre*, I argued that the magnetic inconsistences of Brontë's novel may
be attributed to Jane Eyre's dual identity as both pedagogical and performative figure. I believe that we may see Emilia Gould in the same
political and narrative light. What Conrad embodies in Emilia is both
the late-Victorian woman whose assumption of moral superiority and

identification with what is not material interest marks her as a pedagogical object, helpless and alone in the treasure house of the world at the end of the novel, and the late-Victorian woman who performatively enacts her own agency as a subject through questioning the very structures that have brought her into being. And what is involved in the latter activity is, of course, the moral interrogation of empire. She questions the patriarchal imperialism challenged by Mary Pigot, defended by Maud Diver, worried about by Dickens and Tennyson, and upheld by H. Rider Haggard. In this way, she may be affiliated with all the subordinated creatures of empire (created by empire, for empire) I have referred to in this book, yet she belongs, of course, to the social class that does the subordinating, living a life of sumptuous comfort defined by glittering jewelry, swishing satin trains, and immaculate carriages.

We learn very early in the novel that she knows the history of the mine, which was worked in the early days "mostly by means of lashes on the backs of slaves, its yield had been paid for in its own weight of human bones. Whole tribes of Indians had perished in the exploitation" (52). Incorporating a good-works approach into her husband's way of doing business (an efficient form of the benevolent paternalism associated with the feudal Spanish aristocracy of the campo), she builds hospitals and schools, and becomes a kind of patron saint of the workers. She is able to see the land in ways her husband cannot, and "trudging files of burdened Indians taking off their hats, would lift sad, mute eyes to the cavalcade raising the dust of the crumbling *camino real* made by the hands of their enslaved forefathers" (87). Hers is the vision that plunges to the interior, hers is the "deeper glance" that sees beyond the Indian body as an object "in the search for labour." (86). Hers is the eye that reads the dreadful meaning of heavy stonework of bridges and churches left by the Spanish that proclaims "the disregard of human labour, the tribute-labour of vanished nations" (89). Hers is the knowledge of labor itself, of what so catches her husband by surprise when the bells clang as Montero gets close to the city, and his servants flood the patio: he beholds "the extent of his domestic establishment, . . . a shrivelled old hag or two, of whose existence within the walls of his house he had not been aware" (238). The bells disclose the secrets of labor for the rich, a knowledge possessed by Emilia, which is not to say that she is uncomfortable with this knowledge. Rather, because she is the quintessential woman of empire, it is her job to know about this labor. It is her inheritance to furrow her brow, to be concerned about the slavery that went into the Spanish stonework, to agonize about the historical fact that whole tribes of Indians perished in the working of the mine before her husband came along with his sensible ideas about material interests and laid the ground for decent treatment of the colonized Indian.

The superb power of *Nostromo* is the way it shows through Emilia Gould the built-in interrogation of imperialism often allotted to women throughout the history of Victorian empire. She exists, so to speak, as the invasive figure from within, possessing the alert sensibility of Emily Eden, the domestic perfection of Florence Dombey, the sensible firmness of Jane Eyre. What Benita Parry in her otherwise excellent reading of *Nostromo* terms an "excess of narrative homage" for Emilia Gould (116), should, I think, be read as Conrad's appropriation of the part played by Victorian womanhood in the construction of empire for his own narrative purposes, whether we read this novel as a meditation on history, a moral critique, or a pessimistic look into the future of imperialist expansion. Indeed, one might argue that the multiple meanings of Emilia Gould in *Nostromo* may be linked with virtually all the different critical and theoretical perspectives that have been brought to bear upon this most dense and complex of Conrad's novels: her character does comment on history, does present a moral critique of late-Victorian imperialism, does indict materialism, does suggest a certain "condition of mind" (as Edward Said suggests in *Beginnings* 110). She worries about Holroyd's puritan capitalism and sees him as worshipping "the religion of silver and iron" (71). She seems to prefer the social order of the "ecclesiastical courts" of history rather than the steamers, railways, and telegraph that Sir John promises is "a future in the great world which is worth infinitely more than any amount of ecclesiastical past" (36). For me, what she does most of all, is disclose the questioning of the British empire that is virtually simultaneous with its expansion in the Victorian period. She symbolizes the cultural power that constructs empire, holds it all together, and critiques it from within.

Where is the political and moral meaning of *Nostromo?* It seems to me it resides in something very similar to what keeps Marlow going in *Heart of Darkness.* He does not, as he puts it, go ashore for a howl and a dance because he has a job to do, a steamer to get upriver, a story to tell at the end of it. In *Nostromo,* from the "contact" of the chairman of the railway and the chief engineer, who possess quite different visions of the world, "there was generated a power for the world's service—a subtle force that could set in motion mighty machines, men's muscles, and awaken also in human breasts an unbounded devotion to the task" (41). This is a power to change a town for the better. To be sure, it means that the "worn-out antiquity of Sulaco, so characteristic with its stuccoed houses and barred windows, with the great yellowy-white walls of abandoned convents behind the rows of sombre green cypresses (97)" gets modernized, Americanized, eventually erased. But it also means that the Indians, instead of breaking their backs building stone bridges, get to wear the white and green ponchos of the San Tome Mine and not get beaten up by the police. Certainly, Conrad's depiction of Central American politics is dismal, pessimistic, deeply suspicious of "material interest."[5] But eventually, material interest makes things materially better. And it is material interest, after all that makes possible the presence of Emilia Gould in Costaguana and thus the voice that speaks an ironic understanding of her own history. Throughout the Victorian period, British women who contributed in one way or another to the construction of empire did not always possess this understanding: they got "grilled alive in Calcutta" without knowing what got them there in the first place, or, they were figures of Britannic rule without knowing the cost to themselves and to others of their gendered power. In Emilia Gould, *Nostromo* superbly concentrates the meaning of women, empire, and Victorian writing. And, in an imaginative linking of the end of this book with its beginning, she also inhabits a part of the world that, some sixty years after the publication of Conrad's novel, was busy exporting tropical fruit to be sold in Brixton Market.

---

[5] John McClure argues, in a rather limited way I think, that "if Conrad's portrayal of recent Latin American history in *Nostromo* is anticapitalist, it is also profoundly pessimistic, antidemocratic, and even racist" (161).

WORKS CITED

Achebe, Chinua. "Viewpoint." *Times Literary Supplement.* 1 February 1980.

Ali, Mrs. Meer Hassan. *Observations on the Mussulmans of India: Descriptive of Their Manners, Customs, Habits, and Religious Opinions Made during a Twelve Years' Residence in Their Immediate Society.* 2 vols. London: Parbury, Allen, 1832.

Allen, Charles. *A Glimpse of the Burning Plain: Leaves from the Indian Journals of Charlotte Canning.* London: Michael Joseph, 1986.

Althusser, Louis. "Ideology and Ideological State Apparatuses." *Lenin and Philosophy and Other Essays.* Trans. Ben Brewster. London: New Left Books, 1971. 127–86.

Altick, Richard D. *The English Common Reader.* Chicago: University of Chicago Press, 1957.

———. *The Shows of London.* Cambridge: The Belknap Press of Harvard University Press, 1978.

Anderson, Benedict. *Imagined Communities: Reflections on the Origin and Spread of Nationalism.* London: Verso, 1991 (1983).

Arac, Jonathan. "Peculiarities of (the) English in the Metanarratives of Knowledge and Power." *Intellectuals: Aesthetics, Politics, Academics.* Ed. Bruce Robbins. Minneapolis: University of Minnesota Press, 1990. 189–99.

Arac, Jonathan, and Harriet Ritvo, eds. *Macropolitics of Nineteenth-Century Literature: Nationalism, Exoticism, Imperialism.* Philadelphia: University of Pennsylvania Press, 1991.

Ardis, Ann L. *New Women, New Novels: Feminism and Early Modernism.* New Brunswick, N.J.: Rutgers University Press, 1990.

Arnold, David. "Touching the Body: Perspectives on the Indian Plague, 1896–1900." *Selected Subaltern Studies.* Ed. Ranajit Guha and Gayatri Chakravorty Spivak. New York: Oxford University Press, 1988.

Arnold, William D. *Oakfield; or, Fellowship in the East.* 2d ed. 2 vols. London: Longman, Brown, Green, and Longmans, 1854.

The Asiatic Journal and Monthly Register for British and Foreign India, China, and Australasia 18 (September-December 1835). London: Wm. H. Allen, 1835.

Auerbach, Nina. "Dickens and Dombey: A Daughter after All." *Dickens Studies Annual: Essays on Victorian Fiction.* Ed. Robert B. Partlow, Jr. Carbondale: Southern Illinois University Press, 1976. 5:95–114.

———. *Woman and the Demon: The Life of a Victorian Myth.* Cambridge: Harvard University Press, 1982.

Aynsley, Mrs. J. C. Murray. *Our Visit to Hindostan, Kashmir, and Ladokah.* London: Wm. H. Allen, 1879.

Bakhtin, Mikhail. "Discourse in the Novel." *The Dialogic Imagination: Four Essays by M. M. Bakhtin.* Ed. Michael Holquist. Trans. Caryl Emerson and Michael Holquist. Austin: University of Texas Press, 1981. 259–422.

Ballhatchet, Kenneth. *Race, Sex, and Class under the Raj: Imperial Attitudes and Policies and Their Critics, 1793–1905.* New York: St. Martin's Press, 1980.

Banks, Olive. *Faces of Feminism: A Study of Feminism as a Social Movement.* New York: St. Martin's Press, 1981.

"Barbados." *Macmillan's Magazine* 51 (November 1884–April 1885).

Beeton, Mrs. Isabella. *The Book of Household Management.* London: S. O. Beeton, 1861.

Behn, Aphra. *Oroonoko, or The History of the Royal Slave.* Intro. Lore Metzer. New York: W. W. Norton, 1973.

Bell, Kenneth N., and W. P. Morrell, eds. *Select Documents on British Colonial Policy, 1830–1860.* Oxford: Clarendon Press, 1928.

Bender, John. *Imagining the Penitentiary: Fiction and the Architecture of Mind in Eighteenth-Century England.* Chicago: University of Chicago Press, 1987.

Bhabha, Homi K. "DissemiNation: Time, Narrative, and the Margins of the Modern Nation." *Nation and Narration.* Ed. Homi K. Bhabha. London: Routledge, 1990. 291–322.

———. "Signs Taken for Wonders: Questions of Ambivalence and Authority under a Tree outside Delhi, May 1817." *"Race," Writing, and Difference.* Ed. Henry Louis Gates, Jr. Chicago: University of Chicago Press, 1986. 163–84.

Biller, Sarah, ed. *Memoir of the Late Hannah Kilham; Chiefly Compiled from Her Journal, and Edited by Her Daughter-in-Law, Sarah Biller, of St. Petersburg.* London: Darton and Harvey, 1837.

Billington, Mary Frances. *Woman in India.* London: Chapman and Hall, 1895.

Blackwood, Harriot G., Marchioness of Dufferin and Ava. *Our Viceregal Life in India: Selections from My Journal, 1884–1888.* London: John Murray, 1889.

Bolt, Christine. *Victorian Attitudes to Race.* London: Routledge and Kegan Paul, 1971.

———. "Race and the Victorians." *British Imperialism in the Nineteenth Century.* Ed. C. C. Eldridge. New York: St. Martin's Press, 1984. 126–47.

Brantlinger, Patrick. *Rule of Darkness: British Literature and Imperialism, 1830–1914.* Ithaca: Cornell University Press, 1988.

"Brief Practical Suggestions on the Mode of Organizing and Conducting Day-Schools of Industry, Model Farm-Schools, and Normal Schools, as Part of a System of Education for the Coloured Races of the British Colonies." *Imperialism.* Ed. Philip D. Curtin. New York: Walker, 1971. 191–209.

Bristow, Joseph. *Empire Boys: Adventures in a Man's World*. London: Harper Collins Academic, 1991.

British Empire Exhibition, 1924. Official Catalogue. London: Fleetway Press, 1924.

Brontë, Charlotte. *Jane Eyre*. Harmondsworth, Middlesex: Penguin Books, 1966, (1847).

Brooks, Peter. *Reading for the Plot: Design and Intention in Narrative*. New York: Alfred A. Knopf, 1984.

Brown, Laura. "The Romance of Empire: *Oroonoko* and the Trade in Slaves." *The New Eighteenth Century: Theory, Politics, English Literature*. Ed. Felicity Nussbaum and Laura Brown. New York: Methuen, 1987. 41–61.

Brown, Paul. " 'This thing of darkness I acknowledge mine': *The Tempest* and the Discourse of Colonialism." *Political Shakespeare: New Essays in Cultural Materialism*. Ed. Jonathan Dollimore and Alan Sinfield. Ithaca: Cornell University Press, 1985. 48–71.

Browning, Elizabeth Barrett. *The Complete Works of Mrs. Elizabeth Barrett Browning*. Ed. Charlotte Porter and Helen A. Clarke. 6 vols. New York: George D. Sproul, 1901.

Buckland, Augustus R. *Women in the Mission Field: Pioneers and Martyrs*. London: Isbister, 1895.

Burroughs, Peter. "Colonial Self-Government." *British Imperialism in the Nineteenth Century*. Ed. C. C. Eldridge. New York: St. Martin's Press, 1984. 39–64.

Callaway, Helen. *Gender, Culture, and Empire: European Women in Colonial Nigeria*. Urbana: University of Illinois Press, 1987.

Callaway, Helen, and Dorothy O. Helly. "Crusader for Empire: Flora Shaw/Lady Lugard." *Western Women and Imperialism: Complicity and Resistance*. Ed. Nupur Chaudhuri and Margaret Strobel. Bloomington: Indiana University Press, 1992. 79–97.

Carlyle, Thomas. "Occasional Discourse on the Nigger Question." *Critical and Miscellaneous Essays*. 3 vols. New York: Funk and Wagnalls, 1905. 3:463–92.

——. *Thomas Carlyle: Selected Writings*. Ed. Alan Sheston. Harmondsworth, Middlesex: Penguin Books, 1971.

Carr, Helen. "Woman/Indian: 'The American' and His Others." *Europe and Its Others*. 2 vols. Ed. Francis Barker et al. Proceedings of the Essex Conference on the Sociology of Literature, 1984. Colchester: University of Essex, 1985. 2:46–60.

Carter, Paul. *The Road to Botany Bay: An Exploration of Landscape and History*. New York: Alfred A. Knopf, 1988.

Cary, Joyce. *Mister Johnson*. London: Michael Joseph, 1947 (1939).

Chapman, Mrs. E. F. *Sketches of Some Distinguished Indian Women*. London: W. H. Allen, 1891.

Chaudhuri, Nupur, and Margaret Strobel, eds. *Western Women and Imperialism: Complicity and Resistance*. Bloomington: Indiana University Press, 1992.

Chrisman, Laura. "The Imperial Unconscious? Representations of Imperial Discourse." *Colonial Discourse and Post-Colonial Theory*. Ed. Patrick Williams and Laura Chrisman. New York: Columbia University Press, 1994. 498–516.

Clive, John. *Macaulay: The Shaping of the Historian*. Cambridge: The Belknap Press of Harvard University Press, 1987.

Coetzee, J. M. *Foe*. New York: Viking, 1986.

Collins, Wilkie. *The Moonstone*. Harmondsworth, Middlesex: Penguin Books, 1966 (1868).

——. *Armadale*. New York: Dover, 1977 (1864–66).

Conrad, Joseph. *Heart of Darkness*. London: J. M. Dent and Sons, 1946 (1899).

——. *Nostromo*. London: J. M. Dent and Sons, 1947 (1904).

Cowper, William. *The Poetical Works of William Cowper*. Ed. H. S. Milford. Oxford: Oxford University Press, 1934.

Curtin, Philip D. *Cross-Cultural Trade in World History*. Cambridge: Cambridge University Press, 1984.

——. *The Image of Africa: British Ideas and Action, 1780–1850*. Madison: University of Wisconsin Press, 1964.

——, ed. *Imperialism*. New York: Walker, 1971.

——. *Two Jamaicas: The Role of Ideas in a Tropical Colony, 1830–1865*. Cambridge: Harvard University Press, 1955.

Dabydeen, David. "Eighteenth-Century English Literature on Commerce and Slavery." *The Black Presence in English Literature*. Ed. David Dabydeen. Manchester: Manchester University Press, 1985. 26–49.

David, Deirdre. *Intellectual Women and Victorian Patriarchy: Harriet Martineau, Elizabeth Barrett Browning, George Eliot*. Ithaca: Cornell University Press, 1987.

——. "The Old Right and the New Jerusalem: Elizabeth Barrett Browning's Intellectual Practice." *Intellectuals: Aesthetics, Politics, Academics*. Ed. Bruce Robbins. Minneapolis: University of Minnesota Press, 1990. 189–99.

Davin, Anna. "Imperialism and Motherhood." *History Workshop* 5 (spring 1978): 9–65.

D'Costa, Jean, and Barbara Lalla. *Voices in Exile: Jamaican Texts of the Eighteenth and Nineteenth Centuries*. Tuscaloosa: University of Alabama Press, 1989.

Defoe, Daniel. *Robinson Crusoe*. Ed. Michael Shinagel. New York: W. W. Norton, 1975.

Dickens, Charles. *Bleak House*. Oxford Illustrated Dickens. London: Oxford University Press, 1948 (1853).

——. *David Copperfield*. Oxford Illustrated Dickens. London: Oxford University Press, 1948 (1850).

——. *Dombey and Son*. Oxford Illustrated Dickens. London: Oxford University Press, 1950 (1848).

——. *Hard Times: For These Times*. Oxford Illustrated Dickens. London: Oxford University Press, 1955 (1854).

——. *Little Dorrit*. Oxford Illustrated Dickens. London: Oxford University Press, 1953 (1857).

——. *Nicholas Nickleby*. Oxford Illustrated Dickens. London: Oxford University Press, 1950 (1839).

——. "The Noble Savage." *Household Words* 7 (11 June 1853): 337–39.

——. *The Old Curiosity Shop*. Oxford Illustrated Dickens. London: Oxford University Press, 1951 (1841).

——. *Our Mutual Friend*. Oxford Illustrated Dickens. London: Oxford University Press, 1952 (1865).

——. "The Perils of Certain English Prisoners." *Christmas Stories*. Oxford Illustrated Dickens. London: Oxford University Press (1956).

——. "Slavery." *American Notes and Pictures from Italy*. Oxford Illustrated Dickens. London: Oxford University Press, 1957. 228–43.

Dinnerstein, Dorothy. *The Mermaid and the Minotaur: Sexual Arrangements and Human Malaise*. New York: Harper Colophon Books, 1977.

Diver, Maud. *Awakening*. London: Hutchinson, 1911.

——. *The Englishwoman in India*. London: William Blackwood and Sons, 1909.

Donaldson, Laura E. *Decolonizing Feminisms: Race, Gender, and Empire-Building*. Chapel Hill: University of North Carolina Press, 1992.

Eden, Emily. *Up the Country: Letters Written to Her Sister from the Upper Provinces of India*. London: Muston, 1866.

Eldridge, C. C., ed. *British Imperialism in the Nineteenth Century*. New York: St. Martin's Press, 1984.

Eliot, George. "The Natural History of German Life." *Essays of George Eliot*. Ed. Thomas Pinney. New York: Columbia University Press, 1963. 266–99.

Fanon, Frantz. *Black Skin, White Masks*. New York: Grove Press, 1968.

——. *The Wretched of the Earth*. Harmondsworth, Middlesex: Penguin Books, 1967.

Ferguson, Moira. *Subject to Others: British Women Writers and Colonial Slavery, 1670–1834*. New York: Routledge, 1992.

Foote, Samuel. *The Nabob; A Comedy in Three Acts*. London: T. Cadell, 1778.

Forster, E. M. *A Passage to India*. New York: Harcourt, Brace, 1924.

Foster, Shirley. *Across New Worlds: Nineteenth-Century Women Travellers and Their Writings*. Hemel Hempstead: Harvester Wheatsheaf, 1990.

Foucault, Michel. *Discipline and Punish: The Birth of the Prison*. Trans. Alan Sheridan. New York: Pantheon, 1977.

Froude, James Anthony. *The English in the West Indies; or the Bow of Ulysses*. New York: Negro Universities Press, 1969 (1888).

Fryer, Peter. *Black People in the British Empire: An Introduction*. London: Pluto Press, 1988.

Gates, Henry Louis, Jr., ed. *"Race," Writing, and Difference*. Chicago: University of Chicago University Press, 1986.

Gerin, Winifred. *Charlotte Brontë: The Evolution of a Genius*. Oxford: Oxford University Press, 1967.

Giberne, Agens. *A Lady of England: The Life and Letters of Charlotte Maria Tucker*. London: Hodder and Stoughton, 1895.

Gibson, Mary Ellis. "The Seraglio or Suttee: Brontë's *Jane Eyre*." *Postscript: Publication of the Philological Association of the Carolinas* 4 (1987): 1–8.

Gilbert, Elliot L. "The Female King: Tennyson's Arthurian Apocalypse." *Speaking of Gender*. Ed. Elaine Showalter. New York: Routledge, 1989. 163–86.

Gilbert, Sandra M., and Susan Gubar. *The Madwoman in the Attic: The Woman Writer and the Nineteenth-Century Literary Imagination*. New Haven: Yale University Press, 1979.

——. *No Man's Land: The Place of the Woman Writer in the Twentieth Century*. Vol. 2: *Sexchanges*. New Haven: Yale University Press, 1989.

Gilroy, Paul. *"There Ain't No Black in the Union Jack": The Cultural Politics of Race and Nation*. With a foreword by Houston A. Baker, Jr. Chicago: University of Chicago Press, 1991.

Gooch, G. P. "Imperialism." *The Heart of the Empire*. Ed. C. F. G. Masterman. London: T. Fisher Unwin, 1901. 308–97.

Greenblatt, Stephen. "Invisible Bullets: Renaissance Authority and Its Subversion, *Henry IV* and *Henry V*." *Political Shakespeare: New Essays in Cultural Materialism*. Ed. Jonathan Dollimore and Alan Sinfield. Ithaca: Cornell University Press, 1985. 18–47.

Gurney, Emelia Russell. *Letters of Emelia Russell Gurney, Edited by Her Niece Ellen Mary Gurney*. London: James Nisbet, 1902.

Haggard, H. Rider. *The Annotated "She": A Critical Edition of H. Rider Haggard's Victorian Romance*. Introduction and notes by Norman Etherington. Bloomington: Indiana University Press, 1991.

——. "Black Heart and White Heart." *The Best Short Stories of Rider Haggard*. Ed. and Intro. Peter Haining. Foreword by Hammond Innes. London: Michael Joseph, 1981.

——. *King Solomon's Mines*. Ed. and Intro. Dennis Butts. New York: Oxford University Press, 1989 (1885).

——. *The Private Diaries of Sir H. Rider Haggard, 1914–1925*. Ed. D. S. Higgins. New York: Stein and Day, 1980.

——. "The Real King Solomon's Mines." *The Best Short Stories of Rider Haggard*. Ed. and Intro. Peter Haining. Foreword by Hammond Innes. London: Michael Joseph, 1981.

Hall, Stuart. "Cultural Identity and Diaspora." *Colonial Discourse and Post-Colonial Theory*. Ed. Patrick Williams and Laura Chrisman. New York: Columbia University Press, 1994. 392–403.

Hammond, Dorothy, and Alta Jablow. *The Africa That Never Was: Four Centuries of British Writing about Africa*. New York: Twayne, 1970.

Harris, Abram L. "John Stuart Mill: Servant of the East India Company." *Canadian Journal of Economics and Political Science* 30 (1964): 185–202.

Harrison, Antony H. *Victorian Poets and Romantic Poems: Intertextuality and Ideology*. Charlottesville: University Press of Virginia, 1990.

Heber, Reginald. *Bishop Heber in Northern India: Selections from Heber's Journals*. Ed. M. A. Laird. 2 vols. Cambridge: Cambridge University Press, 1971.

Henderson, H. B. *The Bengalee: Or, Sketches of Society and Manners in the East*. London: Smith, Elder, 1829.

Hobson, J. A. *Imperialism: A Study*. London: James Nisbet, 1902.

Hollington, Michael. *Dickens and the Grotesque*. Totowa: Barnes and Noble Books, 1984.

Homans, Margaret. "'To the Queen's Private Apartments': Royal Family Portraiture and the Construction of Victoria's Sovereign Obedience." *Victorian Studies* 37 (autumn 1993): 1–41.

Horne, James Moffat. *The Adventures of Naufragus. Written by Himself*. London: Smith, Elder, 1827.

Hughes, Robert. *The Fatal Shore: The Epic of Australia's Founding*. New York: Alfred A. Knopf, 1987.

Hulme, Peter. *Colonial Encounters: Europe and the Native Caribbean, 1492–1797*. London: Routledge, 1992 (1986).

Hunter, Sir William Wilson. *The Indian Empire: Its Peoples, History, and Products*. London: Smith, Elder, 1892.

Hyam, Ronald. *Empire and Sexuality: The British Experience*. Manchester: Manchester University Press, 1990.

India's Women. 2 vols. London: James Nisbet, 1881.

"Instructions for the Members of the Unitas Fratrum Who Minister in the Gospel among the Heathen." *Tracts Relating to Foreign Missions*. London: Printed for the Brethren Society, for the Furtherance of the Gospel among the Heathen, 1784.

Jameson, Fredric. *The Political Unconscious: Narrative as a Socially Symbolic Act*. Ithaca: Cornell University Press, 1981.

JanMohamed, Abdul. "The Economy of Manichean Allegory: The Function of Racial

Difference in Colonialist Literature." *"Race," Writing, and Difference.* Ed. Henry Louis Gates, Jr. Chicago: University of Chicago Press, 1986. 78–106.

Johnson, Charles. *Middle Passage.* New York: Plume, 1991.

Joseph, Gerhard. "Tennyson and the Savage." Paper delivered at MLA convention, New Orleans, 1989.

Kanner, Barbara. "The Women of England in a Century of Social Change, 1815-1914: A Select Bibliography, Part II." *A Widening Sphere: Changing Roles of Victorian Women.* Ed. Martha Vicinus. Bloomington: Indiana University Press, 1980. 199–270.

Kaplan, Fred. *Sacred Tears: Sentimentality in Victorian Literature.* Princeton: Princeton University Press, 1987.

Katz, Wendy. *Rider Haggard and the Fiction of Empire.* Cambridge: Cambridge University Press, 1987.

Kaye, John William. *Peregrine Pultuney; Or, Life in India.* 3 vols. London: John Mortimer, 1844.

——. *The Suppression of Thuggee and Dacoity.* Reprinted from "The Administration of the East India Company; a History of Indian Progress." 2d ed. 1853. Papers on India, no. 1. London: Christian Literature Society for India, 1897.

Kennedy, Paul. "Continuity and Discontinuity in British Imperialism, 1815-1914." *British Imperialism in the Nineteenth Century.* Ed. C. C. Eldridge. New York: St. Martin's Press, 1984. 20–38.

Kiernan, V. G. *The Lords of Human Kind: Black Man, Yellow Man, and White Man in an Age of Empire.* New York: Columbia University Press, 1986 (1969).

——. "Tennyson, King Arthur, and Imperialism." *Poets, Politics, and the People.* Ed. and Intro. Harvey J. Kaye. London: Verso, 1989.

Kilham, Hannah. *Present State of the Colony of Sierra Leone, Being Extracts of Recent Letters from Hannah Kilham.* 2d ed. Lindfield: Schools of Industry, C. Green, 1832.

Kincaid, Jamaica. *A Small Place.* Harmondsworth, Middlesex: Penguin Books, 1988.

Kipling, Rudyard. *Complete Verse: Definitive Edition.* New York: Doubleday, 1940.

——. *Kim.* Ed. and Intro. Edward W. Said. Harmondsworth, Middlesex: Penguin Books, 1987 (1901).

Knighton, William. *The Private Life of an Eastern King.* London: G. Routledge, 1856.

Koestenbaum, Wayne. *Double Talk: The Erotics of Male Literary Collaboration.* New York: Routledge, 1989.

Lamming, George. *The Pleasures of Exile.* Foreword by Sandra Poucet Paquet. Ann Arbor: University of Michigan Press, 1992 (1960).

Lang, John. *The Wetherbys, Father and Son; Or, Sundry Chapters of Indian Experience.* London: Chapman and Hall, 1853.

Lerner, Gerda. *The Creation of Patriarchy.* New York: Oxford University Press, 1986.

Levine, George. *The Boundaries of Fiction: Carlyle, Macaulay, Newman.* Princeton: Princeton University Press, 1968.

Levy, Anita. *Other Women: The Writing of Class, Race, and Gender, 1832-1898.* Princeton: Princeton University Press, 1991.

London Quarterly Review 89 (October 1851): 133–43.

Lootens, Tricia. "Hemans and Home: Victorianism, Feminine 'Internal Enemies,' and the Domestication of National Identity." *PMLA* 109 (March 1994): 238–53.

Lorimer, Douglas. *Colour, Class, and the Victorians: A Study of English Attitudes toward the Negro in the Mid-Nineteenth Century*. Leicester: Leicester University Press, 1978.

Lutz, Catherine A., and Janet L. Collins. *Reading National Geographic*. Chicago: University of Chicago Press, 1993.

Lynch, Mrs. Henry. *The Cotton-Tree; or, Emily, the Little West Indian*. London: John Hatch and Son, 1847.

——. *Years Ago: A Tale of West Indian Domestic Life of the Eighteenth Century*. London: Jarrold and Sons, 1865.

Macaulay, Thomas. "Government of India." A Speech Delivered in the House of Commons on the 10th of July, 1833. *Macaulay: Prose and Poetry*. Selected by G. M. Young. Cambridge: Harvard University Press, 1967. 688–718.

——. "Minute of the 2d February 1835." *Macaulay: Prose and Poetry*. Selected by G. M. Young. Cambridge: Harvard University Press, 1967. 719–30.

Mackenzie, Mrs. Colin. *Life in the Mission, the Camp, and the Zenana; or Six Years in India*. 2 vols. London: Richard Bentley, 1854.

Macmillan, Donald. *The Life of Professor Hastie*. Paisley: Alexander Gardner, 1926.

Madden, William A. "Macaulay's Style." *The Art of Victorian Prose*. Ed. George Levine and William Madden. New York: Oxford University Press, 1968. 127–53.

Maitland, Julia. *Letters from Madras, during the Years 1836–1839, by a Lady*. London: John Murray, 1843.

Majumdar, Ramesh Chandra. "Lord William Cavendish-Bentinck: A Revised Estimate of His Administration (1828–35)." *Readings in Political History of India: Ancient, Mediaeval, and Modern History and Archeological Series*. New Delhi: Indian Society for Prehistoric and Modern Studies, 1976. 248–54.

Malcolm, G. A., and M. M. Kalaw. *Philippine Government*. Manila: Associated Publishers, 1923.

Mani, Lata. "The Production of an Official Discourse on *Sati* in Early-Nineteenth-Century Bengal." *Europe and Its Others*. 2 vols. ed. Francis Barker et al. Proceedings of the Essex Conference on the Sociology of Literature, 1984. Colchester: University of Essex, 1985. 1:107–27.

Mannsaker, Frances M. "The Dog That Didn't Bark: The Subject Races in Imperial Fiction at the Turn of the Century." *The Black Presence in English Literature*. Ed. David Dabydeen. Manchester: Manchester University Press, 1985. 112–34.

Marcus, Steven. *Dickens: From Pickwick to Dombey*. London: Chatto and Windus, 1965.

Martineau, Harriet. *British Rule in India: A Historical Sketch*. London: Smith, Elder, 1857.

——. *Illustrations of Political Economy*. 9 vols. London: Charles Fox, 1832.

——. *Miscellanies*. 2 vols. Boston: Hilliard Gray, 1836.

——. *Retrospect of Western Travel*. 2 vols. London: Saunders and Otley, 1838.

Marx, Karl. *Capital: A Critical Analysis of Capitalist Production*. Trans. Samuel Moore and Edward Aveling. Moscow: Progress Publishers, n.d.

——. "The East India Company—Its History and Results." *Surveys from Exile*. Ed. David Fernbach. New York: Vintage Books, 1974. 307–16.

——. "The Future Results of the British Rule in India." *Surveys from Exile*. Ed. David Fernbach. New York: Vintage Books, 1974. 319–25.

Mayhew, Henry. *London Labour and the London Poor*. New York: Dover Publications, 1968. 4 vols. (1861–62).

Mazumdar, Vina. "Comment on Suttee." *Signs* 4 (1978): 269–73.

McClintock, Anne. "Maidens, Maps, and Mines: *King Solomon's Mines* and the Reinvention of Patriarchy in Colonial South Africa." *Women and Gender in Southern Africa to 1945.* Ed. Cherryl Walker. London: James Currey, xxxx 1990. 97–124.

McClure, John A. *Kipling and Conrad: The Colonial Fiction.* Cambridge: Harvard University Press, 1981.

McGuire, Ian. "Epistemology and Empire in *Idylls of the King. Victorian Poetry* 30 (autumn-winter, 1992): 387–400.

Meyer, Susan L. "Colonialism and the Figurative Strategy of *Jane Eyre.*" *Victorian Studies* 33 (winter 1990): 247–68.

Middleditch, Thomas. *The Youthful Female Missionary: A Memoir of Mary Ann Hutchins, Wife of the Rev. John Hutchins, Baptist Missionary, Savanna-La-Mar, Jamaica, of Ipswich; Compiled Chiefly from Her Own Correspondence, by Her Father.* London: G. Wightman and Hamilton Adams, 1840.

Miller, D. A. " 'Cage aux folles': Sensation and Gender in Wilkie Collins's *The Woman in White." Representations* 14 (spring 1986): 107–36.

———. *The Novel and the Police.* Berkeley: University of California Press, 1988.

Mitchell, Sally, and James D. Startt. "Empire and Imperialism." *Victorian Britain: An Encyclopedia.* Ed. Sally Mitchell. New York: Garland Publishing, 1988. 263–65.

Monsman, Gerald. "Olive Schreiner's Allegorical Vision." *Victorian Review* 18 (winter 1992): 49–62.

Moore, R. J. "India and the British Empire." *British Imperialism in the Nineteenth Century.* Ed. C. C. Eldridge. New York: St. Martin's Press, 1984. 65–84.

Mukherjee, Ramkrishna. *The Rise and Fall of the East India Company.* New York: Monthly Review Press, 1974.

Munich, Adrienne Auslander. " 'Capture the Heart of a Queen': Gilbert and Sullivan's Rites of Conquest." *The Centennial Review* 28 (winter 1984): 23–44.

Naipaul, V. S. *The Mimic Men.* Harmondsworth, Middlesex: Penguin Books, 1969 (1967).

Neill, Stephen. *A History of Christianity in India, 1707–1858.* Cambridge: Cambridge University Press, 1985.

Nochlin, Linda. *"Women, Art, and Power" and Other Essays.* New York: Harper and Row, 1988.

Nunokawa, Jeff. "For Your Eyes Only: Private Property and the Oriental Body." *Macropolitics of Nineteenth-Century Literature: Nationalism, Exoticism, Imperialism.* Ed. Jonathan Arac and Harriet Ritvo. Philadelphia: University of Pennsylvania Press, 1991. 138–58.

Opinions of the Indian Press on the Defamation Case, Pigot vs. Hastie. Calcutta: Indian Daily News Press, 1883.

Owenson, Miss. *The Missionary: An Indian Tale.* 3 vols. London: J. J. Stockdale, 1811.

Page, Norman, ed. *Wilkie Collins: The Critical Heritage.* London: Routledge and Kegan Paul, 1974.

Palmer, William J. "Dickens and Shipwreck," *Dickens Studies Annual: Essays on Victorian Fiction,* vol. 18. New York: A.M.S. Press, 1989. 39–92.

Parks, Fanny. *The Wanderings of a Pilgrim in Search of the Picturesque, during Four-and-Twenty Years in the East; with Revelations of Life in the Zenana.* 2 vols. London: Pelham Richardson, 1850.

Parry, Benita. *Conrad and Imperialism: Ideological Boundaries and Visionary Frontiers.* London: Macmillan Press, 1983.

———. *Delusions and Discoveries: Studies on India in the British Imagination, 1880–1930.* London: Allen Lane, The Penguin Press, 1972.

Paxton, Nancy L. "Complicity and Resistance in the Writings of Flora Annie Steel and Annie Besant." *Western Women and Imperialism: Complicity and Resistance.* Ed. Nupur Chaudhuri and Margaret Strobel. Bloomington: Indiana University Press, 1992. 158–76.

Pemble, John Ed. *Miss Fane in India.* Gloucester: Alan Sutton, 1985.

Perera, Suvendrini. *Reaches of Empire: The English Novel from Edgeworth to Dickens.* New York: Columbia University Press, 1991.

Peterson, M. Jeanne. "The Victorian Governess: Status Incongruence in Family and Society." *Suffer and Be Still: Women in the Victorian Age.* Ed. Martha Vicinus. Bloomington: Indiana University Press, 1972. 3–19.

Pollock, J. C. *Shadows Fall Apart: The Story of the Zenana Bible and Medical Mission.* London: Hodder and Stoughton, 1958.

Poovey, Mary. *Uneven Developments: The Ideological Work of Gender in Mid-Victorian England.* Chicago: University of Chicago Press, 1988.

Pratt, Mary Louise. *Imperial Eyes: Travel Writing and Transculturation.* London: Routledge, 1992.

———. "Scratches on the Face of the Country." *"Race," Writing, and Difference.* Ed. Henry Louis Gates, Jr. Chicago: University of Chicago Press, 1986. 138–62.

Qualls, Barry. *The Secular Pilgrims of Victorian Fiction: The Novel as Book of Life.* Cambridge: Cambridge University Press, 1982.

Quiz. *The Grand Master or Adventures of Qui Hi? in Hindostan. A Hudibrastic Poem in Eight Cantos.* Illustrated with engravings by Rowlandson. London: Thomas Legg, 1816.

Ramusack, Barbara N. "Cultural Missionaries, Maternal Imperialists, Feminist Allies: British Women Activists in India, 1865–1945." *Western Women and Imperialism: Complicity and Resistance.* Ed. Nupur Chaudhuri and Margaret Strobel. Bloomington: Indiana University Press, 1992. 119–36.

Reed, John R. "English Imperialism and the Unacknowledged Crime of *The Moonstone*," *Clio* 2 (June 1973): 281–90.

Retamar, Roberto Fernandez. *Caliban and Other Essays.* Trans. Edward Baker. Foreword by Fredric Jameson. Minneapolis: University of Minnesota Press, 1989.

Richards, Thomas. "Archive and Utopia." *Representations* 37 (winter 1992): 104–135.

———. *The Commodity Culture of Victorian England: Advertising and Spectacle, 1851–1914.* Stanford: Stanford University Press, 1990.

Richetti, John J. *Defoe's Narratives: Situations and Structures.* Oxford: Clarendon Press, 1975.

Roberts, Emma. *Oriental Scenes, Dramatic Sketches, and Tales, with Other Poems.* Calcutta: Norman Grant, 1830.

———. *Scenes and Characteristics of Hindostan with Sketches of Anglo-Indian Society.* 3 vols. London: Wm. H. Allen, 1835.

Robinson, Ronald, and John Gallagher. *Africa and the Victorians: The Official Mind of Imperialism.* Macmillan Press, 1981 (1961).

Rosenberg, John D. *The Fall of Camelot: A Study of Tennyson's "Idylls of the King."* Cambridge: The Belknap Press of Harvard University Press, 1973.

Ross, Adelaide. "Emigration for Women." *Macmillan's Magazine* 45 (November 1881–April 1882): 312–317.

Rowcroft, Charles. *Tales of the Colonies, or, The Adventures of an Emigrant.* Edited by a late colonial magistrate. London: Saunders and Otley, 1843.

Said, Edward W. *Beginnings: Intention and Method.* New York: Basic Books, 1975.

———. *Culture and Imperialism.* New York: Alfred A. Knopf, 1993.

———. *Orientalism.* New York: Pantheon Books, 1978.

———. *The World, the Text, and the Critic.* Cambridge: Harvard University Press, 1983.

Sandison, Alan. *The Wheel of Empire: A Study of the Imperial Idea in Some Late Nineteenth and Early Twentieth Century Fiction.* London: Macmillan Press, 1967.

Schlicke, Priscilla, and Paul Schlicke. *The Old Curiosity Shop: An Annotated Bibliography.* New York: Garland Publishing, 1988.

Schreiner, Olive. *The Story of an African Farm.* New York: Schocken Books, 1976 (1883).

———. *Woman and Labor.* New York: Frederick A. Stokes, 1911.

Seal, Anil. *The Emergence of Indian Nationalism: Competition and Collaboration in the Later Nineteenth Century.* Cambridge: Cambridge University Press, 1968.

Sedgwick, Eve Kosofsky. *Between Men: English Literature and Male Homosocial Desire.* New York: Columbia University Press, 1985.

Sharpe, Jenny. *Allegories of Empire: The Figure of Woman in the Colonial Text.* Minneapolis: University of Minnesota Press, 1993.

Shires, Linda. "Patriarchy, Dead Men, and Tennyson's *Idylls of the King.*" *Victorian Poetry* 30 (winter–autumn 1992): 401–19.

Showalter, Elaine. *The Female Malady: Women, Madness, and Culture in England, 1830–1980.* New York: Pantheon Books, 1985.

———. *Sexual Anarchy: Gender and Culture at the Fin de Siècle.* New York: Penguin Books, 1990.

Sinfield, Alan. *Alfred Tennyson.* Oxford: Basil Blackwell, 1986.

Sinha, Mrinalini. "'Chathams, Pitts, and Gladstones in Petticoats': The Politics of Gender and Race in the Ilbert Bill Controversy, 1883–84." *Western Women and Imperialism: Complicity and Resistance.* Ed. Nupur Chaudhuri and Margaret Strobel. Bloomington: Indiana University Press, 1992. 98–116.

Sleeman, Major [Sir William Henry]. *A Journey through the Kingdom of Oude in 1849–1850.* 2 vols. London: 1858.

———. *Report on the Depredations Committed by the Thug Gangs of Upper and Central India from the Cold Season of 1836–37, Down to their Gradual Suppression, Under the Operation of the Measures Adopted Against Them by the Supreme Government in the Year 1839.* Calcutta: G. H. Huttmann, Bengal Mily. Orphan Press, 1840.

Smith, Raymond T. "Race and Class in the Post-Emancipation Caribbean." *Racism and Colonialism.* Ed. Robert Ross. Leiden: Leiden University Press, 1982. 93–119.

Spear, Percival. *The Oxford History of Modern India: 1740–1975.* 2d ed. New Delhi: Oxford University Press, 1978 (1965).

Spivak, Gayatri Chakravorty. *In Other Worlds: Essays in Cultural Politics.* New York: Routledge, 1988.

———. "The Rani of Sirmur: An Essay in Reading the Archives." *History and Theory* 24 (1985), 247–72.

———. "Subaltern Studies: Deconstructing Historiography." *Subaltern Studies,* vol. 4. *Writings on South Asian History and Society.* Ed. Ranajit Guha. Delhi: Oxford University Press, 1985. 330–63.

———. "Three Women's Texts and a Critique of Imperialism." *"Race," Writing, and*

Difference. Ed. Henry Louis Gates, Jr. Chicago: University of Chicago Press, 1986. 262–80.

Steel, Flora Annie. *On the Face of the Waters: A Tale of the Mutiny.* New York: Macmillan, 1897.

———. *Miss Stuart's Legacy.* New York: Macmillan, 1897.

Stevenson, Catherine Barnes. *Victorian Women Travellers in Africa.* Boston: Twayne, 1982.

Stocqueler, J. H. *India: Its History, Climate, Productions; With a Full Account of the Origin, Progress, and Development of the Bengal Mutiny, and Suggestions as to the Future Government of India.* London: George Routledge, 1857.

Stokes, Eric. *The English Utilitarians in India.* Delhi: Oxford University Press, 1989 (1959).

Suleri, Sara. *The Rhetoric of English India.* Chicago: University of Chicago Press, 1992.

Sturge, Joseph, and Thomas Harvey. *The West Indies in 1837, Being the Journal of a Visit to Antigua, Montserrat, Dominica, St. Lucia, Barbados, and Jamaica.* London: Frank Cass, 1968 (1838).

Sturgis, James. "Britain and the New Imperialism." *British Imperialism in the Nineteenth Century.* Ed. C. C. Eldridge. New York: St. Martin's Press, 1984. 85–105.

Swift, Jonathan. *Gulliver's Travels and Other Writings.* Ed. Louis A. Landa. Cambridge, Mass.: Riverside Press, 1960.

Tennyson, Alfred. *The Poems of Tennyson.* Ed. Christopher Ricks. London: Longmans, Green, 1969.

Thomas, Ronald R. "Minding the Body Politic: The Romance of Science and the Revision of History in Victorian Detective Fiction." *Victorian Literature and Culture* 19 (1992–93): 230–51.

Tillotson, Kathleen. *Novels of the 1840s.* London: Oxford University Press, 1956.

Torgovnick, Marianna. *Gone Primitive: Savage Intellects, Modern Lives.* Chicago: University of Chicago Press, 1990.

Trevelyan, Charles E. (of the Bengal Civil Service). *On the Education of the People of India.* London: Longman, Orme, Brown, Green, and Longmans, 1838.

Trevelyan, Sir George Otto. *The Life and Letters of Lord Macaulay.* Foreword by G. M. Trevelyan. London: Longmans, Green, 1959 (2 vols. 1876).

Tytler, Harriet. *An Englishwoman in India: The Memoirs of Harriet Tytler, 1828–1858.* Ed. Anthony Sattin. Introduction by Philip Mason. Oxford: Oxford University Press, 1986.

Vicinus, Martha. *Independent Women: Work and Community for Single Women, 1850–1920.* London: Virago Press, 1985.

Viswanathan, Gauri. *Masks of Conquest: Literary Study and British Rule in India.* New York: Columbia University Press, 1989.

Watt, Ian. "*Robinson Crusoe* as a Myth." *Robinson Crusoe.* Ed. Michael Shinagel. New York: W. W. Norton, 1957. 311–32.

Weedon, Chris. *Feminist Practice and Poststructuralist Theory.* Oxford: Basil Blackwell, 1987.

Welsh, Alexander. *The City of Dickens.* Cambridge: Harvard University Press, 1971.

Williams, Patrick, and Laura Chrisman, eds. *Colonial Discourse and Post-Colonial Theory.* New York: Columbia University Press, 1994.

Williams, Raymond. *Culture and Society, 1780–1950.* New York: Harper and Row, 1966 (1958).

Wilson, Horace H. "Education of the Natives of India." *Asiatic Journal and Monthly Register for British and Foreign India, China, and Australasia* 19 (January–April 1836). London: W. H. Allen, 1836.

Wilt, Judith. "The Imperial Mouth: Imperialism, the Gothic and Science Fiction." *Journal of Popular Culture* 14 (spring 1981): 618–28.

Wolpert, Stanley. *A New History of India.* 2d ed. New York: Oxford University Press, 1982 (1977).

Yelin, Louise. "Strategies for Survival: Florence and Edith in *Dombey and Son.*" *Victorian Studies* 22 (1979): 297–319.

INDEX